MURDER FOR HIRE

MURDER FOR HIRE

MY LIFE AS THE COUNTRY'S MOST SUCCESSFUL UNDERCOVER AGENT

Jack Ballentine

≋

THOMAS DUNNE BOOKS
St. Martin's Griffin
New York

Author's Note: This is a true story,
though many names have been changed.

THOMAS DUNNE BOOKS.
An imprint of St. Martin's Press.

MURDER FOR HIRE. Copyright © 2009 by Jack Ballentine. All rights reserved.
Printed in the United States of America. For information, address St. Martin's
Press, 175 Fifth Avenue, New York, N.Y. 10010.

Design by Kathryn Parise

www.thomasdunnebooks.com
www.stmartins.com

The Library of Congress has cataloged the hardcover edition as follows:

Ballentine, Jack.
    Murder for hire : my life as the country's most successful undercover
agent / Jack Ballentine.—1st ed.
        p. cm.
    ISBN 978-0-312-38452-4
    1. Ballentine, Jack. 2. Police—Arizona—Phoenix—Biography.
3. Police—United States—Biography. 4. Undercover operations—United
States. I. Title

    HV7911.B27 A3 2009
    363.2092—dc22

                                                        2009007592

        ISBN 978-0-312-66777-1 (trade paperback)

        First St. Martin's Griffin Edition: February 2011

*This book is dedicated to my beautiful wife, Patti,
and my two sons, Cody and Geoff, for their endless support,
understanding, and love during my complicated life
as a public servant.*

Contents

Acknowledgments

To Patti, for making my life better and giving me two wonderful boys, Geoff and Cody, who in return gave me both a direction and a new purpose for the rest of my life. Thanks also to Patti for her convincing nudge to write this book as a lasting memory that Geoff and Cody can have when my time has passed. To Geoff, who has grown into a strong and wonderful police officer with integrity and concern for the community he serves. To Cody, for being a major reason I never crossed the line and strived to return home each day with my honor still intact, and being able to provide him a role model to follow. To my father, John, and my mother, Joan, for their love and guidance that gave me a conscience and purpose in life. To my brother, Jeff, and my sisters, Judy and Jana, who have loved me and stood by me throughout my life. To Alex Femenia, Tim Cooning, Jim Wilson, and Ron Sterrett, the greatest law enforcement professionals I have ever had the privilege to work with. They are also lifetime friends I will always admire and treasure. To Tim and Donnie Hallahan, who remain my key to memories of the past. To Jerry and Jo Zeitman for partnering with Patti and convincing me to write this book. Jerry and Jo also provided vision for the story path that helped me find my voice. Jerry found my story with the help of Tom Colbert and has never once lost belief in the value of telling it to the public. Thank to Tom Colbert, who has supported me for nearly twenty years and shares my belief in supporting all the innocent victims changed forever by a criminal act. To my literary agent Bob Diforio, and Rob Kirkpatrick, senior editor at Thomas Dunne Books, who represented me during this process and never wavered in their support. Both Rob Kirkpatrick and his editorial assistant, Lorrie McCann, used their razor-sharp edits and tireless reviews that led to a cleaner final product. Thanks for leadership and unquestionable support from Tim Black, Mike Frazier, and Kevin Robinson throughout my entire career. Gerd and Jerri Kurtenbach supported me as if they were my parents and have continued their support. For all the victims and their families whose strength provided role models to other victims who followed in their path. For the many more I could not name; my life has been shaped by your presence and I wouldn't have realized my success without your support. Finally, to my brothers and sisters in public safety, the Phoenix Police Department and the Phoenix Fire Department. I am a better man for knowing you and proud to have been a part of your life. Success is measured by the lives you save and the good you do. You are all God's gift to the public and will always be special to me.

Preface

I grew up living the life of an unaffected youth in a middle-income family, never dreaming that as an adult I would live the life of a chameleon.

I joined the Phoenix Police Department as a twenty-one-year-old man to make a difference on a larger scale. I always believed that one person can help shape the lives of those less fortunate and hopefully make the world a better place to live. Both my mother and father raised my brother and sisters to have a strong faith in God and serve others who needed your help. I believed there could be no better place to serve others than in public safety. The beliefs instilled in me by my parents led me to champion the rights of those that were beaten, abused, and routinely bullied.

Those beliefs also led me to a life of undercover work. As an undercover operative, I took on the role of a murder conspirator, better known as a hit man. Over fifteen years, I assumed a variety of identities that included biker-gang warlord, Mafia hit man, soldier of fortune, disgruntled Vietnam vet, and Aryan Brotherhood prison convict. In my ever-changing persona, I was contacted by men and women who wanted someone killed—not only eliminated from their lives, but killed in the most gruesome ways known to man.

While playing this role twenty-four hours a day, I fortunately found the woman I had always dreamed of, with whom I raised two boys that grew into outstanding young men. These three people became the balance in a complicated and sometimes disturbing life. Many undercover operatives fall into the very life of crime that they are supposed to be fighting. This is also the story of how love gave strength to a man who many times felt lost in his characters and rose above the pitfalls.

I wrote this book at the request of friends and family to show the life and challenges faced by so many undercover operatives. Never before have you seen undercover operatives in this light, as well as with whom they work. I show the mental makeup of informants, as well as that of the victims of these would-be murders—business partners, spouses, even children. Most of the intended victims are devastated when they learn of the plots against them, while some refuse to believe it and even remain in contact with the very person who wanted him or her killed.

Either way, their lives were changed forever from the moment people in their lives decided that nothing else was more important than themselves and their anger, greed, or jealousy.

Therein lies my story. . . .

1

The Other Side of Hell

This may not be the end of my world, but I sure feel that I'm stuck in hell and can't dig my way out. Here I sit inside a pitiful bar that has dirt floors, located right in the middle of the worst and seediest part of Phoenix, Arizona. Everyone in my world has an insatiable drug habit or an alcohol problem, and most have both. They mostly live on the streets or call a three-hundred-square-foot, roach-infested apartment home. I can't really say too much because I live in the same hole and call most of these people friends. Unfortunately for me, my so-called friends have long histories in the criminal justice system and don't care whom they hurt or what they steal. Even more incredible is their lack of concern for human life. As long as they get their drug of choice to satisfy their addiction, they don't care who gets hurt or dies in the process.

Every drug addict and junkie in the place slithers up to me

and tries to convince me he or she has the best heroin or meth in town. Not one of them can take no for an answer and move on to some other anxious buyer. As they continue to bother me, I begin to think how my patience is beginning to wear thin, and I think to myself how sick and tired I have become of this sorry-ass life I'm living.

All of them are so strung out on their dope that they have a hard time seeing me for who I am. I have hair down to my ass, I'm six feet five inches tall, weigh 285 pounds, and can bench-press 405 pounds without much effort. I've got more muscle than they have brains. I'm definitely not the picture of a drug abuser.

Take one look at them and you see six-foot-tall men weighing one hundred pounds, and the women weighing even less. Teeth are rotted out and their eyes have a hazy cloud around them. Their drug and alcohol abuse has withered their once healthy bodies into walking skeletons. The only thing they respect about me is my overpowering size. It's just enough to make them think twice before they attempt to stab me and then take my wallet as I lie on the ground slowly dying. They have rid their bodies and minds of all morality. Their only thought is the next hit off the crack pipe or draw from a needle full of heroin. Oh, yeah, and the money they need to purchase more "stuff."

They try to sell what drugs they have, but none of it belongs to them. The main supplier has fronted the stuff to them and expects to be paid back immediately. He gives them a small portion of the drug in return for their efforts. They then turn around and purchase more drugs from the dealer for their personal use. It's a vicious cycle that goes on and on.

The sad part about my life is that I fit right into this place even though I haven't become addicted to the stuff that rules their lives. Maybe it's that I haven't bathed in a couple days. Or maybe it's because I haven't shaved for days and absolutely never wash my clothes. It's kinda funny to think about, but most people have never given any thought to how a pair of jeans last about a year before they fall completely apart if you don't get them washed. I haven't washed mine in over a year and don't intend on starting the washer anytime soon. Now, that's a badge of honor to be proud of!

The more I sit here and drink, the more I feel sorry for most of these people. Trigger is a regular in here, and at one time she was a pretty little blonde. She's twenty-five years old and all of five feet, ninety pounds dripping wet . . . on a good day. Because of a severe staph infection and using dope laced with every kitchen chemical known to man, her skin is scarred and the flesh has been eaten away from her limbs. She was telling me a story the other day about when she was born and her mother was addicted to crack cocaine. Her father started raping her when she was nine and beat her if she refused to give him what he asked for. She hit the streets by herself when she was thirteen and has been there since.

As I sit at the bar and watch Trigger, I wonder what it would have been like if she had been born into a good family. One that cared, loved, and nurtured her. Or, just maybe she was born to a loving family and they ran out of ways to help her. Now she sits on a barstool and leans her back against the edge of the bar. Trigger then lies back on the bar top while still seated on the stool. Some freak she calls a friend helps her shaking hands inject a new round of heroin into her body. Suddenly the syringe is emptied and she lies calmly on the bar top and takes it all in. Trigger says it's best for her to get help because most of her veins are ruined from abuse and overuse. The helpers locate which vein is still operational enough to accept the drug and move it through her body. It sickens me to think this girl has wasted her life and probably won't live past thirty. I don't have a lot to brag about myself while I sit and watch her, but I still feel sorry for her.

In a sad, pitiful way she is sweet and innocent. If you look past her sores, scars, and all the track marks, you can see a little girl who had dreams of a beautiful life. She lies back on the bar with her heavy eyelids closed as the dope rushes through her body. It's as if she is in a deep sleep and going to a place where she doesn't hurt anymore. Of course, the heroin is eating away any future they may have had.

Heroin junkies always tell you that the first high is better than anything else they ever experienced or will ever experience again. The next time isn't as good . . . and each time after the first seems to be every bit as anticlimactic. I ask them every chance I can about the "why" of shooting more heroin. They all tell me the same thing. They keep searching for the intense rush they got the first time. Searching and searching for that incredible rush, but never finding it again. They can't stop though. Can't stop because they just know it is around the next corner. They chase until they die.

Thinking about what they often say, I find myself comparing the heroin rush to a first kiss in a new relationship. The fireworks explode and nothing else can compare to the moment. Funny thing is, it never seems to be as intense again. That's what you always hear from the first one to leave the broken relationship. People always say, "It's not the same anymore . . . the fire is gone." They seem to be chasing that first intense feeling with every relationship that follows. The rush is why so many people play the dangerous game of "cheating" and eventually find their way to me and my dark world. Not much difference between the junkie and the cheater. In the long run someone is going to hurt.

After ten minutes pass, Trigger starts to raise herself up from the bar and looks around in a slow, drug-induced manner. Her heavy eyes start to focus on me as she gets off the barstool. She walks over to me, bumping into everything along the way and stops right in front of me. Trigger places both hands on my knees and parts my legs. She walks between my open legs and looks me directly in the eyes. Trigger stares at my face for a moment and makes me nervous as hell. After a moment passes she says, "Do you love me, Jake?" Just as the words come out of her mouth, my pager goes off. The pager distracts Trigger and she slowly walks away to the bathroom.

Leaving this bar is like walking through a minefield. You walk out the front door into the dark of night because there's no outside lighting. Along the way are more junkies and thugs that would think nothing of stabbing or cutting you for a buck. I'm lucky though. As I said, they like me and respect me. Or maybe they fear the hell out of me. Kick one person's ass when the bar is full and the word travels fast. I got their respect early on.

It also doesn't hurt that my transportation for the night is a reconstructed Harley that sits in the parking lot. And more important, everyone thinks I belong to the Dirty Dozen motorcycle gang, and that automatically demands their respect and attention. This whole "motorcycle envy" thing really cracks me up. I own a Harley and look the part of a badass biker so I automatically get labeled a gangster. What they don't know is that the parts to my Harley came from recovered stolen motorcycles and were eventually pieced together to make the mutt of a scooter they are so impressed with. I personally don't have a clue how to hook a gas line to a carburetor or a brake line to a brake system. But my buddies do, and they put together a great ride. If it weren't for them, I would just be another bigger-than-average drunk in the bar.

As I sit on my bike, I shuffle for my phone so I can call the paged number I just got. It's a typical Arizona day . . . hot as hell. The heat rises off the parking lot and up my pant legs as I sit on the bike. You begin to cook, and the smell of sweat mixed with hot booze oozes from your pores. My body odor begins to step up another notch, and people can smell me from across the parking lot.

As the phone rings on the other end of my call, I find myself wondering, what did I do to deserve the life I've chosen? We all have choices and I made this one. It doesn't seem right. I would love nothing more than to wear a good suit and shower regularly. Maybe splash on some hundred-dollar cologne and work in an air-conditioned office. That's not going to happen anytime soon though. When the only thing that loves you is a scarred and infected heroin junkie . . . you're destined for a life of misery and heartache.

The person on the other end of the call answers and claims he has someone for me to meet. That someone brags of having cannibalistic cravings and needs a hired killer to kill a young boy to satisfy those cravings.

Maybe it's time to reconsider my career choice and get a real job.

2

Slaying the Serpent

One of my street contacts had sent me to the back of a bowling alley near the freeway in Phoenix. I was headed there to meet the face of evil.

My source told me a man named Eric Hunter wanted to torture and kill boys and men for his sadistic pleasure and taste their body parts. Eric doesn't have the nerve to do the killing himself, so he needs a hit man. "One more thing," the middleman says. "He has a foot-long penis and likes to play with it." When Eric starts to talk about killing and his sadistic tortures, he gets aroused. As he gets aroused, he begins to touch himself and eventually removes his penis from his pants. Eric then openly plays with himself as he talks about his thoughts.

A hit man, yeah . . . but entertaining a freak . . . not quite what I bargained for. I'm used to getting the order to whack someone and being paid handsomely for my work. I have the hit-man job down to a science, and I'm so good at it that I haven't ever met anyone who didn't believe I am who I say I am and that I mean business. Not bad for a guy whose real job is police officer. Problem is, though, I've lost touch with that guy and have become whomever anybody wants me to be. I'm a chameleon who changes my identity so frequently that it's making me one confused guy. What I really miss is the guy I once was. That guy in a sharp suit wearing hundred-dollar-a-bottle cologne and working out of an air-conditioned office.

I didn't stay in a uniform for long when I first became a police officer. Within a couple years I was whisked off to a sting operation where I made a living undercover buying stolen property from burglars, thieves, and fences. Then came the murder-for-hire business and I was off on another venture. I began changing personalities and appearances regularly so I could appeal to an assortment of clients in need of a killer because they were too scared to do it themselves. I could be in the bar with the likes of Trigger where I looked and smelled like garbage. The next moment I was arriving as a soldier of fortune that had been contracted to kill someone and get him or her out of the client's life. Mental confusion began to permeate every pore in my body, and I questioned my identity.

Many nights I would lie awake trying to remember who I was and how I got so screwed up in my head. Then I remembered what kept me moving forward. Doing the right thing . . . for the right reasons . . . and for those that can't help themselves. I would finally fall back asleep and wait for the next question from my conscience. My mind ran all night long with questions and playing out the day's events. When I woke, I felt as if I had just finished a shift.

I can see it all now. I meet Eric in a hotel room to discuss his plans. My team is next door rolling video and audio for the case. Eric starts to get excited and pulls out this foot-long serpent. The boys next door capture the moment on tape, as my eyes are wide-open and awestruck. The photo then ends up in every police-precinct locker room in the state.

Not going to happen! I decided that when I met Eric, I would be carrying a ten-inch switchblade tucked away in my boot. It would make him think twice about taking his penis out in front of me.

I would always do one more thing before my deals with clients such as Eric. I'd call the foremost expert in forensic psychiatry, Dr. Steven Pitt. I would spend hours with Dr. Pitt discussing interview techniques and understanding the criminal mind. Understanding Eric was going to be much more difficult because what he wanted was so incredibly abnormal. Dr. Pitt helped me understand the mental illness associated with Eric and his cannibalistic thoughts. From our conversation I could then determine how I would approach Eric and gain his trust. Most of all Dr. Pitt gave me a sounding board for my thoughts and plans.

The meeting with Eric happened as planned on a Friday afternoon at La Quinta Inn Hotel. The boys had set up video surveillance under the direction of Sgt. Dennis "DD" Duncan. He was a soft-spoken senior detective sergeant who was loved and respected by everyone. He's a cowboy with boots, chews tobacco, and talks smooth as molasses. When DD is in charge, everything runs like clockwork.

The hotel room is dark as Eric steps inside. He's tall, built thick, and normal-looking, straight out of *GQ* magazine. I remember later hearing a woman say she would gladly have dated him if he would have asked. Of course, that's before she learned he was a cannibal. His regular job was as a commodities broker in Scottsdale, Arizona, and his father was a successful businessman. It was an easy life for Eric, full of spoils.

This meeting was going to be no easy task, and I knew I needed to be someone that Eric believed was more dysfunctional than he was. The only thing that came to mind was a heartless devil worshipper who killed for pleasure and made sacrificial offerings to Satan. I could go completely over-the-top with that character and maybe counter some of Eric's sadistic thoughts and plans. I had seen this character one night while I was watching a late-night television show. I also knew that when people watched television and saw a certain character, they immediately believed the character was the real deal. When they met that person in real life, they expected the same personality as the television character's. That makes it so much easier to develop yourself into someone like a Satan worshipper and be believable.

When we first met, I immediately began to speak of my affection for Satan and how I did all my killing for Satan. In a low, gravelly voice I said, "I don't know what you want, bud, but I know Satan sent me to you. I'll kill for Satan if he tells me to . . . and if he tells me to do it for you . . . consider it done."

With that, Eric began to talk of his "thoughts" to have people killed for his pleasure. He wanted it to be clear that he hadn't acted on it yet, just thought about it. His thoughts were so far outside of what society believes that I was shocked. He dreamed of calling a pizza delivery boy or a paperboy to his house. When the boy got there, Eric wanted to drug him with a drink and cut off his legs. Eric would laugh out loud and tell him, "Now try and make your deliveries." He wanted to find a bus loaded with schoolchildren and set the bus on fire, then he would sit back and listen to all their screams as they burned. He wanted to decapitate someone and defile the body. He would also correspond with other mass murderers and exchange recipes for body parts.

As I sat across from Eric and tried to conceal my utter shock, I had to act as if I had done things just as bad. I needed to act as if I were nuttier than this freak.

The more I listened, and the more I acted like a murdering nut myself, the madder I got at this guy. He was so twisted that I didn't know if it was safe to let him walk out of the room.

It's strange sitting in a room with someone like Eric. As he talks about his sadistic pleasures and desires, you sit back in a mental haze. It's all too much information to mentally digest, and even more difficult to tolerate. One part of my head tries to figure him out, while the other side tries to make sure I convince him that he is sitting with Satan himself. The things that come from my mouth leave me wondering where I came up with such twisted ideas. I'm almost like a closet killer myself.

I had arranged to get a young rookie cop right out of the academy to play the role of a runaway whom I was to kill and give to Eric. He liked the idea, but he also had his eye on the teenage boy next door to his house. This boy turned out to be the son of a police officer.

We agreed that Eric would go home and get some lye, shovels, a tent for concealment, and other miscellaneous tools. The lye, according to Eric, would cover the smell of the dead body. Our final plan was that Eric would bring everything back and we would take our teenage boy to the desert where I would kill him. Eric could then do everything he had been dreaming about. I made him believe my reward would be satisfying Satan with a sacrifice.

All the ideas were Eric's. I just gave him a person he thought would understand him and would do the killing for him. No entrapment on my part because it was all his idea and he provided the means to get it done. He had it planned out long before he met me. I just provided the partner.

The surveillance team readied themselves outside the hotel room as Eric prepared to leave. He left the room in a sexually aroused frenzy, and that concerned me. No serpent had surfaced because I'd pulled my switchblade out as he became more and more aroused with the talk of death and eating people. I sat right across from Eric and carved the sole of my boot as he looked me in the eyes. I stared right back at him and sent the message that I was completely removed from reality and he should be careful. The entire time I was with Eric I felt he figured I was crazier than he was and would kill him as easily as the next person. I later learned from the middleman that Eric had called him after our meeting and bragged I was an absolute nut, but he was really excited that he had found me. I had successfully convinced Eric and he believed I was exactly who I wanted him to think I was.

When Eric left the hotel room with the surveillance team following close behind, rush-hour traffic had filled the streets. The team followed Eric as he drove near schools, unable to stop him for fear of negatively impacting the investigation. The team began to believe that Eric was hunting for his own young boy to bring back for me to kill.

Suddenly, the surveillance leader asked over the radio, "Who has the eye on Eric?" No answer! I immediately realized they had lost him in the traffic around a school. Eric was now alone on the streets to act out his fantasy. As the news worked its way around the command post, everyone's stress level shifted to an all-time high.

Surveillance is incredibly difficult because the team has to blend into traffic to avoid detection. As they tried to blend in, Eric had somehow slipped through their net.

Just the thought of Eric's snatching a young boy to bring back to me sent chills down my spine. I had spent my early years in college studying to be a counselor for abused children. I never dreamed that I could be part of a plan that would lead to the abuse of a child. I wasn't part of the surveillance team that had lost him in traffic, but I was ultimately responsible for the success or failure of this case. It all rested on my shoulders.

We had to find Eric, now. There was no excuse for him to violate a child's life, and no excuse for me if he did. I didn't realize the decision I was about to face.

Every day starts the same for me. I get up and take a quick shower before I head off to the gym. I work out for two hours in a hardcore free-weight gym that plays host to professional football players and wrestlers. After the workout I hurry back to my home and get lunch ready so I can be seated in front of the tube before my favorite soap opera, *Guiding Light*, begins. I'm totally hooked on it.

After *Guiding Light* ends, I scan a few more shows to see what people are buying into as "real," then I'm off to the streets.

I couldn't believe how many people had the same soap opera addiction that I had. We might not be watching the same soap, but we had the same addiction. Sometimes in conversations with people about *Guiding Light* I'd discover they knew every line and every character's bio. That was when I knew I had to model my characters after the soap characters or those on other mainstream nightly shows. People believed in all those shows, and many believed the characters were real. The shows and the characters were societal role models, examples for behavior and personalities.

I followed my daily routine before I met Eric and expected that everything would go smoothly when we hooked up. I never imagined he would get lost, and I definitely never imagined he would be looking for a child victim of his own. This had become a personal nightmare for me, and at the moment everything was out of my control.

Orders started flying from DD and the command post to develop a plan to find this guy. Everyone talked about finding him and continuing with our original idea. Have him come back and we would plan to kill the pretend boy I brought and passed off as a runaway. The more I thought about it, the more I didn't like it and couldn't play along any longer. My mind raced with the thought of Eric kidnapping an innocent child and bringing him back to me. Nothing was worth a child's being scarred for life just because we wanted to make a case.

In Arizona we have a law, known as conspiracy to commit murder, that covers exactly what I was doing with Eric. The only penalty it doesn't include is death. If convicted, you go to prison for life. The earliest chance for parole is twenty-five years.

To make the conspiracy-to-commit-murder charge stick

you have to demonstrate the defendant's commitment and his knowledge he is talking about a murder, not a kidnapping or an assault. The commitment comes with money, pictures, and/or a map. In this case, the tools, tent, and lye he claimed to be getting from his home would be more than enough to show his commitment. These were all tools he said were needed to complete the murder plot and quench his deviant sexual thirst.

My problem lay with continuing to give Eric a chance to come back to me. If they let him continue on his way . . . would he kidnap a boy? What if he evaded surveillance again? He did it once without even trying, and he could do it all over again. Or would he be comfortable and content with my pretend boy. I couldn't live with myself if he kidnapped a child. This case isn't bigger than a young boy's future.

So, my dilemma was, to keep going as planned and take the chance he came back alone, or to pick him up as soon as they found him again. After serious consideration I finally decided and told DD that we should arrest him once they found him. If we took him into custody, we could write a search warrant for his house and recover all the items he'd discussed as needed for the murder. We might never be able to charge him for the conspiracy, but we could put together what we had and let the county attorney decide on charging. After close review of the circumstances in this case they might decide to pursue charges. The charging part was out of my hands, but avoiding a wrongful kidnapping wasn't.

DD agreed with me and ordered the surveillance team to sit on Eric's house. Another team continued to circulate in the area in hopes of finding him.

Several hours passed with no sign of Eric until he suddenly

drove into his driveway. No boy with him, and he was still alone. The surveillance team got the order to take him and completed this task swiftly. As the arrest was made, I felt a rush of relief that he was alone and no child was hurt. Now the work began and the case had to be made to make sure he was unable to ever hurt anyone.

My whole body hurt from the pressure of the past day, and I found myself heading to the Taco Bell for something quick to eat before I interviewed Eric. Walking into the restaurant, I saw a young mother with her little boy standing in line. I walked up behind them and took my place. As I daydreamed and read the menu, I forgot how much of a piece of shit I had become. I stink, I'm huge, and I have hair down my back. I also add to my visual intimidation by always having a toothpick hanging from my mouth, and a pocketful to replace the ones that break apart.

I've been told over and over that people I deal with are incredibly nervous about the toothpick. I move it in and out of my mouth and shift it from side to side. For some reason people seem to think I'm going to pull it out of my mouth and stick them in the eye with it. Nobody explains why they feel that way, but they all think of the toothpick as some kind of weapon.

Most people see me and hold their purses just a little closer or take their kids inside for safety. I forget this, though, because inside my heart I'm that college kid that wanted to help children and set out to save the world. As I stared for a while at the menu on the wall, I snapped out of my daze and looked down at the little boy in front of me. I thought to myself how he could have been a victim of Eric's if we weren't so lucky. I smiled at the boy because it felt good knowing he was safe and with his mother. But my smile changed quickly when he looked back at me and instantly screamed in fear. The mother stared at me and pulled the boy closer. The whole restaurant looked at me as if I had just hit this little guy.

I couldn't have felt any lower. Only an hour earlier I had had this incredible high. And now . . . kicked in the gut. It was one of those days when it seemed I just couldn't win.

3

Love Struck

Things have got to be a little better today because
they can't be worse than yesterday.

I'm just finishing my workout when the phone rings. DD is
on the other end and needs my help to scare a close friend of
his. He doesn't want her hurt, just playfully scared as an innocent joke or prank. His friend, Betty, has known DD since high
school. He meets with Betty and her sister Patti every couple of
months for dinner. They catch up and talk about old times. DD
describes Betty and Patti as incredibly good-looking and even
more incredibly naïve. They are, he says, an easy mark to scare
and intimidate. DD figures that with my appearance, and riding
the scooter, I'll be just the ticket to put the fear of God into his
friends.

Not only am I a hit man, I've now become a damn novelty
item.

I get directions from DD to go to this fancy restaurant located in an exclusive Phoenix neighborhood where communities are gated and crime is minimal. When I pull up to the front door, I'm met by a valet, who thinks he's going to park my bike. In my normal world I would have just given him the keys and thanked him for the courtesy, but that isn't going to happen in my current life. Even though I'm not in my criminal environment, I still run the chance that someone who knows me as a crime figure is within sight of me. If I fall out of character, then I run the risk of being exposed. That's part of the pressure of being in character so much of the time. I always believe someone is watching me when I'm out in public.

I explain to the young valet that he needs to move on or I'm going to ride my bike right up his ass. The youngster has some spunk and explains why he needs to park the bike and I can't. After I listen to him for a few minutes I fire up the bike and drive right to the front door. As the door opens, I inch the bike inside the restaurant until I stop halfway inside. In a squeaky, frenzied voice the valet begs me to stop and directs me to a space near the front door. I park the bike and pocket my keys as I go inside. I give the valet one more hard stare to make sure he understands I mean business. It also leaves an intimidating message with anyone who has watched. Always working on my reputation no matter where I am.

Of course, by this time I have drawn a lot of attention. Not only for my defiance, but how I look. I stand out like a sore thumb. My presence sends an aura of "everything that is bad" throughout the restaurant, and everyone notices as I walk inside.

Whenever I enter an establishment while I'm working and in character, I make a point to do so with a flair and make sure

I'm noticed. Once I break the threshold of the door, I stand for a moment and make hard eye contact with everyone in the place. I make all of them uneasy and also silently convey that I'm confident and in control. I have become the person that everyone sees based on my outside appearance. It becomes more and more difficult to act as if you care when you look as if you don't give a shit. I live in a dirty, dangerous world where everyone has low self-esteem. I dress dirty, smell dirty, and feel dirty. Suddenly, I don't care about anything, just like all the other people in my life.

As I scanned the room, I caught the eye of DD, who gave me a head nod toward a blond-haired girl near the dance floor. I slowly walked toward her as everyone in the place watched. As soon as I was next to her, I closed in and stood deep inside her comfort space. I just stared at her until she flushed and became weak in the knees. Frozen with fear, she couldn't move. She just stood and looked at me as I said, "I want you . . . and want you now!" Betty was close to collapse when DD stepped in and laughed so hard he just about soiled his pants. He told Betty about the joke and invited me back to their table. It was all Betty could do to make it back to the table. All her energy seemed sapped, and she could hardly move her legs and feet.

The table was surrounded by an oval, bench-type seat, and as I approached, I could see that it was full of people. I sat down on the end and did a quick scan of those seated. I suddenly focused on a beautiful blonde with blue eyes and the warmest smile. She looked at me, but almost in disgust. Once again, I'd forgot what I looked like on the outside and how normal people see me. I pulled my hair back, slicked back my eyebrows, and flattened out my T-shirt, hoping to make myself more presentable.

DD introduced me to the five or six people at the table. The pretty, petite blonde was Patti. She owned her own hair salon and also worked as a makeup artist.

When I met her, I found my entire tough-guy image slipping away. I felt strange inside and a bit out of control. For a guy who lives his life with topless dancers and crack whores that don't impress, I thought I might finally have met someone that does it for me. Of course, she only sees a creep and doesn't plan on giving me the time of day.

I have worked so hard to develop an image that intimidates and controls everyone around me. Now I meet someone I like, and the image I worked so hard to get works against me. There isn't any way I can make her believe I'm a good guy trapped in a creep's body. I tried though. I searched wildly through my mind for a way to make her realize I was her type, but no luck. The well was suddenly dry.

We all sat at the table for a while until my pager rang and I was off to meet another client and make another deal. I apologized to Betty and thanked everyone for the great joke, then excused myself from the table. But not before I took another hard look at Patti and made sure she knew I was looking. Of course she probably thought I was once again pulling my intimidation gig.

As I left the restaurant, I told myself this wouldn't be the last time little Patti saw me. Somehow I'd figure a way to make her take another look at me.

Night after night I go into the topless clubs and have half-naked women treat me like a God. Crack whores and heroin junkies follow me around like the pied piper, and I don't give it a second thought. The amazing thing about the underworld is how much its inhabitants fear power and size. But they also respect it and do everything they can to be your friend. In their twisted, little minds they feel protected if they can say they know you and have beers in the same place you roam.

Tonight, though, I had found myself in the presence of a classy woman and it made me feel as if I were home again.

My life has become confusing and I find myself searching for the person I was before I came into this business. My mother was the one woman I respected above all others while I grew up, and she was taken from me shortly after I became a police officer. When I got really confused, I found myself riding to the cemetery to sit and talk to my ma.

Tonight was no different. Even though I had another deal waiting to be called back, when I left the restaurant, I headed toward the cemetery. It had got late and the cemetery was closed, so I parked the bike and hopped the fence to get inside. I went to the spot where my mother lives and took a seat. Sitting, thinking, and talking always seemed to help me figure it all out. I always believed my mother heard me, and in her way she answered back.

I remember the day she was buried as if it were yesterday. I was standing around the grave after the service ended with my older sister, Judy. She always questioned life, and this day was not going to be any different. Judy looked at me and said, "If Mom really hears us and will be protecting us, I want someone to give me a yellow rose. Then I'll believe she is still here." After a few minutes passed, the mortuary assistant walked over to the casket and grabbed a rose off the top. He looked around for a moment, then walked directly to Judy. The man softly handed her a yellow rose and said she looked as if she needed something to remember her mother by. So . . . I'm thinking my mother listens.

As I sat in the dark and talked, I found myself slipping into deep thoughts of how it all got started and when I had my mother with me to help. Everything started to flash back to then, and the memories rushed through me as if it were all happening again.

I began to think about my college days and how great it was at the University of Arizona. I never had a care in the world and spent my time having a good time and getting through school. I always thought when I graduated I would be a counselor for convicts and straighten them out. I believed that abused kids normally turned to a life of crime. If you can help them out early, maybe you can stop the trend. If you miss them, then you get the chance to help them as a counselor at the prison.

Some of the guys at school, including my best friend, Tim Hallahan, decided to go up to Phoenix and take the Phoenix Police Department test. I agreed to go along, and before you knew it I was accepted to the academy.

I remember standing in my mother's kitchen one day after coming home from school and rifling through her mail pocket on the wall in the kitchen while she talked and cooked. I came across a card from the Police Department saying I had been accepted. I looked at my ma and she turned her head away. After a few uncomfortable minutes she fired back at me, "Too dangerous and I don't want you to do it." I tried to explain how much I wanted to help people and how this was the best chance I had to make a difference. "I'm tough, Ma, and I can take care of myself.

If someone doesn't do the job, then the criminals continue to hurt and take advantage of everyone they cross."

She cried and prayed for several days until I came back home for the weekend. She said she needed to talk with me for a minute. We sat at the kitchen table, as did everyone who ever came to my home. She handed me a prayer card and gave me a smile and an affectionate nod to read it:

Holy Michael, the Archangel, defend us in battle; be our safeguard against the wickedness and snares of the devil. May God rebuke him we humbly pray; and you, Prince of the heavenly host, by the power of God, cast into hell Satan and also the evil spirits who wander through the world seeking the ruin of souls.

"St. Michael is the patron saint for all police officers," my mom said. "You have all my support and prayers if you do one thing for me." I asked her in a somewhat suspicious way, "What might that be?" She told me to start each day as a police officer by saying the St. Michael prayer and to carry it with me forever.

I still have the same prayer card, even though it's a bit tattered. I had to laminate it so it wouldn't totally fall apart, but I still carry it and still say the prayer before each shift.

The twenty-two weeks in the Police Academy didn't pass quickly, but left memories that I will never forget. I met two of my closest friends during that time and have trusted them for the rest of my career. My father always told me that in your life you can feel fortunate if you can count your close friends on one hand. Many people will never have that privilege. My inner circle included Alex Femenia and Jim "JP" Wilson from the academy. Tim "Coon Dog" Cooning, who came in later during my undercover years, became another confidant.

The academy day started at 5:00 a.m. and didn't seem to end until midnight. Running, workouts, running, classroom, running, marching, training problems, firearms, and more running. I had never been yelled at so many times in my life and can still hear the voices of the drill sergeant. "Ball-en-tino! What are you doing and who taught you how to march?" That voice came from Sgt. Ralph Griffith, who retired as a marine drill sergeant. I knew he came to the Police Academy to make my life miserable. In spite of everything, he made me tougher than I ever thought possible. I respected him then and respect him even more today.

After graduation I went directly to a patrol car and was trained by a senior officer named Patrick Farmer. My time with Pat lasted about two and a half weeks, but he treated me well and gave me a good jump start. I moved on to the south side of Phoenix after about four months with Pat's squad. There, I started working in a specialty unit that handled street gangs and other surveillance and fugitive activities.

One Friday night I was sitting in briefing when the door to the room suddenly opened and there stood a military-style "high and tight" uniformed police officer. It was as if Jesus himself stood in the doorway and horns began to play and beautiful voices sang to their music. The sergeant sat for a moment in awe, then jumped up from his chair and ran to the officer. They exchanged hugs and slaps on each other's back. With his arm around the officer, the sergeant turned to us in the briefing room and said, "Everyone! This is Officer Tommy Hernandez. He is one of the most decorated Phoenix police officers in our history and has come back to work after a leave of absence. Tommy will be working with our squad from now on. If you're smart, you will attach your wagon to his horse and learn everything you can from him."

You didn't have to tell me anything more than once, and I immediately knew this was the guy I would be a sponge around. I planned to listen to everything he said and watch everything he did. If it would make me better, that's what I wanted. One other thing my father always told me was to respect the older people around you and learn from them. Their years of experience are worth more than any experiences I may have had as a youth. Respect them even if you don't like them. Respect what they have accomplished and experienced. That's what I planned to do with Tommy, who was ten years my elder.

Everyone was so excited to see Tommy that it was as if the president of the United States had stopped in for a visit. You could tell he was special and you could feel his charisma and aura. Tommy was nearly six feet tall and very fit. He looked like Erik Estrada from the television show *CHiPS* and walked with a swagger. His uniform was impeccable and he didn't have one badge or medal out of place.

While I was in the briefing room, I listened to some of the guys talking about Tommy and how he'd left the department unexpectedly after the death of his partner, Gilbert Chavez. Tommy had been gone from the department for over a year, and this was his return to law enforcement. Everyone seemed quiet about why he'd really left, but they all welcomed him back with great excitement.

Gilbert was a young officer killed in the line of duty on June 16, 1975, while responding to a burglary in progress at the Engel and Hoskin Radiator Exchange, 2034 W. Jackson Street.

Officer Chavez found an open door to the building and entered to investigate. He confronted the burglars and was shot in the chest. He then staggered from the building and collapsed in the middle of Jackson Street, where he died from his wound.

Tommy ended up falling in love with Gilbert's wife and they had a child out of wedlock. Everyone described Virginia as a beautiful woman who had eventually been hurt by Tommy. In the police business it's never a good thing to run off with your living partner's wife. It becomes even more complicated when you become romantically involved with the wife of your partner after he is killed in the line of duty. Even if both adults consent to the relationship, emotions run high throughout the department. Most people didn't look favorably upon Tommy for moving into Virginia's life. Maybe a little time between Gilbert's death and Tommy's romance with Virginia would have been better. I'm sure it would have been easier for all those that loved Gilbert.

I always wondered if this was the reason that Tommy took his leave of absence, or if it was the confusion over his love for Virginia. Since many officers didn't approve of Tommy being with Virginia, the workplace surely became a bit uncomfortable. But, Tommy didn't seem to be having any problems with being accepted by the guys when he returned. Maybe the absence made everyone forgive and forget.

As the weeks passed, I followed Tommy around from call to call and watched how he worked. I soon realized that this guy didn't have an ounce of fear in him. What he did was make you stronger and more fearless. I found myself not wanting to show him any sign of fear, even if it was there. We would go on a call with a man holding a gun inside a house and refusing to surrender. Tommy would grab me and we would force our way in the door and tackle the guy. Tommy didn't care if he got shot, and I came to believe I couldn't be shot. It was almost like becoming cowboys and believing we were invincible. If you were with Tommy, you became Tommy.

On a bright sunny Sunday afternoon, after being in patrol for nearly six months, I was patrolling by myself when I heard a call dispatched to another officer for a family fight. I answered the call and said I would follow in as backup. When I got to the upper-class residential neighborhood, I went directly to the assigned house and found I was the first to arrive. I waited for a minute, then decided to go to the front door and handle the fight call until the originally assigned officer arrived.

When I got to the door, I didn't hear any noises or fighting from the inside. I rang the bell, and moments later the door swung open. Standing in front of me was a young lady and an older lady. They were both crying hysterically as they told me, "He's a monster and he's trying to kill us!" I told them to step inside and I followed closely behind. As I stood in the entryway of the house, I noticed something just outside my vision and to my side. It was large, and the room appeared to darken as it quickly closed in on me. Next thing I knew I was hit by something that gave me no chance to react. I was thrown off my feet and through the front screen door. I flipped through a hedge in front of the door and landed in the front yard on my back.

I lay there for a moment and questioned why I had gone inside alone. Then I got mad and decided to go back inside and "take out" whatever had hit me. If waited for backup, I would be considered a coward. Most of all, what would Tommy think?

I picked myself up and went charging back in the door, only

to be met by a six-foot-ten-inch, 280-pound monster. This man had lost his mind and just beaten his wife and mother-in-law. I don't know what possessed me, but I spun him around and grabbed him from behind as we went to the ground in a heap. The fight became furious and I knew if I stopped, he would kill me. Suddenly, another body appeared and I wondered if I was about to deal with two madmen. Fortunately, though, it was Tommy. He slapped cuffs on the guy and I rolled over on the carpet to take a breath. Tommy looked at me and started laughing. "Should have waited, rook, I could have helped. Good job, though, proud of you. Now let's get him booked."

That evening at the end of the shift, I sat in front of my locker and assessed the wounds I'd got from the day's battle. As I changed into street clothes, Tommy walked by me and stopped at the locker. He told me to meet him in the parking lot, then walked away and didn't give me a chance to ask why. Of course, my mind started to go a mile a minute and I questioned what I might have done wrong.

4

Abandoned by the Man

I walked out the locker room door into the back parking lot where Tommy and his tricked-out van were waiting. He sat in the driver's seat smoking a cigarette as if he were making love to it. I opened the passenger door and jumped onto the seat. Tommy didn't say a thing and off we drove. Eventually Tommy said, "I'm taking you some place special. You're going to 'my place,' and I expect you to make a good impression." I asked him where it was, but he just told me to be patient and wait.

We drove several miles until we got to the north side of Phoenix, where Tommy drove down a small road between two buildings. He parked behind a hole-in-the-wall bar with a back door. The building was so nondescript that if you drove past it, you wouldn't have known what it was. I had noticed a small sign on the front that was partially lit and flashed the business name PHYL'S COCKTAILS, so I had some clue.

We got out of the van and Tommy stopped for a minute to light a cigarette and smooth out his clothes. Then we went inside into a dark hallway that led to a long, narrow bar. Feeling somewhat relieved at first, I thought this was just going to be a couple of cold drinks and then on our way. That relief ended quickly as we walked into the main portion of the bar and I thought I had slipped into the cantina scene from *Star Wars*. You know the scene . . . where all the creatures are standing around a bar, long ears, big noses, and giant eyes. Or the hairy creatures with huge muscles and disfigured faces. This seemed like that. There were bikers that looked ready for war. Mafia types dressed in fine suits and slicked-back hair. Women with the look of a prostitute, and a number of other characters that looked like extras for a movie.

I started thinking to myself, what had Tommy brought me into? Was this some kind of joke or was he serious? Then I figured that he must be a regular because everyone treated him like a brother or a lover. His favorite drink, a beer, was handed to him right away, and a pool stick was stuck in his empty hand. The women were all over him and wanting his attention. Tommy didn't disappoint as he worked the room.

After I stood in the bar near Tommy for a while, he grabbed me by the shoulder and yelled to the crowd, "This is my new partner, take care of him." He looked at me and smiled with a chuckle. "These people are ours. They're all cops, and this is our place. Someplace where we can relax and not be 'on.' Make yourself at home, it's safe."

Tommy continued working the room all night, and every chance he had, he would bend the ear of one or more people standing around him. Each time he told them that I had what it took to be undercover, and he wanted them to take me under their wing as he had done. Because of Tommy, I was instantly accepted and became part of the crowd.

Every day when our shift ended, we headed back to the bar and I continued to hear stories and learn the art of being undercover. It was the best training that any cop could ever have received. My credibility with the department soared and my name recognition increased, all because Tommy vouched for me. I was his chosen one. You didn't need any more than that.

Alcohol defined most of the guys who were regulars at Phyl's. At work, they were normally calm and caring. After several hours at Phyl's, they became womanizers and had instant strength. Our shift would end at 10:00 p.m. and we would go to Phyl's and drink until the bar closed at 1:00 a.m. When the bar closed, someone would already have bought a ton of beer, and we would go into the parking lot for "choir practice"—the code for drinking after work. We would drink in the parking lot until the sun came up.

Along with all this camaraderie came additional support from the older officers and supervisors. One of the main people that stepped up as a mentor for me was Capt. Gerd Kurtenbach. He accepted me just as Tommy had and became the voice of reason in my head. He would guide me through the often-troubled waters that lay ahead. I respected him and loved him like a father. He treated me like a son, and so did his wife, Gerri, whom I would forever call Mom.

Working with Tommy, I prepared myself for an eventual assignment into the undercover world. Then Tommy asked if I would like to room with him in a two-bedroom town home. I jumped at the chance and saw it as fun and another opportunity to learn even more from Tommy. I didn't consider Tommy's drinking problem, even though it was blatantly obvious with each trip to Phyl's. His abuse of alcohol never affected his job performance, but it trashed his personal life and relationship potential. He was so much older than me that I didn't want to be disrespectful and bring attention to his alcohol abuse. I just shut my mouth and let him live his life as he chose.

After I moved into the town home, Tommy told me that I needed to bulk up if I was ever going to work undercover. An incredible cook, he began making meals designed for me to pack on the pounds. Every sitting included multiple pounds of meat, dozens of eggs, bread, and protein shakes. A workout program was also designed to add size that would eventually identify my characters. I worked out, ate, and worked until the time came that I was considered for an undercover position. I got bigger and bigger while my hair began to grow longer and longer. One day I even received a call from an older officer worried that I was using steroids. He couldn't have been further from the truth. I always knew where the line was and made sure I never crossed it. Every ounce of size came naturally with hard work—no steroids.

I also promised myself when I went undercover, I would never use drugs to be believable, get tattoos, or pierce my body. Nothing against those who have done all those things (except the drugs), but it wasn't going to work for me. If I couldn't be believable with my own gift of gab, then I wouldn't do the job. My choice was to be the best without ever crossing the line. Break the law by using drugs to be believable and you sell out. Then whom do the people you are protecting have to rely on?

As I was getting deeper undercover, Tommy was becoming

more and more hooked on the booze. He let his auto insurance lapse and started to become an angry drunk. Every visit to the bar would end with Tommy beating someone, but never me. In the heat of a fight I could pull Tommy back, and he wouldn't lay a hand on me. Anyone else . . . they would get sucker punched. My voice seemed enough to tone him down, and he didn't want to disappoint one of his own. He treated me like a son and showed me that same respect.

Most people in Tommy's position would be alienated from the group for all their outrageous behavior, but not Tommy. He had a gift to make everyone love him in spite of his bad-boy ways. They would forgive him within minutes of a fight and brush it off as his being "just Tommy." I don't know of anyone else that could have survived his relationship with Virginia and all the drama surrounding it.

As the months passed, I began to worry about Tommy and found it harder and harder to live in the same house because of his alcohol abuse. I was getting ready to start my undercover assignment and had dramatically increased my size to over 250 pounds. I was bench-pressing over four hundred pounds and becoming a powerful force. All because of Tommy's attention, but it was too tough to continue in that environment. We finally agreed to move into separate apartments, but at the last minute he decided to rent a room from another cop.

While all this was unfolding in my life, I was also dealing with the news of my mother being diagnosed with terminal cancer. I would spend as much time as possible trying to be with her while continuing with my life. It got to be really difficult dealing with Tommy, preparing for the loss of my mother, and growing into my career. The last thing I wanted to do was hurt Tommy, especially after all he had done for me. So I used my mother's illness as an excuse. I told Tommy that I needed to move because my mother had been diagnosed with cancer and I needed some space to cope. He said he understood and would support my decision, but I'm not completely sure he really ever did. I ended up using excuses because I never knew how to confront him and talk about his alcohol abuse. I wish I did though. Maybe everything would have turned out different. I've always shouldered some of the blame for Tommy's behavior because I didn't speak up to him.

My personal life started to become complicated as my mother neared her death. I saw her as a rock in my life and my sounding board in troubled times. When she finally died, I was devastated. At the time of her death I was sitting at home on an early Sunday morning in late August when I heard a knock at the door. The sun had been up for a few hours. I answered the door and was greeted by Captain Kurtenbach.

He told me Tommy had gone crazy after drinking and shot another officer living in the same house where Tommy had rented a room. Officer Ray Shaar had been shot multiple times and died in bed. Tommy was on the run and had robbed a store and kidnapped a family in Scottsdale, Arizona. He was eventually captured at a campground in Camp Verde, Arizona, where police negotiated his surrender.

I was sitting in church overseeing my mother's casket as the church service was conducted. When the service ended, fighting back tears, I walked the casket down the aisle to the waiting hearse. As I neared the back of the church, I almost had to shake

my head to clear my eyes when I saw Tommy seated there. He
had bonded himself out of jail to be at the funeral.

I was already filled with emotion from the almost insur-
mountable loss of my mother; now I had to add the loss of
Tommy. I felt abandoned. The only difference was that he had
come back and it almost seemed like a tease. I knew he couldn't
stay, and I knew he would be out of my life forever. What I really
wanted was everything to go back in reverse and to forget all this
had ever happened. My mother would be back in the kitchen
and Tommy would be showing me the ropes. That never happened because Tommy turned himself back into the jail once the
funeral was over.

Tommy was sentenced to twenty-eight and a half years in
prison and I have never seen him again. I always think about
what he meant to me and remember the good times we had. I
just know "that guy" died the day he killed Officer Ray Shaar.
The guy I knew before Ray's death is the guy I will forever remember. A day doesn't go by that he doesn't flash in my memory. It is so confusing to me that a man who had so much good
in him could turn out to be so violent. I never figured out what
made someone change so drastically. What I do know is that it
scares the hell out of me. Is it the job? Can the job and the undercover work make the animal in all of us raise its ugly head?

When Tommy went to prison, he tattooed his chest with a
dragon. When he was asked why he tattooed the dragon, he
calmly answered, "Everyone has a dragon in them. My dragon
is alcohol. When I wake up every morning and look in the mirror, I want to remember my dragon." Maybe that's the answer.
Identify your dragon and face it every day. You have to fight

the dragon to keep it controlled and never ignore its power and control over your life.

It didn't end there for me though. I had a run of really bad luck that has stayed with me through the remainder of my life. My mother died and left me without the strength and support that I truly relied upon. Tommy left me forever without a chance to ask, "Why?" Another regular at Phyl's was Sgt. Ed Bender. He spent many hours with me grooming my undercover skills. He also used my address as his own so he could live with his girlfriend and nobody would know. At the time, the department wouldn't condone cohabitation. If discovered, you were fired. (The chief believed it was immoral and violated the image of a clean-cut police officer.) Nobody will ever know what happened that horrific evening, but Ed shot and killed his girlfriend. He then turned the gun on himself and took his own life. All this while his girlfriend's children stood by and watched. And last, but not least, my friend Officer Curtis Hildreth found out that his ex-wife was getting married again. In a tragic fit of depression he killed his two young boys and himself so nobody else would be able to raise his children.

All this happened within six months and led my father to pull me aside and question my decision to be in law enforcement. I chose to serve and protect; now everyone I worked with was killing or being killed. I told Dad that I needed to carry on in spite of everything that had happened. I had an opportunity to make a difference, and I needed to seize the moment. He assured me that he would be there and stand with me through it all. He did just that until he died a few years later.

This job as a police officer gives everyone who accepts it a chance to make a difference. The public believes the men and women behind the badge will make all the right decisions and be there when they need them. Unconditional trust is what they give you, and they expect 100 percent honesty and commitment in return. I started to question if that was possible in light of all the events I had been faced with. The only answer I could find was to not quit and to carry on being a difference-maker. I laughed at myself thinking how I might be a little too naïve in my thoughts. The pressure and responsibility might be too much, and that's what drove all those men to mental-health issues and committing unthinkable acts. Or maybe I could be stronger and rise above the pressure. I knew only I could make the choice. And as I saw it, there was only one choice.

A message on my pager snapped me back to reality. I picked myself up from my mother's gravesite and headed back into the world that awaited me.

5

Kristle and the Candy Store

I **got on my bike and reached into the saddlebag for my** cell phone before I drove off. Flipped open the phone and started to dial the number left on my pager. The phone rang and someone answered, "Candy Store." Not recognizing the number at first, I was caught off guard until I could gather my senses.

I constantly battle with who I am and what I should sound like when I get calls. It becomes even more difficult in the early-morning hours when the phone rings and I'm in a deep sleep. I found it best to always answer "Yeah." Then let the caller carry on until I gather myself and I locate the character I need to be. It's a tough transition from biker warlord to Mafia hit man. The phone rings all the time and I hardly ever know who the caller is. Patience on my part and voice recognition helps get me to whom I need to be. I also never changed my dialect with the different people I dealt with. Using the same voice, but offering little conversation until I'm sure whom the caller is looking for, gives me some consistency and avoids my being caught short.

It often becomes funny in the middle of the night when the phone rings with the caller asking, "Who's this?" I respond, "Who's asking who's this?" The caller always seems mystified and either apologizes or comes back with "Who did I call?" At that point I just hang up and let the caller try it all over again.

When I heard the caller on the other end, I knew right away it was Kristie, a dancer from the topless bar called the Candy Store, where they knew me as Jake, a biker. People who worked there also knew that Jake was a regular at the bar and my go-to girl was Kristie. She only knew me as an outlaw biker and a powerful street criminal, but said she was attracted to me because something was different about me. Kristie rarely pushed me for sex and never asked for anything except my attention. She got her power by knowing me and using that to her advantage. Everyone left her alone because they feared my wrath if she was abused.

I made her believe that my "old lady" was a rich real estate broker that took good care of me. She let me do as I pleased and supported my lifestyle. Even though . . . Kristie believed I would eventually come to her when I left my old lady. Until then, she quietly waited and took care of my business at the topless club. At times, though, I would become concerned that Kristie was going to test me and make a move sexually. When I sensed those times coming, I would surround myself with crowds of people and keep her at a distance. She could hang on me and rub on me, but the crowd kept the intercourse issue under wraps. It seems hard to believe, but these girls just want to say they belong to somebody. It doesn't matter how much commitment you give them if they can say, "That's my old man."

At times I would also gather up some undercover women who would pose as prostitutes and take them to the Candy Store. Kristie's fear of losing her power by not being associated with me kept her jealousy under control. Instead of getting upset, she would ask if she could go home with all of us and party together. I'd just laugh and tell her I wanted her all by myself and our day would be soon. Kristie was like all the girls in the club, incredibly beautiful but insecure. They needed constant reassurance and would accept any behavior from the man they had their heart set on. It didn't take much to keep them happy, and even less to hold their attention. Just promise something and wait awhile. When they ask again, make another promise. You never fulfill the promises and they just keep hanging in there.

All my pretend behavior made me feel guilty, though. I didn't go around using people to get what I needed. But in this world I had to be an insincere asshole that used everyone around him. What would happen was, in spite of my efforts to be a tough guy, my good side always rose to the top and the people recognized it. If it didn't, then Kristie might not have been so accepting of a fruitless relationship.

Kristie was my credibility in the bar and vouched for who I was, and that I had been around for a long time. I could take clients into the club and be instantly greeted by half-naked women who handed me and the clients drinks at no charge. The clients got attention immediately, and any questions they had about me were instantly gone. Business progressed and I was believable. All it takes to confuse another man and distract him is to throw a half-naked woman in his face and do it for free.

I told the doorman at the Candy Store when he answered the phone that it was Jake and someone had called for me. He respectfully asked me to hold, and after a few moments Kristie got on the other line and said, "Jake, a regular in here by the name of Harry wants to talk to you. He asked if you could stop by." I told Kristie that I was too busy and to put him on hold, but she said that might not be a good idea. Harry was anxious to meet me and had been bugging her for weeks to set up the meeting. He was starting to get irritated. I told her to tell Harry that I would meet him when I was ready, not a minute sooner. "And warn him, Kristie," I said, "don't fuck with me!" She agreed and said she would hold him off a little longer. The call then ended abruptly.

I fired up the bike and headed to the safe house, where I could find out what was next for me to do. The safe house was a warehouse located in a commercial district that blended in with every other business. The panel doors opened as I drove up and rolled inside.

The warehouse was an interesting place with another six undercover cops all scurrying around working on deals and writing reports. I was the only one doing the hit-man thing, but they all had their own special talents and clientele. Ricky Lo worked with Colombians, while Gary looked like an old, gray-haired man who was a stolen-property dealer. Or as the crooks knew him, a fence for stolen property. My closest friend at the warehouse was Tim "Coon Dog" Cooning. He looked exactly like Charles Manson and was the best undercover cop I had ever met, believable and incredibly talented. I also knew I could trust him with my life because he had proved that on a couple of occasions.

You see, I had the benefit of size and strength, but not fire-power. I didn't like guns and rarely carried one. But that didn't stop others from trying to shoot me.

When you got inside the warehouse, you found a whole new world that had many moving parts. One room was designed for all the video and audio equipment used to capture the deals or transactions on tape. Another room was office space for paperwork, and attached to it was a "down room" for rest and a shower. Yet another room had weight-lifting equipment, arcade games to hone your skills, a pool table, a basketball court, and an archery range. All to help the guys unwind. Nobody except the undercover cops was allowed in the warehouse. It was a safe house for only those in the program.

With the bike parked away safely, I headed into the office space at the far end of the building. DD grabbed me by the arm and told me that I needed to get ahold of Sgt. Bill Wren because he had another hit for me to do. I've known Billy for my entire career and have always respected him. He's easygoing and a friend of everyone he has ever met. Billy stayed in patrol and moved through the ranks of supervision, and his supervisory skills matched his interpersonal skills.

I agreed to call Billy the next day and find out what he had come up with. For tonight though I needed to get some sleep and start planning how I was going to win over Patti. The way my luck with women ran, I'd finally get a date with Patti and be out somewhere in public. Probably laying my best stuff on her when I got a tap on my shoulder. I'd look up and it would be Kristie, dressed like a million-dollar hooker. Nothing new for her, and she would climb in my lap and start running her hands up and down my body, kissing my neck, and rubbing herself as she moaned in my ear. Then I'd look at Patti and she would stand up and walk away. That was another nightmare for me to worry about, and with my luck it would have a great probability of happening.

6

Gun for Hire

It's beginning to feel like each day is the same as the previous day as I get up and head off to the gym for an early-morning workout. All the guys I work out with are great, and they take each session seriously. One of the guys just retired from the Pittsburgh Steelers and warms up by pressing 225 pounds twenty times. Another guy is still with the Jets and trains as hard as he plays the game. As for me . . . I'm just glad to be in the group and have all this motivation around me to get bigger and stronger with each lift. This group fits me perfectly because I eat up the challenge of training daily with incredible athletes.

After a couple of hours passed and the session was over, I sped back to the house and got ready for *Guiding Light*. I know I could miss a month of this show and be caught up within minutes, but that still doesn't stop me from watching every day.

When the show ended, I picked up the phone and called Billy. As soon as he answered the phone, he gave me shit about not calling a day earlier when he was trying to get ahold of me. Then he got serious and said he had a "strange one" for me. Leigh Wilson owned a business by the name of Guns for Hire, on the east side of Phoenix. The business was both a gun store and an office for a western stage-show company contracted for corporate parties. Leigh and his wife also double as private investigators.

An unknown female called Leigh and said she was hoping he could take care of a problem she had. She was vague, but told Leigh that she wanted to hire him to "kill someone" and the murder had to be done in Canada. He asked her to call back the next day and he would see if he could make the arrangements for her. Leigh finished by saying that he knew a lot of people who could take care of "things."

Leigh said he thought she was joking at first. Nobody would be that bold and open about a murder. He also thought at first she was trying to book one of his western stage shows and was joking with him. That thought changed the longer the call continued. He soon realized the lady wasn't joking around and was serious.

The second time the lady called Leigh, he recorded her call on tape. She told Leigh that her name was Jenny. Leigh told her that he knew several people that could take care of different kinds of problems, but he wasn't going to say any more than that. He told me that he had decided to play with her and see just how far she would go.

Jenny questioned if Leigh's phone was safe to talk on and what would be best for her to say. He told her to talk in generalities and not to discuss the facts. She agreed and began talking almost in code. She spoke of Canada and "the sooner the better." Funds would be at the airport in a safe-deposit box, and she would send the key as soon as everything was complete. Jenny didn't want face-to-face meetings so she could avoid any obvious connection with her and the hit man.

Leigh arranged for Jenny to call back later and they would finalize the deal. She agreed and called back two days later when I was seated at the phone next to Leigh.

I follow the same steps each time I enter a murder-for-hire case. I try to get a phone conversation with the client before a meeting. That worked 95 percent of the time and would give me a huge insight into what they wanted, how committed they were, and whom they were looking for to do the job.

As I said earlier, people watch television and believe everything they see on TV. They go to the movies and also believe those to be true. How the directors develop a character is how the public believes that person should act in real life. That's why I always watch television and develop my character from the eye of the director.

When I spoke to clients, I listened closely to all they said and I considered the type of people they were. All factors, such as education, financial status, gender, race, age, and conversation were considered in my character development. I wanted to give you everything your confused mind believed I should be. If I got into your head, I knew that I had won half the battle. The rest was easy.

I had always made it a point to understand what makes the people around me tick. I wanted to know their birthdays and favorite foods. What made them the happiest and who inspired them. Then I could be a true friend who showed he cared through actions and not just words. If I was going to be your friend, then I was going to know everything I could about you and your world. I transferred this same ambition to my hit-man clients. I learned everything I could before I even had the first meeting. That was one way to make them comfortable early on and accept me for who I said I was.

My planning for the call with Jenny was going to be no different from any other preparation I had ever done for a hit. I made sure I learned everything about her from Leigh before we met and before we spoke on the phone. My goal was to analyze the type of person doing what Jenny was about to do, and to try to understand what makes a woman sacrifice everything for one single moment. I have learned over time that all the women who have hired me have similar traits. You don't even have to know them before you meet them. You just have to know one, and the rest will mirror that one. Greed was always their common motivator. Feed the greed and they will follow you and believe in you. Almost like being an evangelist.

Leigh told Jenny that he had found the person she was looking for. He described me to Jenny and told her that I had worked for him before and had done several things for him. She believed that with my reputation and the kind of person I was, it would make a difference in how things were done.

Then it was my turn.

I got on the phone and immediately took control and put Jenny on the defensive. Our conversation started as a chess match and continued the same throughout. She would question my commitment and whether I would set her up. I questioned her sincerity and whether she was a cop.

Jenny operated from a totally incorrect premise. She said she had long ago learned that if you ask someone if he is a cop and he says he isn't, then you are safe if he turns out to be a cop. Sounds good, but it doesn't work that way in Arizona. Police officers can lie and continue to do their job if acting in an undercover capacity. The mere job of undercover is a lie. Hell, my whole undercover life was developed from one lie after another.

I had recently heard from one of the guys that many of the women in my real life didn't believe a thing I said. They'd look at me and know what I did for a living and assumed I couldn't tell the difference between the truth and a lie. What they'd apparently been saying was that if I didn't know the difference, then I couldn't expect them to trust me. I couldn't catch a break. Here I stood with low-life women hanging on my every word and believing everything I said. On the other hand I had the women in my real life doubting my every word and questioning all my actions, all because I pretended and lived a lie. And my life was being lived so other people could be safe and secure.

All Jenny wanted from me was to trust that I could do the job she hired me to do. And when I finished her job, I would never contact her again. Most important, if I got caught, I would never tell about her. Jenny also said she wanted everything done over the phone and never to meet face-to-face. That definitely wasn't going to happen. If she continued to demand the no-meet clause, then I would tell her to move on and find someone else. I told her I wanted to see her face-to-face. I wanted to know exactly whom I was dealing with so I could find her if she turned on me.

I always play hard to get. I make you believe that you want me more than anyone else. No matter what I say or do, you stay with me and don't go anywhere else. Of course, unless you aren't really that committed to having someone killed. I get inside your head immediately and get you to know you shouldn't be with me because I'm really bad, but you like and want me so much that you won't let me go. People have told me over the years they had been searching a lifetime for someone like me. That's when I know I totally have you believing my act.

We continued to banter back and forth until Jenny seemed to become comfortable with me. She told me the person I was to kill was her current husband, who lived in Vancouver, Canada. She had already decided how she wanted him killed and explained it to me when I asked. Her plan came from crime novels that she had read, and she wanted him blown up when he was in his car.

Crime novels and soap operas—I already knew exactly how to deal with this gal. I'd watched enough soap operas to realize what she was looking for in a hit man and how she expected everything to work out. Her world was nothing more than a dangerous fantasy.

We talked about their neighborhood in Canada and where would be the best location to have him blown up. Jenny then offered to pay me $10,000 for the entire deal. That would be all she could get off the books from her husband's business without attracting attention. I agreed to the $10,000, but demanded $2,000 more for expenses. She agreed as long as she didn't have to put up a large amount in the beginning. She wanted to pay part now, then the rest when it was over. She had known someone that paid $7,500 up front for something and the person never completed the job.

I'm sure she never knew anyone that was ripped off for the

money in a deal similar to ours. She probably read it in one of her romance novels. My guess is that everything she came up with was from those books.

Jenny's husband was selling his masonry-supply business, and she wanted his murder to look like a mob hit that was related to the business sale. Both Jenny and her husband lived on a yacht in the marina, and she didn't want him killed there. Someone at the marina would suspect her if it happened there.

Tough life for a rich girl who had obviously had everything provided for her. She had so much and needed so little that boredom had set in. Her only alternative in her pathetic life filled with family, friends, money, and the respect of the community was to "off" her husband. Then she could run off with another man. And here we go again, she gets immediate gratification until the initial rush of her new relationship wears off.

I finally convinced Jenny to meet in the parking lot of a Black Angus restaurant in Mesa, Arizona. The meeting would be the following day, and this would give her plenty of time to rethink her decision. A decision that would impact the rest of her life . . . and the life of her family.

From my conversation with Jenny I had learned so much about her that I immediately knew the character I was going to be. She was obviously rich and spoiled. Lived on a yacht in Vancouver, Canada, and had access to her husband's business and money. Her husband traveled around the world making deals for his masonry business and probably paid little attention to his high-maintenance princess. She'd read too many crime novels and her mind was twisted from the trash written in those fiction books.

I decided to give her a character right out of a crime novel.

Jenny was going to meet an ex-convict who killed for a living. Everybody believes that's real-life stuff, especially "little Jenny."

Jenny had the same belief as so many other people that have only read about Arizona and never visited. John Wayne lived in Arizona and hundreds of western movies have been filmed throughout the state. Travel guides and history books tell stories of how the Indians and cowboys pioneered Arizona and developed it into the great state it is today. Visitors from other countries tour the many tribal reservations and attend western shows like the one's produced by Leigh. People still think they will come to Arizona and find cowboys and Indians fighting in the streets.

Jenny's skewed knowledge from all she had read led her to check the yellow pages to try to locate a "gunslinger" from the Wild West. When she found "Guns for Hire," she was sure she had located a company with contract killers. It's funny how the mind can be so confused by reading novels. Jenny's imagination had run away with any responsible thought she may ever have had.

I researched Jenny's life through numerous criminal searches when she finally told me her real name was Sharleen Bath. She was forty-six years old and lived in Vancouver, Canada, with her husband, Jim, and one daughter and one son. Sharleen and Jim had been together since they were thirteen years old and had developed a major masonry business from the ground up. They lived on a yacht, and Sharleen had fallen in love with the marina manager. When she started to act strangely while at home, Jim became concerned and thought she might be getting sick. He never considered she was having an affair. Jim took her to the doctor, who diagnosed chronic fatigue syndrome. Jim then decided to send her to Mesa, Arizona, after her doctor recommended warm weather as the path for her recovery.

Jim's main mistake was that he loved Sharleen so much he would do anything for her. Because he worked so many hours in a day to provide a special life for her, she became bored and started playing with the "marina boy." When Jim took Sharleen to Mesa, Arizona, to recover, he never thought she would spend her time planning his death.

Sharleen saw the trip to Mesa as being exiled. She couldn't be with her new lover and felt abandoned by the family. She turned to reading crime novels, and Danielle Steele romance novels. All her reading led her to hatch a plan to kill Jim so she could go home and be with her lover. Her first mistake was having an affair. Her second and final mistake was believing everything she read in those romance novels that had begun to define her life.

The following morning came and I readied myself for the meeting with Sharleen. She had told me she would be wearing a hot-pink jacket. It would be hard to miss that. The team that was going to tape the meeting had concerns that I might be set up in this deal. Sharleen had seemed unusually sure of what she wanted and asked questions that left us wondering about her true motives. I also wondered if a real hit man had discovered who I was and wanted to take me out. The more you live the complex life I had entered, the more unsure you become of your surroundings. Everyone looks suspicious, and everything people do appears to have an ulterior motive.

We became so concerned about a setup by another hit man,

or another police department, that we arranged to have the SWAT team on the roofs of buildings and at different locations in the area. If it was a setup, then we were definitely going to be ready.

I arrived in the parking lot of the Black Angus restaurant and stood back in the shadows of the building. I watched as a maroon 1989 Lincoln with British Columbia plates arrived in the parking lot. At the wheel was a small, blond-haired woman wearing a hot-pink jacket and driving suspiciously through the lot. I watched her for a while, then decided to make her wait and build some suspense that would make her nervous and give me an edge. I also began checking the area and surrounding rooftops for any other activity that might be out of place. When people are so desperate they want to have someone killed, anything can happen; anything is possible.

After Sharleen was parked for a while I went over to her car. She got out of the driver's seat and asked if I was Jake. When I said yes, she pulled a pad of paper from the car and said she had several questions for me. Little did I know this was going to be a job interview.

Before I let Sharleen intently question me, I asked her how much money she had. She told me she had $1,900. Some of it American money, some Canadian. She told me about the money with such confidence I knew we could continue with our deal.

"I've got questions for you too as to how much money you got that you're gonna be able to pay me," I told her.

"Today?" Sharleen asked.

"Yeah! Today."

"I have two thousand . . . minus one hundred. I went to the

bank and took what I needed and then found out I'm a hundred short."

"But you got damn near two thousand dollars?"

"Yeah."

Sharleen seemed to be as calm as a mother nursing her newborn. She didn't really act as suspicious as I thought she should be during our negotiations. It made wonder if she had medicated herself before our meeting.

"Okay, you tell me if this sounds good to you. I want the rest of the money in a locker at the Vancouver airport. You leave me the key and I'll collect the remainder when I'm completed."

As we continued to talk, I kept looking around and watched as a landscaper turned on his weed blower. The noise concerned me. I needed to capture the audio from Sharleen's conversation. If the noise from the weed blower was too loud, the audio would be compromised. I decided to stand a little closer to her, but not so close that I intimidated her too much. While I was getting a better position, I noticed a suspicious vehicle drive through the parking lot with tinted windows. The vehicle drove by again, and again, which fueled my concern about a setup.

I didn't show Sharleen any concern over the car, but the SWAT team immediately redirected their attention to the suspicious vehicle and its occupant. My job was to stay focused on Sharleen and ignore everything else. If she had set me up and I was going to be hit, then so be it. I wasn't going to worry about it. Let the team take care of things around me and I'd focus on Sharleen.

Sharleen held a piece of notepaper in her hand. She had drawn up a number of questions about how she would be protected if I was ever caught. The questions seemed to flow from her mouth as if she had practiced their delivery over and over before we met:

"Have you ever done this before and been successful? Or been fingerprinted, and did you ever get a criminal charge? . . . How do you know that there will be no trace to you? . . . If you get caught and turn state's evidence and plea-bargain, you could accuse me and get a light sentence for yourself and the max for me. What do you have to say about that? . . . There, of course, will be an investigation. You can't leave any leads. From your experience can you tell me what form this investigation will take?"

I had to convince her that I was good at what I did and would not get caught. If for some unforeseen reason I did get caught, then I would do my time in prison. I had no problem doing time, and that was where I was the most comfortable. It was nothing for me to go back to prison. Sharleen believed everything I told her about my time in prison and success at murder.

All Sharleen wanted from me was to have Jim killed while he drove his car, preferably away from work. She gave me a hand-drawn map of how to get to Jim's workplace and a description of his business. She also handed me a picture of Jim to make sure I didn't kill the wrong person. One of her biggest fears was that I would accidentally kill her son after mistaking him for Jim. I suggested that I just shoot Jim, but Sharleen thought a bullet could easily be traced back to her.

She provided everything I needed to find Jim. She had done her homework and knew what she wanted. She just didn't have the nerve to do it herself. Someone might suspect her so she needed distance from the killing.

As Sharleen told me of her perfect murder plan, I watched one of the SWAT vehicles race through the parking lot. They were obviously onto something, but I didn't know what until later. Even with everything happening around me, I stayed in the game with Sharleen. The SWAT team was the best in the state, and I was confident they would take care of any threat. The threat turned out to be another police agency, which had received a call about suspicious activity in the parking lot. The SWAT team jumped on it to stop the police from acting, which would have blown everything.

Sharleen thought she wanted Jim drowned in the marina. The only problem with that was it could be traced back to her and her boyfriend, who also lived in the marina. Sharleen then shocked me when she said that she had already contacted another individual to murder Jim. That person talked too much though and would eventually lead police back to her.

In that one moment Sharleen confirmed what I have always said: people who are committed to murder will get it done one way or another. *If they don't find me, they will find someone else.*

The only thing that Sharleen cared about was herself and whether she would be caught and sentenced to prison. I tried to convince her to consider divorce. She told me divorce was absolutely out of the question. Her family could never deal with a divorce, but they could get over the murder of Jim. Sharleen was a socialite in Vancouver and a Sunday-school teacher. The faith that she and her family practiced prohibited divorce.

Sharleen questioned my chances of getting caught and the police being led directly to her. I told her over and over that I wouldn't be caught, and they couldn't locate me because I didn't live in Arizona. No ties to Arizona, and no identification making me a resident.

I jokingly told her that I would eat a bug if I got caught. She stood a little taller and looked at me in a peculiar way. "What do you mean eat a bug?" Sharleen asked. I responded, "Eat a bug!" She asked again, "What's 'eat a bug,' I don't know what that means, some sort of code?" I had to become more assertive with her and settle her down. Once I did that, we were able to talk more about money and the specifics.

I thought this was the moment my deal with Sharleen would end. She was so incredibly suspicious that anything I said could cause her concern. When she backed off after I got into her personal space, I was really relieved. I can only believe that her greed outweighed her suspicion and kept me in the game.

Sharleen was an odd little lady who looked as if she should have been at the tennis club and not with me talking about murder. Everything I said left her with another question and her continued concern about being caught. I normally watch my intimidation with a woman, but she left me no choice but to get in her space and constantly reverse her inquisitive questions to take her off guard. It eventually worked and she handed me an envelope saying that everything was inside.

I opened the envelope and found 675 Canadian dollars and 1,309 dollars in U.S. currency. She also included a Canadian dollar coin. The loonie was Sharleen's little gift to me, and she thought herself a bit cute giving it with all the other money. The balance of the money was to be paid after Jim was killed and could be found in a Vancouver International Airport locker.

A description of Jim's 1990 blue Bronco was also provided and where it would be parked.

All the conversation and exchange of items were captured under the careful eye of a camera surveillance team. They sat literally yards away from me as they filmed every minute and word with Sharleen. When it was time to give the surveillance team a code alerting them to make the arrest, the film crew passed it on.

The prearranged code to arrest Sharleen was for me to walk away from her to my car to count the money. When I knew that I had everything necessary to make a strong case against Sharleen, I walked away and told her I would return after I counted the money. Once away from Sharleen, I watched out the side of my eye as the SWAT team swiftly moved toward her and grabbed her before she could run. She looked surprised and calmly lay on the hood of her car as the police handcuffed her.

The SWAT team members escorted Sharleen to the awaiting police car, where she was placed behind a screen in the backseat. After fifteen minutes had passed, I walked toward the vehicle to give further direction on where she was to go. As I looked in the window, she looked me in the eyes and said, "If you weren't so good, I would have never done this. You made me believe!"

The oddest part of this whole investigation was Jim and his commitment to Sharleen. He never believed that she could have done this. His explanation was that her sickness forced her into the odd behavior. He didn't want to prosecute her and also paid for her attorney, Alan Bickert. Jim flew in from Canada and came to see her every weekend while she was in jail. Eventually, though, he divorced her several years after she was released from prison. Jim was a caring, loving man who never wanted to believe all this was possible. The whole mess destroyed Sharleen's family, and she eventually died from cancer. Her boyfriend, Dal Young, also died, of heart disease, and her son died of cancer as well.

7

Deadeye and the Shark

Months had passed since my meeting with Sharleen, and I continued to do one murder for hire after another. Boston Jimmy came to me as I was drinking a beer one evening and offered me $10,000 to kill his boss at the car dealership where he worked as a lot boy. This was the same boss that had given Boston a job when he was released from prison after serving twelve years for armed robbery. Now he hated the man and wanted him killed because the boss yelled at him for not detailing one of the cars on the lot. Mortimer Hylton hired me to blow up a restaurant with seventy-five people that included his business partners. They had left him to defend himself on a fraud charge and he felt disrespected. When told there would be collateral damage and huge loss of life after two pounds of C-4 were used in the blast, he just responded, "A message has got to be sent." Roosevelt July was in jail on an assault and robbery charge. He beat and robbed an elderly woman in her home and got caught. Roosevelt wanted me to kill her so she couldn't testify against him. The requests went on and on, and I met each person to determine his or her level of commitment and to decide if I was willing to negotiate a deal.

The upcoming Friday night was going to be a big night for me because I had to hang out with my insane informant Deadeye, but first I was off to a party at Phyl's for a detective who was leaving undercover work and going to be a pilot for the Air Support Unit. Mike was a guy I admired and really liked. Always funny, he knew something about everything. You always hear about people that act as if they know something about everything, but Mike really did!

As soon as I walked in the back door, I was greeted by everyone along the hallway into the main area. It's interesting how times had changed. Not so long ago I'd walked in the same door with Tommy and he'd got the same exact greeting. I was just a puppy following in his footsteps hoping to pick up some scraps. Now here I was getting the same attention he had. The difference was that I didn't fight the people I cared about the way Tommy did, and I didn't start any trouble in Phyl's. I still respected the old guys and still listened to everything they had to say. I continued to be a sponge, hoping for that nugget of information that would make me better than any other undercover cop had ever been.

When I got inside the main area, I spotted Patti sitting at the bar with her sister and DD. I felt a shot of adrenaline upon seeing her and found myself out of sorts again. I went to the table where my close pal, Alex Femenia, was seated. I asked if he knew Patti was in the bar, and he laughed as if to say, "Hell yes, I know." I told Alex I wanted to talk to her, but wasn't sure how to do it. My whole persona of confidence had escaped me, and I was like a little schoolboy with a crush and completely frozen in one spot.

A drink or two had been served to Alex's table before I decided I could make my way over to Patti and start up a conversation. When I finally walked over, I stumbled with words and looked like an idiot. She seemed pleasantly surprised to see me, and her gentle voice made me relax while I was with her. Patti stayed seated at the bar while we talked, and I stood next to her while everything around me seemed irrelevant. There could have been naked women dancing throughout the bar and I wouldn't have noticed them. Finally I summoned up the nerve to ask Patti on a date for the following night, and to my surprise she accepted.

Since the first time I had met Patti, she must have asked DD or someone else some questions about me. I just knew this had to be true because when I asked her for her phone number, she refused to give it to me. She said, "I'll tell you what. You give me your number and I'll call you. You're a single guy, right? Shouldn't be any problem with me calling you at home."

Even though I was a bit surprised at her offer, I was good with her calling me at home and told her so. I later learned that some of the other women in the bar had told Patti I was a difficult man to be with. Hard to catch and even harder to hold down. If you hooked up with me, it wouldn't be for long. Now that's just the reputation I needed when trying to catch a girl who was already difficult to impress.

I finally gave her my phone number at the house, then set a date for 7:00 p.m. the following evening. In addition to Patti, I was also going to get a date that evening with her ten-year-old son, Geoff. She told me that if I went out with her, then I went out with her boy. That was quite a change from my nights out at the strip clubs.

After securing the date for the next night, I left the bar and headed out to be with Deadeye. I felt like a million bucks when I left Phyl's because I thought I might just have a chance with someone who seemed really special. In my crazy way of thinking, she would just have said no if she didn't like me. She didn't say no, so that told me I was good to go. I hadn't experienced an opportunity like this for a long time and didn't plan on messing it up.

I had driven my old International pickup truck for the evening just in case I would have to tow Deadeye around town. The truck was primer gray and had an old-time three speed with the stick shift on the floor. It wasn't fast, but you could drive over a Mack truck and come out the winner. Deadeye and the truck had a lot in common. He was about as beat-up as the truck, and probably just as slow.

As I drove down the road, I found myself daydreaming again and feeling a confused anxiety starting to consume me. The only thing I could figure out was that being around Patti had brought me back to my "comfort place." That place was fighting internally with whom I had become and the world I now lived in. More and more I would realize the "character" that was me had become my dominant personality and I found that I didn't like that guy. But I had to be that character to survive in my world. I couldn't go back to the person I once knew because everyone saw me for what I looked like. What people saw is what they believed they were going to get.

I remember my father always lectured me about never asking for things you don't really want and need. Apparently I didn't listened too well because I definitely asked for this assignment and now I wasn't sure if I wanted it any longer. How to make it work and not lose my mind was going to be the challenge.

I would go to either of two places when I needed to be Jack and to leave Jake at the curb for a while. The first place was always the cemetery, where I could talk to my mother. The other place was back to the old neighborhood and my Little League field. I could sit at the field and watch as the young kids played their games. Nothing felt better to me than the smell of the grass and to hear the sounds of a game being played. It was like home and brought back a rush of feelings, all of them good. When I would ride away, I would almost feel new again.

So many great memories had come from my playing in the Cartwright Little League, and here I was years later trying to recapture those feelings. I've always felt when you find yourself getting lost, it serves you well to go home. Go back to where it all began and search for those feelings and smells of happiness. The sounds and smells will trigger something inside you and bring you home again. Then it will ground you and give you a chance to recover.

Of course, I had to stay totally away from the field and sit in the dark away from everyone else. I didn't want people to stare or to worry about their kids being grabbed. I almost felt like the creature from *Beauty and the Beast*. I could have stayed away and not enjoyed the feeling I got from the park, but then where would I turn since nobody was there to fill that void?

Patti seemed to make me think about all of this. She was the first person that had confused me and made me wish for my normal life. But then I kicked myself and reminded myself why I was doing what I did and how I had a chance to make a difference. Self-evaluation was a constant for me and was how I survived. A day didn't ever pass that I didn't evaluate myself from the inside and remember who I really was and what my mission was.

I was sure I would know by the next day if the feelings stirred up by Patti were for real or if I was just feeling sorry for myself.

Deadeye had called and told me to meet him at a hole-in-the-wall bar located in Glendale, Arizona. The bar had enough room for fifteen people, and when full, it was crowded. Deadeye was an ex-convict from the Arizona State Prison. While in prison he joined the Aryan Brotherhood and was considered one of the most dangerous and temperamental inmates at the facility. He had spent so many years in prison that he had become antisocial and didn't know how to acceptably interact socially in society. He had no fear of death and definitely had no respect for the life of others.

The Aryan Brotherhood is a white supremacist group that operates both inside and outside prison. They are most powerful inside the prison walls because dope isn't as prevalent inside as it is on the streets. They control the dope in prison and that lends them power. When members get out of prison and go back to the streets, they normally begin to use their drug of choice, and that leads them straight to heroin abuse and addiction. Once on the heroin they can only think about their next fix. They are so consumed with drugs that they forget about everything else and become a minimal threat to law enforcement. The only time they become a concern is when they are cornered and react like a caged animal or rattlesnake. They strike quickly, violently, then get away by slithering into the darkness.

After being in the prison for many years Deadeye was contacted by a young girl who worked for her father, a minister. She believed she could change Deadeye, and while working with him, she fell in love. Or so she said. She was a naïve Southern Baptist who had been protected by her father her entire life. She was also beautiful, and that made everyone wonder what she saw in Deadeye.

When I walked into the bar, I saw Deadeye playing pool with a group of men that were clean-cut and appeared to be college students. They didn't seem to belong in that dump, but I didn't give it another thought. Deadeye was an evil man with an equally evil face. While in prison he told other Aryan Brotherhood members that he had fallen in love with the minister's daughter and had found the Lord. He didn't want to be in the Aryan Brotherhood any longer and wanted to do his time quietly until he was released.

The Aryan Brotherhood is governed by a set of rules they enforce themselves. The main rule is "blood in, blood out." This means that you kill or seriously hurt someone before you become a member. If you want out, your blood will be spilled.

The members waited until Deadeye least expected it and used a prison-made gun to shoot him in the face. The gunshot scarred Deadeye's face, and his right eye was so damaged it had to be removed. The doctors sewed the eye socket shut, and Deadeye was given his new nickname.

Deadeye couldn't get along with anyone. He was forever getting into fights and seemed to seek out people he could agitate and fight with. I was surprised when I walked into the bar because he seemed to be playing well with the group at the pool table. As I got closer, I realized that Deadeye had been betting with the group and had taken most of their money in pool games. The more he won, the more he made fun of them and embarrassed them by loudly proclaiming that they "sucked." After being in the bar for about thirty minutes, I knew it was time to go or we wouldn't get out alive.

I waited a bit too long to leave because all of a sudden the group turned into a mob and demanded all their money back. Deadeye told them to play with each other in the bathroom because that was the only thing they were going to get. He wasn't giving the money back. As the group became more upset, I decided to step in and save Deadeye from a beating or, more important, save the group from being stabbed by Deadeye. He couldn't lose his prison ways even on the street and always resorted to stabbing someone when he didn't get his way. Almost like a two-year-old who gets mad and bites. Well, Deadeye had the mentality and social skills of a two-year-old. Once he stabbed you, then he was all better and calmed right down. No remorse though . . . just recovered from the moment of anger.

I walked into the group and told them to back off because Deadeye was on his way out. I threatened to hurt each of them if they followed us outside, then grabbed Deadeye by the arm and pulled him out the door to my truck. The group was really unruly and I wasn't sure that we were going to get outside. When we did, we got into the truck and Deadeye began laughing hysterically like a madman. I sat and watched Deadeye for a moment until I felt the barrel of a gun pressed against my left temple. I heard an angry man yelling that he wanted his money back or I was getting shot in the head. Deadeye was yelling,

"Shoot him, motherfucker, he don't care." Deadeye kept telling the shooter to shoot me, escalating the moment until it was unstoppable.

The emotional pressure was incredible as I felt the gun against my head on one side, and Deadeye yelling at the shooter on the other side. For a moment I felt as if my mind was in slow motion and I could hardly think. I knew that at any minute the shooter would react to Deadeye's taunting and pull the trigger. The only choice I had was to quickly reach up with my left hand and grab the shooter's wrist. The move would be risky because a sympathetic reflex might cause the gun to fire. But thanks to Deadeye's big mouth, I had no choice.

I quickly grabbed the wrist of the shooter through the open window and pushed the gun forward. Then I pulled back and forth on his arm until he seemed to be losing his balance. I knew that at any minute the gun was going to fire, but that didn't stop me. After one more forward push the shooter fell to the ground, and I quickly reversed the truck out of its parking space onto the street.

Once I put the truck into gear to go forward, I watched as the shooter got off the ground and turned toward me. He raised the gun toward me and leveled it, readying himself to shoot. I told big-mouth Deadeye to lie down on the seat, but of course he had a death wish and wanted to see the shooter fire the gun. He yelled that he wanted to see the bullet if he was going to be shot.

With the truck pointed directly at the shooter, I accelerated quickly at him. He bailed out of the way, and as I drove by, he began firing his gun. To my surprise none of the windows were struck and he missed the entire truck.

Deadeye sat in the seat and counted his money as we drove

away. None of it seemed to faze him. He just counted away and acted as if we had never experienced any of the past fifteen minutes. Meanwhile, my heart was racing and I had visions of a gunshot to the head. All I could think of was throwing Deadeye out of the truck, but I giggled to myself and we moved on to another pool hall for the rest of the night. As I giggled, though, I thought to myself how I had become somewhat like Deadeye. I was almost killed and here I sat laughing.

In my early years as a patrolman I worked for a man whom I learned to respect early on, Sgt. Dave Pennington. He was cut from the same cloth as an old television cop named McCloud. Dave was tall and thin and claimed to be a Southern man who had relocated to Arizona. He spoke slowly and with a Southern drawl that forced you to pay attention. We always waited to see what he would say next and how he would say it. I remember one time when we were running out to the convenience store and asked if anyone wanted anything, Dave piped up, "Get me a Moon Pie and an RC cola." He was completely serious, but all I could do was laugh and walk out the door.

I always sat around and listened to Dave while he told his stories of the early policing days. If you listened long enough, he would throw out a nugget of information that would serve you well the rest of your career. "Always listen to the convicts and learn what makes them tick. Pay close attention to their tattoos because they will tell you a story," Dave would say. I remembered those words and stored them where I could find them when the time came for their use. Dave went on to be my sergeant for a time while I worked undercover. His words and leadership were invaluable.

On Dave' suggestion, I hooked up with Deadeye to play the role of an Aryan Brotherhood member from prison. This was no easy task because it meant that he would be killed if other members found out. Without the member's guidance, though, I could never be as believable as I needed to be. If I wasn't believable, I would surely die. Dying was never an option I considered.

In the criminal world where I operated, this membership meant instant respect. The only people that didn't get the respect thing were the college kids at the bar who tried to shoot me. The problem with Deadeye was that he never had enough sense to guide me and train me. He was just a good cover.

I could never have convinced Deadeye to trust me if not for Aryan Brotherhood leader Mark "the Shark" Scibillia. Mark told Deadeye that he could trust me, even though I was a cop, and that I would treat him fairly. Mark had come to me when he decided he wanted out of the Aryan Brotherhood. He is dead now, but he died making a difference as an informant for me, and not being the cold-blooded murderer he once was.

Mark told me after I agreed to let him work with me that I would someday be proud of his life change. He said, "I know words are cheap, Jake, so I won't ramble on about how I really intend to turn my life around. Just let me say this. When the day comes that you can see with your own eyes that I have beat the odds and made something of my life, I will be a happy man."

He called me right before he died and wanted me to know that he had removed all his white supremacist tattoos and opened a restaurant. He had some black people in his restaurant as employees. Quite a change for a man who hated African-Americans for the twenty years he was in prison.

I remember Mark telling me that the murders committed in prison were the most heinous and brutal murders that one could imagine. It was not uncommon to see someone stabbed to death or to watch someone's head turned to mush by a steel pipe. Mark said more things were happening in the prison than murder. There were beatings, rapes, and extortions. There were also riots and racial wars daily and a constant flow of drugs. Guards were classified by Mark as good or bad. The bad ones would turn their heads for racial reasons or for a price.

Mark remembered the first day he went to prison and the lecture he got from the head guard. The guard said, "Now listen, and listen good. Only people have names, and you are no longer a person. If you were a person, you wouldn't be here. You lost your right to be a person when you killed your daddy or raped your mother or chopped up the little baby next door or whatever the fuck you did. You're what the State of Arizona shit out its asshole. And when they shit you out, they didn't want to leave you out in the cold with nothin'. So, to keep you company on those long, lonely nights, they gave you your own precious little number. And your number is . . ."

The old convicts told Mark to stay away from the other races. Eat where the white boys eat, exercise where the white boys exercise. If you ever see a white boy in trouble with members of another race, help him. An Aryan Brotherhood member is never wrong. Even if he is wrong, he is right.

With Mark's guidance I became surprisingly believable as a white supremacist having served prison time in upstate New York. Deadeye also believed it, even though he knew I was a cop.

Because he was comfortable with how I pulled off the character, he told everyone we saw that I was a "brother." It feels good to convince the real thing that you are one of them, even when you are pretending. It is also comforting to know you are believable as the character when one mistake in this group can mean the end of your life.

The problem with living my new character was that it wasn't even close to who I really was. I didn't have a single racist bone in my body. I didn't see color when I walked with my friends or question other ethnic lifestyles. Now I lived the extreme and had to pretend I hated every race except the white race. Taking on new characters has to include the believability factor. You looked the part, dressed that way, and spoke that language. It became you and eventually you risked getting lost in that persona. The risk was worth the reward when I had to play the role of an Aryan Brotherhood gang member, and I became so convincing that it led to the successful prosecution of a murder conspiracy.

I found myself constantly questioning how I could be so believable when it went against my very core. I exhausted so much energy in pretending to be full of anger and hate that I quickly tired of the misery that came with the lifestyle and the display of hate for so many people. It became a difficult character to summon out too often for a murder conspiracy.

After I explored all my personal angst with playing this character, I began to wonder what had gone so terribly wrong with all the people who belonged to these groups. Who taught them at their early ages to hate and hurt, and what was done to make them so heartless? If you ever want to fix the ills of the world, start right there.

What I learned from my time with Mark and Deadeye made

me more complete as an undercover agent playing roles in my murder conspiracy cases. I didn't even have to play the role of Aryan Brotherhood member to be believable. It gave me an edge knowing the prison system and culture when I tried to convince clients that I had been to prison, as with Sharleen when she questioned my time and experiences in prison.

If you lie, then you better know everything about what you are claiming to be the truth. Otherwise, you will be caught in the lie.

8

Can't Run Fast Enough

Saturday began like Friday with a trip to the gym and a chance to work off the booze from the previous evening. As I sweated and pushed myself to exhaustion, I found myself questioning the damage I was doing to my body with my current lifestyle. I didn't have long to think about it though because I was a novelty item in the gym and everyone kept trying to talk to me. I was the freakish-looking big guy that had some kind of criminal history. That's what they all said to each other and apparently decided it was best to keep me as a friend. Who knew, they might need my help someday.

I hadn't planned on answering the pager or the phone on this day and risk getting called out on something that would force me to miss my date with Patti. She already had concerns about me and surely didn't totally trust me. How could she? Just take one look at me and you'd think thief, thug, or rapist. Not a good recipe for a first date. But of course the phone rang and I answered it without a thought, hearing the sweet voice of a girl I knew as Tia.

"Uncle Jake?" she said, using my nickname from the Candy Store. Most of these bar girls and topless dancers and addicts have low self-esteem and get little attention from their family. If you're older than they are and treat them kindly, they call you things like uncle. It makes them feel special.

"Ya, Tia, it's me. What can I do for you, girl?"

She explained how I needed to help her with her sister, who was being abused by her husband. Tia cried hysterically and at times I didn't understand a thing she said.

"What do you want me to do, Tia? I'm in a hurry today and don't have much time."

I've known Tia for some time now because she is a bartender at a nice club where I visit when I'm trying to display my mobster character. I'll usually dress in some nice clothes and slick my long hair back and put it in a ponytail. I don't play like a high roller, just a bone-breaking thug. It's difficult to get me too dressed up, so I stay with the muscle role and not the mob-boss character. Everyone in the bar knows me as Jake and believes I'm muscle for the mob.

Tia said her sister Tiffany wanted to have her husband killed. If I could spare a few minutes, Tia would get her sister to tell me everything I needed to know. She said she would forever be indebted to me if I would just take a minute of my time for her sister.

Had I ignored the phone, I could have spent the rest of the day getting ready for my night with Patti. But that's not how I conduct my business, so now I needed to rush and put something together for a quick meeting with Tia and her sister. First thing I did was get ahold of one of the guys to drive a dark-colored Suburban I had available. Then I dressed in the way Tia knew me to dress and slicked my long hair back with a handful of pomade.

We had agreed to meet behind a shopping center in the northern part of Scottsdale. Tia said they would come in her red Corvette and park around the front. As we pulled into the parking lot, I noticed Tia's car in one of the front spaces. Not too hard to see since it was a bright candy-apple red. I could see Tia walking under a store awning with another woman who looked just like her. They continued to walk along the stores until they turned the corner toward the back, where I had my driver park the Suburban and wait.

I stayed seated in the backseat of the Suburban while Tia and Tiffany approached. The driver got out of the front seat and opened my back door. Without saying a word he motioned for the girls to get inside and sit with me. Tiffany got in the farthest backseat with me, and Tia sat in the middle seat. After introductions were made, Tiffany started to cry as she told the story of her abusive husband.

When her sad story ended, I looked her straight in the face and said, "What do you want me to do, Tiffany, kill him?" She looked scared and stumbled with her words. "I don't know what I want. Tia just said you can help."

Many times clients are afraid to use the words *kill* or *murder*. They beat around the bush as if they're afraid to put a name to what they want done, so I have to make sure they understand that's what we're talking about. I explained to Tiffany that I killed people for a living. I don't kidnap or beat them to send a message. "If I kill your ole man, then I'm going to do it quickly and you are going to keep your mouth shut. If you don't keep your mouth shut, I'll kill you too."

Tiffany began to shake at the thought of my killing her and cried even harder as I gave her an empty stare that seemed to last forever. Suddenly her crying turned into chest heaves and she quickly darted her head to her sister, then back to me. Her head moved back and forth for a moment until she looked at the door handle. Without saying a word she grabbed the handle and quickly opened the door. With a swift leap like a cat she jumped out of the Suburban and ran lightning fast until she disappeared around the building. Tia looked at me and said, "Guess she's not serious."

I warned Tia to never take unnecessary time from me again, and she apologized as I gave her a hug. Then she headed off to find her sister. Tiffany never knew how lucky she was because of her indecision. I would continue to keep my eye on her through Tia, and Tiffany had given up the idea for good after our meeting.

Once I got back home, I did the best I could to make myself presentable and not embarrass Patti on her first night out with me. Checked to make sure I had my money, then pulled my hair back in a ponytail after all the grease had been washed out. But good clothes, a shower, and cologne still didn't make me acceptable for someone like Patti. I just did the best with what I had to work with. I only hoped that she would see past the outside and into my heart for the real me.

It didn't take me long to find her house. It was in the middle of a nice neighborhood where people would lock all their doors and hide the children if I drove the Harley onto the street. As I pulled up, I noticed a cute blond-haired boy out front riding a skateboard. As the truck rolled to a stop just a few feet from the boy, he immediately made eye contact with me. He stood frozen for what seemed to be an eternity, then broke into a dead run toward the front door of his house, all the while screaming for his mom.

Maybe I didn't clean up as well as I first thought.

I got out of my truck and knocked on the front door. After I waited a few patient moments, the door flew open and a giant dog ran swiftly past me, followed by the same boy, who was now screaming at the dog to stop. Next came Patti, flying out the door in an all-white outfit, yelling that she would be right back. They chased the dog down the street until they captured it and safely returned her home. I just stood outside the door while all this was happening and thought to myself, "And they think I'm some kind of freak?"

As Patti took the dog inside, she greeted me and said they would be out shortly. Once again no invitation to come inside for the freak. "Just wait and the homeowner will be with you shortly," I sarcastically thought to myself. It was almost like being a door-to-door salesman that nobody wants to deal with. About five minutes passed, then Patti and her son, Geoff, came outside ready to leave. As we walked down the driveway, Geoff stared at me as he clung tightly to Patti.

Patti sat in the passenger seat of my truck with Geoff in the middle. He had calmed down and seemed to somewhat accept me because his mom was with him. We had a wonderful dinner at a little Italian place called Red Devil, then went back to Patti's house. For some odd reason it didn't seem that strange for me to be out to dinner with a small boy and his mother. In fact it was really fun. We laughed and played kid games, and he constantly wanted to see my policeman's badge. When we realized he and I had the same birth date, I was good as gold. Patti's eyes lit up with that bit of information. I thought to myself, "I got to her and wasn't even trying." Just maybe now I had a chance.

The ride home turned out to be really good, and as I walked them to their front door, Patti told Geoff to thank me and head inside for a bath. He politely thanked me and asked to see my police badge one more time before he went inside. After looking at the badge he ran inside and the door shut behind him.

Patti stood outside the door for a moment making sure Geoff stayed inside, then said, "I'm surprised, Jake."

"You are? What about?"

"I would have never guessed in a hundred years that you were this nice, and you even have manners! I've heard some scary things about you that made me consider saying no to tonight."

"Give me another chance to see you again and I can surprise you even more. I might look like a bum, but deep down inside I'm just a regular guy."

She laughed as she continued to kid with me and quickly gave me a kiss on the cheek.

"Hopefully just you and I can get together again soon," she said.

"I would like that. But just a second! What have you heard? Give me a chance to defend myself."

She just looked at me innocently and tilted her head to the side. "Call me," she said, then disappeared inside.

I sat in the truck and wondered what the hell had just happened to me. I wasn't allowed past the front door, yet she wanted to see me again. I had never met anyone like this before, but I knew right then I liked it.

9

Four Eyes Are Better than Two

I **learned early on in my undercover career that two** sets of eyes were much better than one. I could be on the streets doing my thing and hookin' up business, but by myself I was missing all kinds of other business. With the help of a strong stable of informants though, I was good to go. I learned that from the old-timers. Work up a good group of informants and set them free to bring the business back to you. Then you are left to develop other cases and not feel pressured to meet some predetermined number of cases. A predetermined number that the sergeants and lieutenants selected to identify those undercover operatives who were successful, and those that weren't.

I always struggled with my decision whether to use an informant. I used a weighted system and incorporated personal beliefs when making my decision. I would never work with a child molester or habitual criminals that couldn't be controlled or stop committing crimes. No illegal activity when working with me, and no carrying firearms. Most of all I asked myself, is what this person's giving me more valuable than having him locked up? The answer would always lead my decision. By the grace of God, it never failed me either.

I was raised to know the difference between right and wrong. If you did something wrong, then you paid the price for your actions. Now here I was deciding whether a particular person got to avoid a jail sentence by working with me or was denied the chance and went directly to prison. Many of the informant candidates wanted to work off pending charges by turning in other criminals. All informants had to be evaluated for their usefulness and risk.

Interviewing potential informants, I began to see the same faces over and over. They had discovered they had enough power and influence in the criminal world to get out of almost anything. When I discovered someone was skirting the system and making deals each time he got caught, I refused to work with him. No matter what he had to offer. Most of the wannabe informants got to the point of having no fear when they got caught committing a crime. They felt they could make a deal, do what was required of them to avoid jail time, then go right back to committing crimes. You had to stay away from these individuals and not empower them to continue a life of crime. The idea was to give them an opportunity to atone for their mistakes and do something good. Then they were expected to leave the life of crime and become good and productive citizens. I would always have to satisfy my own conscience with the repeat offenders and refuse their help, even if it meant losing a great case.

It became the challenge of good versus evil and right versus wrong. I also knew that the victims of these potential informants deserved respect and consideration when I was deciding whether to use one. Many nights I would lie awake and wonder what I should do. My whole insides would turn and I would wrestle with the right decision. I also had the added pressure of the informants' behavior once I decided to use them. Not only for the time they were working for me, but for years later.

One detective I knew had an informant that was also a bounty hunter. Years after they worked together, the informant went into a house under the pretense of hunting a fugitive. While inside, the bounty hunter's team killed two people and were eventually convicted of murder. The press had a field day with the fact that the bounty hunter had been an informant. They neglected to mention how many years had passed since he'd worked as an informant. They also failed to report that he had had no instances of illegal behavior while working with the detective. Sometimes it doesn't matter what you do during your management of these characters. They are hell-bent to get into trouble, and your best management skills won't keep them straight.

I knew I had to use informants, but I hated every minute of it and constantly questioned my decisions. I always knew that no matter how much time had passed since my use of an informant and a possible crime they would commit, I would still be held accountable. Just like my detective friend and the bounty hunter.

The art of informant management came in identifying the right informants and what motivated them to give you information that might lead to their being killed if discovered. Once

I identified their motives, I could manage them and glean information pertinent to cases. I could also see into their reasoning and prevent any illegal behavior they might engage in. There are several motives for becoming an informant.

Monetary gain. Everyone who falls into this category is easy to spot from the beginning. In most cases I pay my informants for their information. Monetary-gain informants want the money for personal use and don't normally expect a lot. They aren't doing this as a profession, just for some spare change to pay a phone bill or fill a gas tank. They would use it to buy food for the family or diapers for the baby. It was also used for children's birthday gifts or Christmas gifts. This type of informant would tug at your heart. I always found myself bringing them clothing or furniture from my house. In their eyes, what I was getting rid of was like high-dollar stuff. They always appreciated it and were in return motivated to work harder for me.

Eliminate competition. Joe Shit the Ragman is selling dope on one corner. Mickey the Mope is selling on the other. Joe wants Mickey out of the picture so he can control all the dope business in the area. So he calls the local undercover officer and gives up on Mickey. They do a couple cases on Mickey and arrest him. He's off the street, and Joe is running the dope business for the whole neighborhood. Sounds like a normal business venture.

Revenge. This is the most common motive for women. A woman's husband, boyfriend, or lover betrays her and hooks up with another woman. She is so upset that she thinks only of having him suffer. She will make him pay for her broken heart even if he has to go to prison. When he is in prison, he belongs to her again. Only this time he is much more humble. On one occasion, a young girl called me with information on her father. I had always wanted to arrest her father because he was a top-ten criminal and gang leader in our community. The girl said he had beaten her mother the night before and she couldn't take it anymore. She said he had a quantity of drugs in his glove compartment and would be leaving at a certain time to sell it. If I hurried, she said, I could stop him and arrest him for transporting the drugs.

We started surveillance on the guy, and sure enough he left the house at the time his daughter said he would. Just as she said, he had drugs in his glove compartment when he was stopped. The only problem was that the drugs included a cigarette wrapper full of marijuana stems and seeds and a small amount of meth. I knew right then his daughter had made this packet up and set up her father. Nobody has a "personal use" stash made of stems and seeds. I later interviewed the girl and she admitted to the setup. I couldn't arrest or hold her father any longer, but eventually I did get a case on him and he also became an informant.

Getting a highly respected gang member to be an informant is like hitting the lottery. They can give you all the inside information and operate with confidence and unquestionable support within the organization. Nothing is better than this when trying to take down a gang of thugs. This was always my ticket into all the gangs I became a part of. The informant opened the door and I walked right through.

Fear. I have seen fear motivate both the men and women to the point where they would do anything to get someone out of their lives. Most of my people have drug problems and purchase drugs regularly. Many times they are broke and get the dope on loan, only to never pay back the debt. Then the dealer threatens and abuses them until they pay the debt or die. The users believe that if they get rid of the dealer, then their lives are theirs again. They don't give any thought that their debt is usually transferred to someone else when the dealer is in jail. That person is collecting the outstanding money to get an attorney for the dealer.

The professional source. This type has always been my biggest nightmare. Thanks to the federal government, this individual is difficult to manage and has high expectations of what he should be paid. The feds always paid their informants a portion of the take. Get a recovery of $10 million and the source gets 10 percent. Once informants get a taste of that kind of money, they're impossible to satisfy by any local agency. Not enough money, never enough perks, and less attention paid to them. Local agencies have little money to pay informants so they can't compete with the money available to a federal agent.

The good citizen. These informants were similar to the ones that were working off charges for themselves or others in that their motive was normally simple and easy for me to identify. Good citizens have lived in their neighborhood their whole lives. Seeing crooks destroy the neighborhood doesn't sit well with them. They will do whatever it takes to rid their neighborhood of the scum and live comfortably again. The important thing with these people is to protect their identity so they can continue to live comfortably. If the gangsters don't know where the information that led to their arrests came from, then the informants are safe forever. Or as long as they keep their mouths shut. Unfortunately they tend to tell other people what they did or that they are working with the police.

Working off charges. This is the usual informant that comes to the undercover officer. These informants want to make a deal to avoid going to prison for years. They would turn in their own mother if it meant a free ride for them. You have to carefully manage these people to avoid any entrapment issues or threats by the source directed at your target without you knowing about it. Tricky path to walk down, and one where I always felt I was walking with the devil.

Rambo. This informant is the guy or girl who watches too much television and was most likely denied a position in the Police Academy. These informants may secretly carry guns or handcuffs and have watched every episode of *Miami Vice*. You have to keep a short leash on them or they'll take you down with them.

One evening my buddy Coon Dog and I were headed to one of the sleazy bars on Van Buren Street, which is known for its prostitutes and drugs. It's a tough place to hang, but has a covey of assholes to choose from. We were talking back and forth and I was at the wheel of my old El Camino. I looked around as most people do when they drive and saw another detective's informant driving alongside me in the other lane. We made eye contact. He didn't know who I was, but I knew who he was because I had seen him on several transaction videos. A few moments later he pulled in behind me and threw a flashing red light on top of his car. He either stole the light or bought it from some store that dealt in police gear. All I knew was that he wasn't supposed to have it. Next, he hung a high-beam light out the window and motioned with the light for me to pull over.

Dog and I started laughing. I told Dog we were getting

pulled over by this nut informant and I was going to play along. This was one that needed to go away so he couldn't play cop with a normal citizen who wouldn't know any different.

He positioned his vehicle the way a highly trained patrolman would, pulling up to our vehicle at an angle and coming to a stop a few car lengths to the rear. Using a microphone attached to his car, he ordered me out of my car, telling me to throw my keys out the window. By this time I had had enough and got out of the car and took him down to make the arrest. As I did this, he began to cry like a big baby. The informant had handcuffs on him, a police scanner, and a carload of other items he used while out pretending to be a cop—the very definition of a Rambo informant.

The main thing I watched for when dealing with informants was the setup. Keeping in mind they would snitch on their own mother made it crystal clear they would do the same to me. I never totally trusted them and never confided in them for fear they would use that against me and jeopardize my safety. I did treat them fairly and with respect, hoping to gain their trust and loyalty. In return I demanded the same respect, loyalty, and honesty. If I didn't get it, they were fired or sent back to prison. My rule was zero tolerance when it came to violating the rules we'd agreed upon or committing a crime while working for me. No second chances if you made a deal with me.

Getting informants is a whole other task that takes a great deal of effort and trust by those that help provide them. Most police officers are leery of defense attorneys because they work against each other every day in court. I found that if you could identify decent attorneys and befriend them, they would provide you a wealth of information that would make you a better cop. They would also give you many of their clients who could make good informants. All they wanted was a deal to stay out of prison or a deal for their loved ones.

10

The Karate Kid

My two favorite defense attorneys who schooled me for years have since died of heart-related illnesses. I respected and often confided in Tom Thinnes and Michael Vaughn. These two men were instrumental in teaching me how to think like a defense attorney and investigate at a higher level. I talked with them about a number of cases and learned how they defended those clients. When you learn the different defense techniques, it forces you to become more thorough in your investigations. Having knowledge of how a case can be defended gives you insight into evidence you must collect and statements needed for a conviction. The main thing they did for me was make me operate like a defense attorney preparing for trial as I worked through the cases. Along with that came patience and avoiding a rush to judgment.

Both Tom and Michael represented their clients with great

expertise, but they also believed in the Constitution and wanted it enforced correctly. If they could help me, then maybe other officers would follow my lead. I miss both of them a great deal and owe them for all the help and support they gave me.

Before Tom died, he came to me with a client who had information about a murder for hire. The client was an Italian drug smuggler who wanted a few years off his sentence if he arranged a meeting with someone trying to hire him to do a murder. We'll call Tom's client Vito for now because release of his true identity would surely lead to his death.

Vito was a smooth-talking leader of a Mafia family in Italy who came to the United States and started smuggling drugs. He had a heavy Italian accent and seemed as if he came straight from some of the best mob movies. Everyone in the jail knew who he was and gave him a huge amount of respect for fear he would have them killed. Vito had his way in the jail and did whatever he wanted. Everyone put money on his books and had family members send him things so as to stay on his good side. Prisoners even came to him regularly to get his permission for something they wanted to do in the jail. He was the leader, and also an ear for those who wanted to talk.

All I needed to do was make sure that Vito was telling me the truth and didn't force the guy into his decision. I didn't want Vito planting any ideas and messing up my case when we came to trial. I needed to take control before he ran with this on his own.

For the first time in Vito's adult life someone else was going to be controlling him. He wasn't calling the shots this time.

Tom arranged my first meeting with Vito, and we all found it to be a memorable experience. Vito started the meeting by introducing himself and explaining what he wanted in return for his cooperation. He was expecting to get at least twenty years in prison and wanted that dropped to somewhere between eight and fifteen years. He wasn't asking to get out of prison, just to have a chance to get out while he had some years left to be with his family. If I agreed to his terms, then he would arrange to have his guy call me and explain the murder for hire. If I didn't agree, then he was finished with our conversation. He made his offer with arrogance and confidence, believing that I would fall all over him and beg for his help.

I stood up from the attorney's table and looked Vito directly in the eyes. With a slight smile I stood for a long moment and stared at him with increasing intensity. Then I turned toward Tom and nodded my head as if to say, "Thanks, but no thanks." As I turned to walk from the room, Vito became confused and started squirming in his chair looking back and forth from me to Tom. It was as if he expected Tom to stop me, but that didn't happen. Tom knew how I operated and knew this guy had just pissed me off.

"Where the hell are you going?" Vito said.

"I'm out of here and thanks for taking time to speak with me."

Vito then said in a high voice, "What about my deal?"

I stood for a minute with my back to him, then slowly turned around. "You can stick your deal up your ass. I don't work with someone in your position telling me what to do."

"Hey, don't get your pants in a bind. I was just trying to make conversation. Come back and tell me what you need."

I looked him in the eyes again and told him that I was in charge and I made the decisions. If he wanted to help me, then we could talk later about his needs. I wanted to know what he had first, then I would evaluate his information and his reward.

Vito quickly agreed and sighed in relief as I came back to the table. Shaking his head in disbelief, he turned and looked at Tom. Tom looked back at him in a way as if to say, "Be careful, dumb shit."

When I sat back down, I warned Vito one more time. "My rules, my deal, and you do exactly what I say. Change one thing . . . we are finished."

Vito agreed and apologized.

I never had any problems with Vito after our first meeting, and he turned out to be a valuable source. Every so often he had to be touched up and straightened out, but it wasn't any big deal.

Vito had a podmate who had been telling him about his case, which was getting ready for trial. He was accused of beating and kidnapping his girlfriend and was looking at prison time. Vito described the podmate, Armando Aros, as a stupid Italian kid. I later found out that Armando, who was twenty years old and lived on the north side of Phoenix, wanted to have his girlfriend killed so she couldn't testify against him. That's where I came in.

Vito agreed to have Armando call me and meet with me to explain his dilemma and arrange to hire me. Vito didn't ask for anything in return at the end of our meeting, and I didn't make any offers. It was later decided that I would write the judge to make him aware of Vito's cooperation and leave sentencing to the court. I wouldn't make any recommendations.

After returning to my office, I checked the records for Armando and found that he had kidnapped his girlfriend, Gwen

Riggins, and threatened to kill her. As I sat at my desk, I started to feel an incredible pain in my back unlike anything I had ever felt before. I went into the bathroom as I started to sweat and hoped that whatever it was would pass and I'd feel better. That didn't happen, so I decided to go home and get away from the office before I started to draw some attention.

I didn't want anyone to see me sweating and acting strange because I was worried they would think I was doing something I shouldn't. I already knew they were worried about my taking chances and hanging around scumbag bars that were obviously too dangerous for one person to go into alone. There was some talk of my taking a break and leaving the streets for a while to cool off, and I didn't want that to happen. My mind raced with the pain I was feeling, and the only thing I could think of was the bosses would accuse me of using drugs or excessive drinking.

The sergeants and lieutenants were always watching you at the safe house and looking for signs that you might be going over the edge. At any indication of trouble, they would take you off the streets and try to bring you back to reality. At the time I thought it was unfair, and it made all of us in the program suspicious and uncomfortable. Today, though, I think it really helped in keeping me focused. It always helps to know that Big Brother is watching.

When I got home, I rolled onto the couch and lay there in pain that seemed to be getting worse and worse. After about an hour my father called to see what was going on in my world. It seemed odd that he called me at home when I was supposed to be at work, but he did and I was glad. I told him about the pain and he said he would be right over to see what he could do. "No, no, you just stay home and I'll be fine," I said. His only response was "Right, I'll see you in a few minutes."

A short time later the front door opened and in came my dad. He got me into his car and whisked me off to the emergency room. None of the staff seemed to really know what was going on with me except that I was suffering from some intense pain. Their only answer for the pain was morphine, and that was all I remembered. Several hours later I woke and looked at my dad staring down at me. "Kidney stone," he said. "Looks like it may have passed, and the doctor said we can leave and head back to your house as soon as you wake up." I had always been told that kidney stones were a male's equivalent to giving birth. After experiencing the passing of a stone, I had a whole new level of respect for women who suffer through childbirth.

We left the hospital and got into my dad's car for the ride back home. I was totally worn-out from the ordeal, and my dad seemed to be lost in his own thoughts. Finally he turned toward me and said, "I've got throat cancer." He told me that he might not have long to live, but would do whatever he could to fight it. I was so stunned that I didn't even know how to answer him. The only thing I knew for sure was that he would need me to be there for the biggest fight of his life.

I returned to work the next day, and nobody at the warehouse even realized what I had been through. I got back on the computer and started looking into Armando again, whom I found to be a complete nut, and a dangerous nut.

Armando had taken Gwen to the desert against her will after an argument and threatened to kill himself and her. According to Gwen, he was out of his mind and jealous that she might have been with another man. He would point a gun at her and threaten to kill her, then put the gun in his mouth and threaten to take his own life. This went on for a considerable amount of time until Gwen convinced him to go home and have sex with her. Armando agreed and they went back to her apartment, where the trouble continued.

Armando was five feet ten inches tall and weighed 205 pounds. He worked out religiously and had been taking steroids to increase his size and strength. In addition to his exceptional strength, he was a black belt in karate and considered by many to be dangerous and unstable. Gwen was petite, five feet tall and ninety-five pounds soaking wet. She wasn't much of a match for Armando.

They met while hanging out at a dance club. Armando was strikingly good-looking and Gwen was equally beautiful. On the outside they looked like a great couple with his *GQ* style and her model looks. Everybody wanted to be with Armando, and he took advantage of the attention. Armando was incredibly jealous and had a bad temper that was hard to control. He was popular in the dance-club scene, where popularity comes from fear and intimidation or goes to the person with the most money or access to drugs.

When Armando and Gwen got back to her apartment, they continued to talk about what had set off his tirade. Gwen thought she was safer by bringing him back to her apartment, where she could eventually call for help. She was right to get out of the desert, where she was sure to die, but she failed to understand Armando's bipolar behavior. She didn't expect him to recycle when they got back to the apartment and become even more jealous and suspicious.

Armando grabbed tiny Gwen and dragged her to her second-story apartment window. He grabbed her by her feet and dangled her out the window by her ankles. He kept her there long enough that the screaming caused the neighbors to call the police. When the officers arrived, they watched Armando leaving the apartment, walking down the stairway. As they tried to contact him, he took off running and was eventually caught and taken into custody. Being charged with the kidnapping and jailed made Armando even more upset and wanting revenge against Gwen.

While I was looking at the police report and contemplating my move with Armando, I got a call on my cell phone from Patti's sister, Betty. Patti's boy, Geoff, had fallen from the playground equipment at school and broken his arm. Not just any break, but a compound fracture. They were at the hospital and Patti was wondering out loud if I could come by and cheer up Geoff. I couldn't believe my ears when the call came. Just think . . . maybe I had broken through and she did really see something in me. This was definitely a big chance and one that I wasn't going to miss out on. Of course, I thought to myself, Betty might be screwing with me after what I had done to her.

But I couldn't chance not going and then having Patti upset because I decided not to show up. I could always get back at Betty if she was setting me up. And if she wasn't, I could do my best to make Geoff happy. We had had such a great time the night we went out, and he was incredibly impressed with my police shield. I knew that I could instantly cheer him up if I let him see the shield again and hold it. Sounds like a small thing, but to a boy who wanted a man to care and show him some attention, it would mean everything. Even if Patti didn't really care for me,

I knew I would be helping Geoff through his pain. It was a win-win situation for me.

As I grabbed my keys to the bike and started to run out the door, my phone rang again. It was Armando.

"I'm in a hurry right now," I told him. "Can I get back with you?"

"No problem, I just need your help in keeping my girlfriend from court when I go to trial. Vito told me to call you for help."

I didn't want to act anxious, so I told him that I was going out of town for a week and he needed to call me back when I returned. Armando thought that would be a good idea because he wanted to meet in person instead of just talking over the phone. I was so quick with him on the phone that I'm sure he worried it was a brush-off. Of course it wasn't because I really wanted to do the deal, but I also needed to see Patti and Geoff. This was probably the first time that something else mattered more to me than the job. I hadn't experienced that feeling in a long time. Fleeting moments like this are times that bring you back to reality.

You have to try to understand how confusing this was. I had a chance to be there for a girl I thought was incredible, be there for her when she needed someone the most. At the same time I was pretending to be a killer for hire that fit a murder into his schedule when it was convenient. I was a psychiatrist's dream patient. If they could figure out what was going on in my head and how many different people were playing up there, then they deserved all the money they asked for.

I hung up the phone and hustled off to the hospital, which turned out to be the best decision of my life. When I walked in, the hospital staff wanted to call security to keep me out, but that didn't stop this long-haired biker from trying to do a little good for a child. When security came to Geoff's bed in the emergency room, I calmly pulled them aside and showed them my badge. They all gave a sigh of relief and went about their business. Unfortunately for me, I made a grand entrance wherever I went, and the hospital was no different. Because I didn't ask for help and barged into the room, I should have expected to draw attention from security.

Being in character all the time is the safety mechanism that protects you from unsuspecting contacts and saves your life. On one previous visit to a hospital where I planned to visit a friend who had just had surgery, I got the surprise of my life. The male nurse in another room was one of the motorcycle gang's members. Immediately concerned about my friend's safety if he was connected to me, I quickly turned around and left. A standard practice for gangs is to place members and close associates in places where they can obtain personal information. Those places often include hospitals, law firms, courts, DMVs, and even police departments. With this always in my mind I rarely found myself out of character.

When Geoff was released, I took him outside and placed him on my Harley. Then I gave him my badge and stuck it in his pocket. I told him, "Okay, buddy, this is your chance to be undercover and get all the bad guys. Don't tell anyone our secret and you can be my partner." He was so excited that he totally forgot about his arm, and Patti stood back and watched with a twinkle in her eye and a beautiful smile on her face.

We left the hospital and went out for dinner that night. Patti and Geoff drove in her sports car and I followed on the bike. We didn't look like much of a match when we were together, and people watched our every move, obviously wondering what the hell Patti was thinking and how could she subject her son to someone like me. For some reason it didn't seem to matter anymore. Until we got back to her house and I was once again left standing outside the door with a "Good night" and "Thanks for a wonderful time."

I really felt this was the turning point for Patti and me. A point when she saw me for something other than what I looked like. It felt good for once.

Armando called a week later and said he wanted to meet. We both played hard to get until we decided to meet in the parking lot at the Denny's restaurant located at Dunlap and Interstate 17. He called me, then tried to act as if he were too busy to meet. I countered his evasive behavior by being even more difficult for him to meet. This seemed to go on forever until the location was finally set. This one phone call gave me a great deal of insight into Armando's personality and how difficult he was going to be.

A day later I went to the Denny's restaurant and waited in the parking lot for Armando to arrive. I waited for about fifteen minutes and was never contacted by Armando, so I loaded up and left. As I drove down the freeway, listening to my stereo, I heard my phone ring over the loud music. It was Armando, and he said that he was in the parking lot and waiting for me.

Just as I expected from everything I knew about Armando to this point. He was suspicious by nature and didn't trust me. He was most likely in the parking lot long before I arrived and watching all my moves. Trying to catch me short or see if I was a cop. It made me a bit mad, but also got my competitive spirit stirred up. *Game on!*

I always expect that the person trying to hire me has some disbelief in me and what I can do. That's always my first hurdle to get over. In fact, I relish the opportunity to make someone who doesn't trust me come to have complete trust in me as a killer. I was concerned about Armando though. He had a reputation as being mentally unstable, and now he was trying to hire a hit man. If he could hang Gwen out the window threatening her death, then he would have no problem killing me.

The Denny's parking lot was located behind the restaurant on the west side of the building. On the east side of the restaurant was the front door and a freeway access road that ran north and south through Phoenix. The freeway access road was eighteen feet above the freeway so the noise was minimal. Armando could park anywhere in the parking lot and not be detected because it was so large. The parking lot was shared with an adjoining shopping center that partnered with Metro Center.

Metro Center was the community's first multichain and multilevel indoor shopping center, with movie theaters and restaurants. When it first came into the community, it was the crown jewel and chronicled around the country. Over the years it had aged, and by the time of my meeting with Armando it had become gang-infested, as had the neighborhood. Armando could park anywhere in the parking lot, stand inside any number of stores, or watch from the top of any surrounding building. He could come when he pleased and never be detected as he watched me. The next time I met with him would be different though. I would have people in all those places, arriving hours

before he did. I was sure "pretty boy" wouldn't come so early that
he might sweat and stain his shirt or just get bored watching.

I knew Armando right when I saw him waiting for me in the
parking lot. He knew me too because I looked exactly as he had
imagined. He was told by Vito that I was a member of a motorcycle gang and had done prison time. I was from Vito's inner circle and therefore trustworthy. I guess trusted by everyone except,
at this point, Armando. I had a lot of characters to choose from.
Motorcycle gangster, convict, disgruntled Vietnam veteran, mobster, dying restaurant owner with nothing to lose, transient, or
construction worker just out of prison. The motorcycle gangster
with extreme size and muscles bigger than Armando's seemed to
be the best fit, especially with Armando being a bodybuilder and
weight lifter and being obsessed with size.

We exchanged greetings; he acted suspicious and kept looking around.

"You want to call this thing off?" I said, challenging him. I
was bigger than he was and I used that to my advantage. Armando understood intimidation because he used it throughout
his daily life. I was just giving him some of his own medicine. I
had to get control of this guy early on or he was going somewhere else to get the job done—or he would do it himself.

"What?" he asked, suddenly off guard.

"You want to call this off? You are wasting my time!"

"No, I just needed to check out the cars. Some of them
looked suspicious."

"You want out? I'm thinkin' I want out now! If you're serious about it, then let's do it. If not . . . fuck it!"

"I'm serious about it," he said gravely.

During a deal, I routinely assess myself to determine if I'm doing the case for the right reasons. In a case such as Armando and Gwen's, I ask myself, *Is Armando so committed to this deal that if not for me, someone else?* If my answer comes up yes, then I'm going to be patient and make sure I'm the one he chooses. On the outside I'm going to give him the impression that I'm uninterested and a bit aggravated by his actions. I'll let him believe I can take or leave his deal, but I'll fit it into my schedule if he decides to cooperate. It's a fine line with people like Armando, and you have to avoid presenting yourself as too anxious.

I started questioning Armando about the murder-for-hire job, asking what problem he needed corrected. He opened up like a floodgate and started telling me about a "broad" that was giving him problems and how he wanted her out of the picture. He knew the girl well because she had been his girlfriend, and he knew that she was in Denver, Colorado, and he had her address.

This would have been a normal conversation for two guys talking about murder, except Gwen had been relocated. The county attorney had relocated her and had her in protective custody and out of harm's way from Armando. I had to hide my shock hearing that Armando had been able to find Gwen and she was in harm's way without even knowing it.

There's a fine line in conversation between "getting her out of the picture" and "murder." I had to find out what he wanted and decide if I could do it. I wanted to avoid his dancing around our conversation and being afraid to say *murder* when that was what he truly wanted. He knew I was a killer and not a babysitter, so tell me exactly what you want.

To understand what Armando was looking for, I asked him one more time to specify his desire.

"So you want her dead or kidnapped?"

"Right now I just want her out of the picture until my trial is over."

"You have to make your mind up for sure, bud. I'm not a babysitter and won't be kidnapping your old lady."

"Yeah, I get it."

"You think about what you want for sure and let me know in a couple of days. If you decide you want her kidnapped, call someone else. I don't need the headache of that drama. Want her killed, then we can talk."

I didn't want Armando to think I was willing to do anything he wanted, least of all kidnapping. I had presented myself as a killer, and he had originally told the informant he wanted his girlfriend dead. Either he had changed his mind, or the informant lied. I needed to find out where his head was at right now and not go any further. If he decided he only wanted to have her kidnapped, then we would eventually deal with that. But for now I'd give him time to think and determine which way he intended on going. No entrapment on my part, just determining what he really has planned.

What Armando said was that he wanted her out of the picture until after the trial. He didn't believe she wanted to testify and thought she was being manipulated by the prosecutor to testify against him. His arrogance was so inflated that he couldn't believe Gwen would ever testify against him. He had completely washed from his mind everything he had done to Gwen. In his mind, she still loved him and wanted him. But he was also convinced that he wasn't safe if she was around to testify.

"How much you willing to pay for this?" I asked.

"How much you want?"

"I charge anywhere from five thousand dollars to twenty-five thousand dollars, depending on the effort."

"I don't have twenty-five thousand dollars, but I can go five thousand dollars."

"All right. How you going to pay me?"

"I can pay you in payments of a thousand dollars a month and give you five hundred dollars right now."

I told Armando that I definitely wanted the $500 up front if I chose to take the job, and he had to go with me to Colorado to show me where Gwen was at. As I watched his face and listened to what Armando said, I became convinced we were talking about murder, but I played his game for now. I went along with the kidnapping scenario, but kept informing him that in the end I would take no part in that action. He said he understood and would have the money by tomorrow, but needed to go to court before we left and make them think he wasn't going to take a plea agreement. That would continue the process and buy enough time for us to get to Colorado and get rid of Gwen before the trial even began. Armando left knowing our agreement would only be for a murder, not a kidnapping. Even though he tried to speak in riddles and avoid the *murder* word, he definitely wanted Gwen killed.

Before I had met with Armando I learned from the prosecutor in Gwen's case that Armando had convinced the courts that he would enter into a plea agreement. He knew he could back out of it at any time and ask for a trial, so that would give him plenty of time to get Gwen killed before the trial.

Armando agreed to call me in a few days and make arrangements for us to go to Colorado. We both left, and I felt pretty good about where I was at in Armando's head.

A few days after my meeting with Armando, Assistant County Attorney Joanne Garcia called me. She told me that Armando had changed his plea agreement and asked for a trial. A trial was set for two weeks from the date of his requested change. This was an obvious act by Armando to conspire to kidnap or kill Gwen, and confirmation that he believed me and who I said I was. Even if he continued to be suspicious.

Shortly after Armando got his plea changed and trial date set, he called me on the phone, excited. "I've decided to change what we talked about and I want her killed. I can't afford to have her come back on me. I thought about this since we talked. What is this going to change for us?"

Nothing changes for us because I was all about murder and didn't like the idea of kidnapping. That would only bring confusion and make it too easy for me to get caught when she was let go. I wanted my $500 up front and wanted to leave and get it done next week. I had business elsewhere and didn't have much time to spare. He also had to go with me and point out where Gwen lived so I wouldn't make any mistakes. No problem for Armando, except he wanted out of the area before "it happens" so he couldn't be tied to the murder.

Easy enough for me. I have Armando committed to the murder, ready to take me to see Gwen, and planning on paying me money. All I need to make the case is an overt act and the commitment to have someone killed. Armando satisfied everything and added more when he showed he had thought it all out on his own and decided he needed her killed. He had the chance to never come back to me, but instead he stepped the game up another notch.

Three more days passed and I got another phone call from

Armando. "I got everything together and I'm ready to go," he said. "I could go tomorrow, but I got something else to take care of, so let's plan on early Wednesday morning." Leaving on Wednesday would be fine for me I told Armando, but I wanted to see the money before leaving. Armando responded, "That's fine, I got it right in my pocket now."

We agreed to meet at 9:00 a.m. in the morning and take off from the Denny's restaurant. In the meantime I had the county attorney relocate Gwen again for her safety in case Armando changed his mind and attempted the murder himself. Who knew with this nut? He might decide to save $500.

I showed up on the day Armando and I had agreed upon, but this time I had friends. The film crew was tucked away in the parking lot and had arrived early so they could keep an eye out for Armando. I also had an entire SWAT team positioned throughout the parking lot and ready to pounce on Armando when I gave them the sign I was ready.

I arrived around ten minutes early, then waited and waited until about forty minutes had passed. By this time I figured he had come to his senses or was suspicious of me and had decided to back out. I also worried that he was already on his way to Colorado, planning to do it himself. It always worried me that I might empower someone to do the murder by him- or herself. People see me and think they can do the same thing, and for a lot less money.

The Hells Angels have a saying: *Three people keep a secret if two are dead*. The same could apply here with Armando. He was street-smart and could possibly have felt it was bad business for him to partner with someone else. Do it by himself and nobody else would be alive to testify against him or snitch on him if caught. A clean getaway and only himself to worry about. The problem with that philosophy is that most people are too scared to do it themselves. They want something so badly they will kill for it, but don't want their hands dirty with the murder.

Three hours after I had gone to the Denny's restaurant, I had returned to my normal routine. Hit the gym, rushed home for lunch, and got ready for *Guiding Light*. I just loved that trash. At about 12:50 p.m. my phone rang and it was Armando. He was sorry for not showing up, but he'd had to take care of some court business. Tried to call me several times but couldn't get me to answer. He wanted to reschedule for tomorrow at the same time as today. I wasn't real happy when I spoke with Armando and made him very aware of it. I agreed to give things one more shot, then I'd be out of town and moving on. No more changes for me. Of course, I would have caved in if something happened, but he didn't need to know that.

Same routine for the next day. We arrived a little earlier than the day before and watched closely to see what game Armando would play this day. My patience with this boy was wearing thin. I was trying to be believable as a hit man, yet make sure I got my case completed. He was challenging me around every corner and I didn't like it.

I pulled in behind the restaurant and parked at about 8:50 a.m. No Armando in my view, and nobody on the arrest team had spotted him. This wasn't going to be Groundhog Day again so I called his phone to see if I could get an answer. He answered and said he was running about ten minutes late and was just getting out of the shower. "Hurry your ass up!" I said. "I don't have all day to wait for you."

Thirty minutes later my phone rang again and it was Armando, saying he was driving around and spotted some police officers parked in the lot. No doubt he'd spotted some of the surveillance team, but I wasn't going to let on. I talked and talked to him until I eventually convinced him that he was seeing things and I didn't see one cop in the parking lot. He finally agreed to come on in and hung up. By this time my patience was just about pegged with all his bullshit, but I didn't want to lose him when we were so close. I was wrapped in a body bug so the video people could hear everything I said, and I warned them to get the surveillance team out of his view or we were going to lose him and the case.

A few minutes passed and Armando walked into the back parking lot on foot. I was later told that his girlfriend, who continued to drive around the parking lot, had dropped him off around the corner. Not only did I have to negotiate with a nut, but also I had his "Bonnie" acting as his backup.

I acted pissed as he walked up to me, and I got irritated when I realized he didn't have any luggage. He was wasting my time and I wasn't playing his game any longer. If I did, he would have lost all respect for me and I could no longer be believable. Armando knew I was upset, and I'm sure he saw his opportunity going out the window.

"Let's forget about this whole thing, man!" I yelled. "I've had enough of your bullshit."

"I'm serious about this, man, I just needed to check out the parking lot."

I gave him a chance to end this whole thing and told him that I wanted out now! If he wasn't serious, then walk; if he was, then let's do it! He quickly told me again how serious he was and that he wanted to keep things going. For the first time

I saw some anxiety in his face. His nervousness told me he knew he might have pushed me too far.

I didn't let up on Armando as we sat on a flower planter and discussed what he wanted to have done. As we talked, he continually looked around and paid close attention to everyone and everything. We talked money again, and he agreed that he was going to pay me a total of $5,000 and make $1,000 payments each month. When I asked to see the $500 that he owed me before we left, he said his girlfriend was holding the money. He walked away from me and went to another parked vehicle north of where we were talking. Before he left, I made sure he knew I was giving him a discounted deal as a favor to Vito. I was also more patient than normal because of my respect and commitment to Vito.

As Armando got to the car, he leaned inside and kissed the female in the driver's seat. Then he grabbed his luggage from inside and walked back to me. As soon as he walked back to me, I demanded to see the money. I wasn't going anywhere until he proved he had the cash he'd agreed to bring. Armando reached into his back pocket and pulled out a wallet that held several hundred dollars. He counted out $600, but I could see many more hundreds were still inside.

Armando stood by the passenger door of my truck while I opened the driver's side. The plan was to get him with his back turned to the arrest team and distract him at the door by talking before we got inside. I did this by pretending to get my gun from under the driver's seat and talking to him at the same time. As he stood at the door and looked at me, I saw everything suddenly go into slow motion.

The arrest team, suited up in tactical gear, came out from

a panel van and started quietly creeping up on Armando. He looked at me through the window, then looked in the tint of my backseat windows. When he did, his eyes opened like giant saucers, and he watched in the tint as the arrest team closed in on him. Armando was wearing a pair of weaved-leather shoes with no socks. He jumped straight in the air and the shoes lay on the ground empty. Like a bullet shot from a gun, he ran north from the arrest team and started dodging other surveillance officers coming to help. When he kept evading the other officers, I started running after him and chased him toward the freeway. Along my side was another SWAT member, named Skip.

The chase was difficult for me because I was wearing heavy-duty biker boots and Armando was fast as a rabbit. As he ran around the side of the Denny's restaurant, Armando was hit by an oncoming car and flew over the hood and onto the ground. He bounced right up and continued running toward the freeway. When Armando reached the access road to the freeway, a car was coming into the restaurant parking lot and didn't see him. The car hit Armando, and he was once again knocked to the ground after rolling off the hood, then bounced to his feet.

I continued the chase him and almost laughed at the bad luck he was having trying to escape. I knew that if I stayed with him, he would soon tire, but Skip and I wouldn't. Too much partying and too many drugs for pretty boy was about to catch up with him.

When Armando got to the side of the freeway embankment, he looked over the fence into the oncoming rush-hour traffic eighteen feet below. I just knew he was going to surrender, but he proved me wrong. Armando looked back at Skip and me and jumped over the fence, disappearing into the freeway. I got to the fence with Skip a few seconds later, and we both looked at Armando as he tumbled down toward the freeway traffic, then jumped after him.

It seemed as if we tumbled and slid down the embankment for an eternity until we stopped short of the traffic on the emergency lane. That we didn't get hit was a surprise to me. Armando was running against the traffic down the freeway emergency lane, periodically looking for a spot to cross without being hit again. Both Skip and I chased Armando as he tired and began to slow. The closer and closer we got, the slower and slower he became. When we were a few steps behind, both Skip and I dove toward Armando, knocking him to the ground. Brakes started screeching and we could feel the wind from the cars brushing right by us.

Armando struggled for a moment or two, but he was so tired that we easily cuffed him and pulled him out of the traffic lane. Cut and scraped up from the roadway, Armando sat on his butt and gasped for air.

As we all three sat on the side of the freeway and looked at the cars that had nearly killed us, we looked at each other. Suddenly, all three of us broke out laughing hysterically, relieved that we'd survived this adventure.

Armando Aros was charged with conspiracy to commit murder and went to trial. In Arizona the sentence if found guilty is life with a possibility of parole at twenty-five years. The only thing the defendant can't get is death. Gwen testified and did a wonderful job in spite of the pressure and grind of a trial while Armando sat in front of her.

He was found guilty by a jury of his peers and is currently

serving a life sentence with possibility of parole in twenty-five years.

After Armando was arrested, I located his new girlfriend, Gina Reed. I questioned her about Armando's intentions and she denied having any knowledge of what he'd planned. She told me a story about Armando and explained how much in love she was with him.

One evening before Armando was arrested for the conspiracy, she had to go to the store for some milk. She knew that Armando was incredibly jealous, but found that sweet and attractive. When she returned home, Armando was in a rage about how long she had been gone. He started accusing her of seeing another man and having sex while out at the store. Armando ordered Gina to pull her pants and underwear off and spread her legs. He then checked her for evidence of intimacy with another man.

Gina looked me straight in the eye with a sincere and sweet loving look on her face and said, "Isn't that the sweetest thing you have ever heard?"

11

The Inner Circle

My father always told me that you are a lucky man if at the end of your time on earth you can count on one hand the number of true friends you had in your life. I found myself always thinking about the number 5 from that point on. In fact, 5 has always been my lucky number. I can count myself one of the lucky ones because I have those five true friends that have always been there for me through everything I have encountered. Those men include Alejandro "Alex" Femenia, Tim "Coon Dog" Cooning, Jim "JP" Wilson, Ron "Ronnie Red" Sterrett, and Tim Hallahan.

Tim Hallahan and I grew up together in the Maryvale community of Phoenix. He was like a son to my parents as I was to his. We grew together through elementary school, high school, and off to college at the University of Arizona, where we roomed together. I took the police exam with Tim and he was hired a year after me.

Through all my changes, Tim was a link to the past where I knew everything was good and right. In Tim I could see a mirror into the past that would lift up my spirits. I had fond memories of my youth, and he represented everything that was good about those days. If I couldn't find Tim to talk with, then I always found his brother, Donnie. Donnie was also like a big brother, and he always seemed to be there with a helping hand. My problem with both Tim and Donnie was that I didn't reach out to them enough because I felt it was a sign of weakness.

Tommy Hernandez had finally gone to prison after his conviction, and when he arrived, he had a tattoo of a dragon put on his chest. His explanation to his family was that he had a dragon in him and his dragon was alcohol. He wanted to look in the mirror every day and remember what his dragon was. I had a dragon too.

My dragon was never wanting to show fear or signs of weakness. To combat this dragon I confronted any sign of personal weakness. If I experienced fear about something, I would run into it head-on. For example, if I was driving down the street and saw a bar that looked as if it might need some attention, I would drive through the parking lot and get a feel for the place. If I got a funny feeling that the bar was dangerous and a bit too risky to go into by myself, I forced myself to go inside. Taking those chances was normal for me, but always seemed to put me in dangerous situations that I didn't need to be in. I didn't want anyone to think I was afraid of anything, even if I was. This led the bosses to thinking I had become a risk-taker. Their concern led to my paranoia and how I behaved when I had a kidney stone for the first time.

Even though I didn't reach out to Tim and Donnie as much as I should have, I always knew they would be there. It was almost like a crutch. With Tim around I knew I had someone that could see through me. He knew me from my early childhood days and couldn't be fooled. I had to play straight-up with Tim or he would call "Bullshit" before I could finish a sentence. He was truly a great guy who will always be my emotional vision to the past.

I met Jim Wilson on the first day of the academy, and we became friends from that moment forward. He is a quiet soul that finds good in everyone. Jim has been that way his entire life and always looks for the good in everyone. The crooks have it made with Jim because he will always try to find a way to fix whatever they may have done wrong.

Jim is a lot like Ross from the television show *Friends*—he's smart and kind to everyone, but naïve and emotional. I made a plane trip with him one time during which I'm sure the other passengers thought we were either gay or he was my caretaker. He wore a fanny pack that had hand wipes, disinfectant soap, snacks, gum, and a number of other items, and he was always asking if I needed anything, then handing me a hand wipe after we ate. As we pulled out from the gate, I watched as the ground crew motioned for the pilot to follow a particular path. As they motioned, Jim watched, then turned to me and said, "Isn't that nice." I asked what he was talking about and he said, "That man on the ground is waving good-bye to us."

When Tommy killed Ray, Jim was also renting a room in the same house. He worked late the night Ray died and returned home after Tommy had left. Jim walked into the home tired from a long day and night on the street as a patrolman. As he walked down the hallway, he noticed that Ray's bedroom door was open, so he quietly closed it so he wouldn't disturb Ray, never realizing that Ray was dead in the bedroom. The next morning, Jim got up to go to church and saw that Ray's door was still closed. It was late for Ray to still be sleeping, so Jim opened the door to wake him and wish him a good morning. That's when he found what Tommy had done and called for help. After finding Ray, it took Jim a long time to recover emotionally from this tragic incident. Jim suffered more than others because he was so truly sensitive.

Everybody needs someone in his or her life that can kick some ass anytime and anywhere. That's the role of Ronnie Red. He's been described as a big ol' redheaded, power-lifting ex-college-football-player that means business. But he is a lot more than what you see on the outside. I soon learned that he was probably the best writer I had ever met, and when he wrote a police report, it sang. I later learned that Red had school administrators for parents and had majored in history at college. He was a lot more than a pretty face that would beat your ass in a minute. He soon became my muscle and bodyguard for all my Mafia murder-for-hire jobs. Every mob guy had his bodyguard as show. That's exactly why we used Red, and he played the role perfectly.

At one point in my career I left the Dirty Dozen motorcycle-gang world and started doing enforcement on the gang right in their faces. The position I took, in the Organized Crime Bureau, allowed me to oversee the motorcycle- and prison-gang enforcement section. I no longer did my gang enforcement by making cases undercover. Now I openly followed them around and went to their functions. With the use of informants in the gangs I could track all their activities and quickly take action on their criminal behavior. This meant I had to develop even more characters for my murder-for-hire cases because I was now exposed in the biker world.

One afternoon I began looking for a fugitive member of the Dirty Dozen after he had disappeared when charged with weapons violations. Little did I know that the gang had suspected he might be an informant for me so they shot him in the head. After shooting him they put him in a fifty-five-gallon oil barrel and burned him until he was nothing but ashes.

Another member had been killed in a motorcycle accident about the same time, and a big funeral was planned. Not knowing that Louie was dead in a barrel, I decided to watch the funeral and see if he showed up to pay his respects. I also asked Red to come along and hang out just in case something happened.

I drove a red Isuzu Trooper that was known to all the gang members after I had become public with my enforcement of them. So when I parked across the street in an open field, everyone at the funeral took it as a slap in the face. A sign of disrespect. Never mind they had already shot Louie and burned his body; my presence sent them over the edge. They hated my name, any talk of me, and the sight of me angered them.

We parked about three hundred feet from the cemetery on the south side of Beardsley Road and began watching the funeral. The president of the Dirty Dozen, Gumby, began yelling, "Fuck you, pigs," about twenty minutes after our arrival. He clenched his fist and waved it in the air as he got more and more agitated. Another member by the name of Hoover also got involved and started inciting all the other twenty to thirty people already at the funeral.

In the motorcycle-gang world the president is a god and receives respect from everyone around him. If he does something, you follow his lead and never allow him to go alone. You must be ready to die for your president or move along. There will always be ten more people behind you that are willing to die. That ideology was in place on the day Red and I went to the cemetery. Gumby knew that and took full advantage of his position as president to incite the crowd into a frenzy. He knew that he could act a fool and never have to dirty his hands. All the other members and wannabes would do the dirty work for him. That dirty work at this place and time was to "kill Jake." All Gumby had to do was start yelling profanities and scream like a madman. The more he yelled, the more his members yelled along with him. Before too long they were all so worked up that they took on the mob mentality.

Gumby started challenging Red and me to fight as he became more crazed. He pulled the handgun on his hip out of its holster, then started moving toward the fence to cross over to our location. When he brandished his firearm, all of the people at the funeral did the same thing and followed his every move. Gumby started to climb the three-foot fence that separated the cemetery from the street. All the other attendees began to do the same thing and continued to mirror everything Gumby said or did. That was the scariest time in my life. For the first time I felt that I was about to die and there was nowhere to run.

I couldn't call in reinforcements because they would be

ambushed as they drove into the area. Besides, there wasn't enough time to get anything set up. It was like the shoot-out at the O.K. Corral and you had to suck it up and ready yourself for the ride.

Red looked at me and said that we needed to get out of there, but I told him that was no longer an option. If I left at this point, then I would be considered a coward and would never have any respect from the gang. I would lose any respect I'd earned from all my years undercover. I told Red to grab his gun and get ready, because if they continued coming at us, then someone was going down with us. Red just looked at me and said, "Let's do it."

As the mob of gang members followed Gumby across the street, we prepared our guns and laid out additional ammunition. The crowd grew closer and closer until suddenly Glaze came from the circle of people and grabbed Gumby. Glaze was a past president of the Dirty Dozen and had huge respect from all the members.

He told Gumby to stop what he was doing and put his gun away. After several minutes of yelling back and forth, none of it intelligible to Red and me, Gumby followed what Glaze was saying and went back across the street. The crowd followed and stood together inside the cemetery.

We survived that day, and the gang still talks about how we refused to back down and they had to regroup. Those kind of moments and events make me wonder if I have a death wish. It's also the kind of moment that made me appreciate the friend I had in Red.

In this group of five lifetime friends is Tim "Coon Dog" Cooning, the greatest undercover cop I ever met. He never disappointed me in the twenty-five years that I knew and worked with him. He had a great undercover look with his Charles Manson features and facial expressions. His never backing down on anything made this ex–Airborne Ranger a treat to have with you on the streets. He was also a friend like no other because he was always there no matter the day or the time. Dog was the most reliable friend I had ever had. He was honest, trustworthy, and a warrior in every sense of the word.

On a dark winter evening one December in 1985, I had invited several of the Dirty Dozen members to a bar called Cheers in central Phoenix. I had been going to this club for over a year and had become a regular. It's funny how that works. You can frequent a new bar for a couple weeks and suddenly you are a regular. Everyone knows your name and people have been drinking with you for years. Great way to become believable to your new customers. I had also told Dog to stop by for a drink later in the evening and meet some of the gangsters.

Cheers has a huge area where tables are set and the patrons can sit and get drunk. A large stage in one corner rises above the crowd, and the entertainers look down into the club. A waist-high pony wall separates a long bar from the tables on the other side.

This was talent-show night, and people came from all over the city to sing, play an instrument, and sing some more. Some were better than others and some just stunk. I was sitting at the bar with the owner, who was also the talent-show judge. He and I were joking and drinking the whole night while the talent show rolled on. Of course, he thought I was drinking, but I was really dumping drinks or giving them away. That was the only way I could stay sober, but appear as if I were a heavy drinker. The last thing I needed was to be totally drunk and have to defend myself in a fight.

A fat lady was next on the stage and planned to sing and play the guitar. When she got up and started singing, I almost fell out of my chair because she sounded so bad. I laughed at her for a moment, then turned my attention back to the judge for a couple more stories and a couple more lies. When the talent show ended, the fat lady didn't win, and she walked back to the crowd dejected and upset. How she thought she would win was beside me.

The judge and I continued laughing and drinking until I heard a voice from behind me in the crowd. "Hey!" I listened to the voice, and for some funny reason I knew it was for me. The hair on my neck stood up and I knew something was about to happen. Once again I heard, "Hey!" This time I turned around to see a skinny, little man reach into the waist of his pants and draw out a machete. "You made my old lady lose, and now you're going to pay!" I just knew this wasn't good at all. I don't like to carry a gun, so of course I was unarmed. All the gang members were there and wouldn't stand for my backing down. I didn't know what to do, so I looked around and grabbed a barstool.

I could see the headlines for the next day: UNDERCOVER COP DIES WHEN HE TAKES BARSTOOL TO A KNIFE FIGHT. What choice did I have though? I wasn't going to look like a coward or give up my identity. I had to fight because the whole gun thing didn't "burn my skirt." I respected guns, but never liked them and rarely carried one. If trouble broke out, then I'd just as soon beat your ass and walk away.

I looked the guy in the face and started laughing out loud

like a crazy man. Looking around the room for some support made me look even crazier. I challenged the man and told him, "Bring it on." I said I was going to break every bone in his body with the barstool, then stick the knife up his ass so he would know where to find it when he woke up.

"Let's go, big boy! Bring it on!" I yelled at him.

"You made my old lady lose and now I'm gonna make you pay!" he said.

I repeated once more, "Come over here and I'm breaking every bone in your body. You know what next, asshole? I'm going to stick that knife right up your little, scrawny ass!"

The more I ranted, the more freakish I became. My fear of the situation had taken over any common sense I may once have had and turned me into a loon that no longer cared. I became Hulk-like and didn't really care what the consequences were. I suddenly didn't believe I could die. I was invincible.

While I continued my rant, I noticed the front door of the club open and in walked Dog. He stopped dead in the doorway and assessed the situation. Man with a machete and me with a barstool in hand. Bad combination, but a good time for Dog to come out and play. He slowly walked through the crowd until he was up against the back of the man with the machete. I watched as he whispered in the man's ear and watched as the man's head began to nod up and down. The man slowly put the knife back in his pants, then ran out the door with his fat old lady running closely behind.

Dog stood in the crowd for a moment and quietly placed his 9 mm semiautomatic handgun back in his pants. Everyone in the place screamed because I had backed the nut down. They didn't realize Dog had saved my life.

Years and years passed with Dog by my side and me by his. I always felt he was a bit of an angel in my life, and one that I was thankful for every day. He never backed down from anything and was always there when I needed him. I never questioned if I could count on him; I knew I could.

Finally we come to the man I have partnered with for my entire career. The only time we didn't share a patrol car or an office was while I was undercover at the warehouse and he was on the SWAT team. We still worked closely together during that time because I knew I could trust him with my life. Alex did all the surveillances I needed and made or arranged most of the arrests.

Alex was a back-East guy who was a standout basketball and football star in his hometown. He got a scholarship to play football for Bowling Green University and came to Arizona shortly after he graduated. For some unknown reason he decided to try a career in law enforcement and applied for the Phoenix Police Department. Picture him on the first day of the academy arriving in clothes straight out of the movie *Saturday Night Fever*. Tight Angels Flight pants, platform shoes, and a silk shirt that was unbuttoned to midchest. He wore gold chains and had hair down to his shoulders. The face still sported a Fu Manchu mustache that extended below the chin. Nothing new for Alex. This is how he and his friends in New York always dressed. He thought he looked pretty damn good for the first day.

Everyone else at the academy had gotten the memo on short hair, dark dress slacks, and a white shirt with a tie. When Alex arrived at the formation area for the morning inspection, he looked like mob central. It didn't take long for Sergeant Griffith to make Alex his personal project for a quick exit from the academy. By the end of the first week, he not only owned Alex, but Alex had returned to the barbershop for thirteen haircuts, never once totally pleasing Griffith.

Alex survived the academy and Sergeant Griffith, and by the end he had also gained a great deal of respect from everyone around him. Amazingly, Alex is without a doubt the funniest person I have ever met. He can tell a story like no other and makes it more interesting each time it is told. No story is ever told the same way twice. His sensitive side also makes him unbelievably compassionate for the underdog. While working the streets, he would give the homeless man money and drive the drunk to a place where he could sleep for the night. His goal was to make sure that no person was ever wrongly charged or had their constitutional rights violated.

The funniest thing he ever did happened after he spent a long night out with a bunch of older cops that included our friend Buck Brown. Buck was a retired marine drill sergeant and drank Old Grand-Dad whiskey as if it were punch. He taught Alex how to drink and it left Alex a bit queasy the next day. When shift assignments were handed out, Alex was hooked up with Chuck Billingsley, a high-strung cop who drove as if he were a Formula One driver. The faster he drove during the shift, the sicker Alex got.

As they were racing to a family-fight call, their speed exceeded eighty miles an hour. The streets were dark and it was difficult to see what was around every corner, even if you drove slowly. Suddenly, Chuck slammed on the brakes but nearly hit a four-hundred-pound Native American man standing drunk in the street. Chuck honked his horn to get him to move so he could continue on the call, but the man refused. Finally Alex got out of the patrol car and walked over to the man, telling him to get out of the street. The man still refused, so Alex got closer.

As he did as, the man wrapped his arms around Alex and belched out some of his native language. The smell of rotten booze belched into Alex's face sickened him far beyond the sickness he had been feeling all night, and he vomited into the face of the Indian. They both stood for a minute and looked at each other in utter surprise, then Alex turned around and got back into the car. The Indian male walked away talking to himself and wiping the vomit from his face.

When Alex arrived at the family fight, he had his shirt unbuttoned and was covered in his own vomit. As he stood at the door, he could hear loud arguing in the house, so he knocked loudly and rang the doorbell. As the door opened, Alex stood there in all his glory. The woman answering the door stopped in midsentence and curbed her anger. She stared at Alex for a moment, then asked if he was all right. Despite being in the middle of a fight with her husband, she was now concerned about Alex. She brought him inside, sat him down, and got him some water.

Just another night and another family fight ended.

I **have** my five friends for life and thank God each day for what they have brought to me and my life. The only way I could ever survive in this world of mine was to reconnect with those five and ground myself, even if for one evening. I always knew they would be honest and tell me the truth.

I always reminded myself to do a self-evaluation, then check with the fellas. Hopefully that would keep me floating.

I constantly thought about those friends and what they meant to my life. I never wanted to disappoint them, and I never wanted to lose their friendship, which meant so much to me. If I ended up like Tommy, then those friends would never again be a part of my life. That was true motivation. I also never wanted to disappoint any children that might look up to me, such as Geoff, or all those children that had been abused in their young lives and needed me for support. When I found myself slipping into the darkness, I would remind myself of a caption on a poster that once hung in the halls of the precinct:

"A hundred years from now it will not matter what my bank account was, the sort of house I lived in, or the kind of car I drove. But the world may be different because I was important in the life of a child."

If you can't stay straight and do the right thing for a child . . . then you have lost everything that matters in our world.

12

This Was the One

Every day and every night followed the same path. I had to continue my trips to the gym each morning to keep the size that had become my identity . . . and possibly my crutch. It became harder and harder to work out for two hours each day after drinking all night and hanging out in the smoky clubs. And I was finding myself drifting further from the reality that I once knew and loved.

Each day before I left for the streets, I crawled around the engine of my truck and then rolled on the ground. A quick stop through the liquor store and a purchase of some cheap whiskey for my cologne of choice. After pouring the whiskey down my back and over my chest, I would hop on the bike and drive around town. I hit all my local stops, including the topless clubs, pool halls, and sleazy bars. I would even go to the housing projects and anywhere I could peddle myself as a criminal looking for business. My being out there all the time kept my name on the street and business coming my way.

I would also stop every single day at a small deli owned by a German guy named Bob and his Russian wife, Ifei. I was constantly eating so I could keep my weight up and support my intense weight-lifting sessions. I would try to eat at least every three hours. When I went to Bob's deli, I would order the same thing every time, and soon Bob would start it as I walked in the door: A bacon, lettuce, and tomato sandwich with a freshly baked cookie and a glass of tea. The bacon had to be extra-crispy and the cookie fresh. Every day I would ride up to the deli and walk inside looking like shit. Bob and his wife would treat me as if I were their finest customer and even comp my dinner periodically. For seven straight years I ate the same thing day in and day out, never tiring of the food or the company. If I showed up early on the weekdays, they would make sure the television was tuned to *Guiding Light*. I think I even got them a bit hooked. After I finished the meal, I headed back to the streets.

I kept returning to the deli because my visits there helped keep me centered. They treated me like a regular person and didn't see me as some big slug that would eventually rob them. I'm not sure why they acted the way they did, but it was special. They were both immigrants and hadn't been in America for long. Maybe they had experienced people mistreating them and decided never to behave that way. Or maybe they just liked my money. Either way, I got a good meal and had some comfort from the street and the creeps that lived there.

Some of my most active suspects (and unwitting) informants were the prostitutes on Van Buren Street. I made it a point to connect with them at some point each day. I would always buy a wallet or credit card they had stolen, then move on to the next stop. The prostitutes were always good for credit cards after giving blow jobs to the truckers who were their routine customers. The girls were busy working the trucker as he lay back with his eyes closed and enjoyed the experience. When the moment was right, the girls would reach in the trucker's pocket and rifle through his wallet. Grab a couple of cards, then get back to work. The truckers never missed the cards until the girls were long gone. Then they were too embarrassed to report them stolen. They never wanted to upset the little lady waiting at home. The working girls loved me because I never beat them and always paid them well for their stolen property.

I finally got tired of the heat coming off the pavement and made a run inside the Candy Store to check out Kristie and the girls. When I walked in the door, it was as if somebody with presidential clout had arrived. Everyone started coming over to me as I sat in my normal seat, and a drink would follow as soon as I finished the one before. Kristie didn't have to chase me like the other girls because she believed she was the chosen one, so she made her way over as soon as the crowd went back to work.

I would often find myself thinking about Kristie and how a girl could end up with a life like hers. She spent her days dancing nude in front of a bunch of guys who thought she only had eyes for them. In reality, she only had eyes for their money. Then at night she was a mother to her children, and by all accounts a good mother. I always believed she only liked me because I gave her clout and a perception of being protected. Other dancers and customers who knew of me didn't mess with her for fear they would be paid a visit by me. It was purely an illusion, but one that worked well for her.

The lights were down, the music blared as one of the girls made love to a brass pole. Drug deals were going on all around me, and trades for other illegal services were being discussed. I leaned back in my seat and started daydreaming about nothing special . . . didn't have a care in the world. Then it hit me. I had become completely comfortable in this world. I was "Jake," the dirty rotten ex-convict looking for the next ass to kick and the next deal. It seemed as if I owned this place.

I looked around the club at the girls, who looked hot to me despite their being hooked on cocaine and meth. What the hell was I thinking? I asked myself. Right then I knew I had to get out and get some fresh air. Maybe ride away for a while and clear out my head. At that very moment, I knew something had gone seriously wrong in my head when meth freaks and cocaine addicts looked good to me.

When I got outside, I was almost hyperventilating, and the only thing I could think of was to call Patti. She'd called me when she needed support after Geoff broke his arm; now it was my turn to ask her for some relief. I didn't have to tell her why; I just needed to hear her voice. Something sweet and pure. Not the smell of cheap stripper perfume and second-grade conversation.

The phone rang three times, then Patti answered in a voice that kind of gave me a comforted feel.

"Hey, this is Jake."

She really seemed excited to hear from me and asked what I had planned for the weekend.

"Nothing but work, and maybe some yard work at the house."

Patti said she had some friends with a cabin and they were having a big party this weekend. "Would you like to go with Geoff and I?"

Would I like to go? She didn't need to ask twice!

The ride up to the cabin the next day was absolutely fantastic with nothing going wrong and our conversation really easy. It was as if we had been friends for our whole lives as we talked through one topic after another. Geoff would chime in with some little-boy stuff about his friends and school, and we would laugh at his sense of humor and what a little boy thought was important. Everything about the trip was about as perfect as it gets.

Most people who don't live in Arizona don't know that it can get pretty damn hot in town in the winter—ninety degrees at times. Then drive an hour and a half to the mountains and you will most likely find snow. That's exactly what we found as we drove into Christopher Creek, just outside Payson, Arizona. Snow on the mountains and snow on the ground. Not only that, but more snow was also expected throughout the weekend.

When we got our truck empty of luggage, Geoff ran off to play and Patti and I started for a walk. Just then, one of her friends offered us an ATV to ride for a while and play in the snow. Things just couldn't get any better. All of Patti's friends were a breath of fresh air for me. Quite a change from the regular group of thugs I had been hanging around with. Her friends included farmers, salesmen, construction workers, and more hairdressers. They told normal stories and sat around laughing and drinking while they took turns cooking incredible meals. Something about a meal that is cooked in the mountains is special. You can smell it as you eat it, and you never seem to get enough. Everything you do has a memory attached to a smell.

We rode through the snow on the ATV for over an hour until we came to a clearing that looked over a canyon. The view was spectacular, and the air was fresh and crisp. As we sat looking over the canyon, we continued to talk, about nothing in particular. She finally inquired about my job and undercover lifestyle, so I told her what a normal day included. What I didn't tell her was how dangerous everything I did really was. I didn't want to scare her off and make her unnecessarily concerned. I never believed in making my life sound dangerous, and I wasn't going to start with Patti. All she needed to know was that I had fun doing what I did and I could take good care of myself.

At one point during our talk I turned my head around and back toward Patti, and she suddenly snuck a kiss. We looked at each other for a few seconds and kissed again . . . and again. It seemed as if an eternity had passed when we stopped, laughed at each other for a short time, then realized it was getting late and we had better head back to the cabin. I started up the ATV as the sun was setting. I felt a lot of love and that teenagelike emotion that comes with a new relationship. You know the one, where fireworks seem to be blasting off inside your stomach and your head is all in a haze. That's exactly how I felt at the moment she began to kiss me. I also felt a sense of relief to know that she seemed to care for me as much as I cared for her.

As we drove down the road that had been plowed clear of the snow, the ATV began to sputter. We were out of gas. Here we were with no phone, the sun setting, out in the snow, with no chance to survive the night if someone didn't find us. We started to laugh and Patti jokingly blamed me for the empty tank because I surely wanted to spend more private time with her. I suggested that we start pushing the ATV back to the cabin. She laughed and said, "You can push, but with me still sitting on the seat." So push I did as she sat on the seat and we tried to work our way back. Once again we started laughing hysterically, but this time at the predicament we had got into.

We probably walked for a mile or so until one of Patti's friends came along and snatched us from the snow. The rest of the weekend was really special and seemed to be the point at which we could really start to date and trust each other. At the end of the weekend I took Geoff and Patti back to their house and unloaded their luggage from my truck.

Patti's house was located in a typical Arizona neighborhood. Most of the yards were green with beautiful grass and several trees growing. The most prominent tree in most of the yards was the palm tree. This tree is almost as popular to visitors of Arizona as the storied saguaro cactus. Intermittently placed around the houses with grass yards were houses having yards with desert landscape. In these yards you could find cacti throughout, including every variety from barrel to saguaro. Patti's house was a frame-stucco construction with a tile roof and a number of windows throughout. The weather is simple in Arizona and brick homes aren't prominent.

Geoff carried a bag in from the truck, and Patti grabbed some of her stuff, leaving me with one more suitcase. They disappeared into the house before I got to the front door, only to return and grab the one remaining bag. Once again I stood outside and listened as Patti told me how much fun she'd had. I didn't even get a chance to go inside and see what the place looked like because I was always left outside.

As I found out later, Patti was incredibly protective of Geoff and didn't want him influenced by someone who wasn't going to be around for a long time. She wasn't in the habit of bringing men into her house and kept the home a special place for her and Geoff. I completely understood this and made a point to respect what she was doing. It reminded me of my own mother when she wouldn't let me bring divorced or strange women into the house for fear that it would be a bad influence on my younger brother and sister. Those types of things made me begin to fall in love and try even harder to make a relationship. It wasn't easy, though, because I had a reputation that could be tough to deal with and could make a good girl squeamish. Most of it totally fabricated because it was part of my many undercover personalities.

You're damned if you do and damned if you don't. I worked hard to be believable as a hit man with multiple personalities and a reputation for toughness. But in my being so believable, everybody thought it was real. Even my friends and family began to believe I had become the multiple personalities I played. It's hard to shake that kind of reputation and convince a respectable girl that you are something different. You know what they say: if it looks like a duck and quacks like a duck . . . it must be a duck.

We continued dating for a long time and I stayed outside for many more months patiently waiting to be greeted and then to be sent off home. Topless dancers wanted me in the worst way with plans to do nasty and bad things to me. Instead, I chose to wait outside a house and be greeted with a kiss and a gentle caress. I was like a 280-pound puppy.

13

Ma and Pa Kettle's Revenge

Walking into Shorty's Bar is a lot like walking from high noon into the dark of night. It's a small joint with one long, narrow bar table that runs the length of the business. No separate tables can be found in the open area where people walk from their barstool to the bathroom, but there is a pool table and an arcade game called Centipede. The only lights in the entire place shine from under the liquor bottles behind the bar or the backlights of the arcade game. Walk from the outside daylight into Shorty's and you have to stop and take a few moments to let your eyes adjust to the black of night they call mood lighting. If you leave before the sun sets, then you are greeted with an overload of light to your eyes and you are once again blinded for a minute or two.

I always knew when I went to Shorty's that I needed to stay inside if trouble broke out. I wasn't going to get lured outside and be met by someone who had clear sight and a baseball bat or knife. It was like that on the streets—people would attack you for no clear reason. When you're the "big dog," other people try to knock you down to bump themselves up. I would never have had a chance to recover because it would have taken my eyes too long to adjust. That would have been just enough time for someone to give me some of my own medicine and ball-bat me to death. I always bragged during my meetings with potential clients that my weapon of choice was a baseball bat. A few swings to the knees, one to the lower back, then a home-run slug to the head. It became a chilling thought for those who were. considering hiring me.

I played a few games of Centipede when I first arrived, then played a couple games of 9-ball by myself until boredom set in. Walking slowly to the bar, I swatted the pool balls around the table, and then took a seat at the end of the bar, sitting snugly against the wall. I didn't have to order a drink because Sara knew what I wanted and had already placed one on the Centipede machine when I first arrived. As soon as I sat down on the barstool, she slid another drink in front of me, then gave me a bowl full of popcorn. I stared at my drink thinking about nothing in particular and feeling quite comfortable with only me, Sara, and "old man Phil" in the bar. As I daydreamed, I began to play a game I routinely played when I was by myself. Guess the number of unpopped kernels in the bowl, then begin the count. Instead of just pouring everything on the table, I dropped each counted kernel into my drink glass and slowly watched as it sank to the bottom. At times the game could take hours and was always totally meaningless. I did it in the beginning because I thought it made me look crazy to onlookers.

But now it has become somewhat interesting and more than anything else a habit.

More time passed than I can really recall until the door opened and a young man with a shaved head walked in the door. Sweating from being out in the summer heat, he took a seat at the other end of the bar and ordered three beers. All three arrived at the same time, and he took them one by one and drank each until the bottles were dry. When he finished, surprisingly he stood upright and walked over to where I was sitting and sat down again, in the stool next to me. "Sonny?" he said.

For a brief moment I continued to watch my kernels float to the bottom of my glass and then stop. Tilting my head to one side, I looked up at him and replied, "Who might be asking?"

The bald young man stared back at me as if surprised, then looked around the room. He looked back and forth until he stopped and gazed at me again. "Waterhead told me to come and see you. Did you get the message or is he messing with me?"

"No," I said as I laughed, "I've been waiting for you but wanted to make sure you were the right guy. You're Billy, right?"

My informant Waterhead had a friend, Billy, he had been working with at the homeless shelter. Billy confided in Waterhead and told him about his crazy neighbors at the trailer park who wanted him to kill their kid. Billy was young, but had spent the better part of his life in juvenile correctional centers and prison. Since getting out of prison this time, he promised his wife he would turn his life around and start doing the right thing. So Waterhead sent Billy to me. I'm sure this was difficult for Billy since his whole life included running from the law and hating everyone with authority. But if he truly planned on changing his life, then this would be a great start—and he said it would make his wife proud of him. Billy told me he felt that Waterhead was a brother to him, and if he trusted me, then Billy would do the same.

Billy's neighbors are an uneducated husband and wife who live in a trailer with their teenage son. Pa is a professional tree trimmer, and Ma stays at home as a questionable homemaker. Dillon is their son and has an incredible temper and apparently terrorizes everyone in the trailer park. Because all the neighbors fear Dillon, the family has been ordered to move. The only way they can stay in their trailer is if Dillon is evicted. The park managers have ordered Dillon off the property, but he refuses to leave and threatens them if they try to evict him. He doesn't mess with Billy because he fears him and respects his prison reputation.

Ma and Pa tried to get an order of protection against Dillon by going to the courts and filing a complaint. In the complaint they wrote:

> *Today cops was called on him. Went into our trailer was not there broke our fence—cussed the neighbor out and myself if not put on him we have to move. Husband not working right now because of wrist and surgery. Doctors care yet afraid if he has place to go. Not allowed on property.*

Billy explained that Ma and Pa were trying to get him to kill Dillon for his $1,000 stereo they gave him as a Christmas present. "If you can help me out and do this one thing," Billy begged, "I won't ask for anything in return." I had to call Ma and Pa right away or they were going to find someone else. They refused to leave their trailer, and the eviction hearing was at 8:00 a.m. the following morning. Their plan was to have Dillon killed before they went to court—then there would be no eviction. If Billy didn't introduce me as the hit man, they were killing Dillon themselves or finding some heroin junkie to do it for them. However it happened, Dillon was going to die, and they were not going to be evicted.

I told Billy to go back to the trailer and tell Ma and Pa to meet me in two hours behind the hotel near McDonald's. "You know where I'm talking about, Billy?"

"I know, Sonny, and trust me, they'll be there."

As I walked out the door, I tried to figure out exactly how I was going to make this work. I have a standard in place for every client I meet. Each is given an opportunity to walk away and never come back. If people change their mind overnight or over the following few weeks, then I know they weren't really committed. In this case I had no choice but to meet with the parents and finish the deal on the spot. What I had to do was to push harder during my conversations with Ma and Pa and make sure they convinced me of their commitment, just as they'd convinced Billy.

Instead of showing up late for the deal as I had always done, I arrived early and stood in a dark hallway to watch the overall area. The surveillance and arrest team had quickly been assembled and a video platform tucked into the shadows of the hotel. Everyone knew his assignment and also knew to watch the entire area for suspicious activity. Billy may have seemed sincere and Waterhead had told me he was "solid," but I had a hard time believing this was really true. No real reason, except maybe I was uncomfortable with the quickness of the setup.

Ma and Pa had hounded Billy to do the murder because they

believed he was a convict with a bad reputation. I didn't have to give much thought to my character because I knew my best role was someone just like Billy. So I became an ex-convict with bad intentions and someone they would be comfortable telling their story to. If I looked the part and they believed a killer ex-convict was their best choice, then I wouldn't have to hurdle the trust issue before getting right to the deal.

As the deal time drew near, I moved from the hallway into the parking lot where the camera could best capture our meeting. I found a light pole by a parking space and leaned against it while I waited for Ma and Pa. Patiently waiting, I pulled a knife out of my pocket and started trimming my fingernails. Then an old Nova with primer-gray paint rolled into the parking lot with a middle-aged man at the wheel and a middle-aged, plump woman in the front passenger seat. The driver drove by me and nodded his head as if he already knew who I was. He slowly backed his car into a parking space near me and rested his arm outside the window.

I continued to cut my nails and looked around for a moment as if I didn't really trust the two. Out of the corner of my eye I saw Pa's arm out the window, and it was completely wrapped in a thick castlike bandage. The beat-up car continued to run and I stared at the two as they stared back at me. A few minutes passed, then I began to walk over to the driver's side of the car. The closer I got, the louder the car seemed. This definitely wasn't going to work as I'd planned on capturing their audio. "Arm looks bad dude," I said as I neared the car. He said something I couldn't quite make out, so I asked him what the hell he'd just said. Pa sat up straighter in his seat and said, "Cut it off trimming a tree." I told him to shut the car off or I was leaving. He quickly reached a screwdriver to where the ignition had been popped off and turned the junker off. It chugged and spit for a bit, then was quiet.

I knelt down outside the car so I could look him in the eyes. Then I looked across to the passenger side and acknowledged her: "Ma'am."

"Are you Sonny?"

I ignored her and looked at the old man's arm as he continued to hang it out the window. When I asked him what had happened, he explained how he was a professional tree trimmer and partially severed his arm while trimming a palm tree. He described how the doctors had tried to reattach the severed arm, and he was waiting to see if it would take.

"So let me get this right. You got your arm caught in the chain saw while you were cutting a branch?"

"That's right," he responded in an almost embarrassed way.

I turned my attention back to the chubby lady and slowly said, "Yeah, I'm Sonny. Billy says you need me to make your kid disappear." With that one statement she opened up and babbled for nearly ten minutes about her son. He was incorrigible and wouldn't listen to a thing they said. "Runs around the trailer park and harasses everyone. Nobody can go outside their trailer when he's home." He wouldn't move and they couldn't afford to be evicted, so he had left them no other choice but to have him killed.

"There has got to be another way," I said.

"No," said Ma. "Either you do it or we gonna get it done with someone else."

Pa started to chime in after Ma finally quit talking and said he had tried everything to get Dillon under control. "One day I had it with him when he smart-mouthed me. I grabbed a pair of pliers and from my toolbox and marched right back to him. Then I grabbed his lips and squeezed and squeezed." Then Pa threw his hands in the air, spit at his windshield, and said, "That didn't even stop him!" When everyone stopped talking at the thought of Dillon getting his lips squeezed by a pair of pliers, Ma looked long and hard at me and said, "It has to be done by eight a.m. tomorrow morning."

First thing I needed to know before I could move forward was how they wanted it done. They both agreed I could do it any way I wanted as long as I made sure he was dead. If I didn't kill him for sure, then he would be real mad and everybody was going to pay. "Okay, I'm going to shoot him in the head when he goes to sleep tonight. Everyone will blame it on one of the neighbors he harassed." Both Ma and Pa thought I had a great idea, but once again reinforced that it had to be done right away.

Then I asked how much they were willing to pay. Ma handed me a picture of Dillon and offered me his $1,000 stereo after he died and $200 right now. I told them I planned on taking everything he had in his room that was worth selling at a pawnshop, and Ma agreed that would make me more money than she could outright pay.

With the picture in hand and $200 neatly tucked in my pocket, I assured Ma and Pa that their little boy would die between now and early morning. Then I pulled a bandanna out of my pocket and wrapped it around my head, the agreed tip-off for the arrest. As SWAT members converged on the dumpy Nova, Pa reached for his screwdriver and began to start the car. I quickly grabbed his injured arm and said, "Start the car, old man, and I'm ripping your arm off." Pa slowly pulled the screwdriver out of the ignition and sat defeated.

The SWAT members pulled Ma out of the car and placed her hands on its hood. She unknowingly looked directly into the eye of a concealed camera and with her round, pudgy mouth whispered, "Oh, shit."

Uniformed officers then went over to the trailer to get Dillon and bring him to meet me at the police station. When they arrived and told him what had happened, he freaked out and began assaulting the officers. Once they'd subdued him and got him into handcuffs, they brought him to me. I walked into the holding room where Dillon was sitting and took a seat next to him. He looked at me and said, "Are you Ballentine?" I told him I was and he started to cry like a little child. "Did my mom really want you to kill me?" When I told him it was true, he cried and cried for probably the better part of fifteen minutes.

14

Coming in from the Outside

Summer months painfully came to an end and we headed into the Christmas holidays. With winter settling in, I was pleasantly surprised by my first-ever invitation into Patti's house, to join her and Geoff for dinner. Never having been inside her house left me a bit skittish when I first arrived at the front door. To my surprise, when I knocked, I heard Patti's voice from inside: "The door's open, come on inside." I stood stunned for a minute, then walked inside. As I stood inside the doorway, I felt a rush of emotions both through my soul and sense of smell. Candles were lit and the aroma was soothing, while food cooked in the kitchen. Everything was in its place, and the décor was country-style.

I couldn't get myself to move or talk. I just took it all in and thought to myself, "I'm home again."

We continued to date and see each other with every spare

minute I could get away from the job, and our relationship grew deeper with each passing month. It seemed as if it had taken an eternity to get to this point, so I made sure to appreciate everything we did with each other. I never took anything for granted and always made her realize how special she was in my life.

While I was dating Patti, Geoff once again asked me to show him my undercover identification. Up to this point everything seemed to be going so well, but I didn't realize a big explosion was waiting for me around the corner. The driver's license I pulled out and showed Geoff had my undercover name of Jake and a fake birth date making me three years older. Patti looked at it with Geoff and I never suspected that she would believe the information contained on my undercover license was my true name and my real birthday. Unfortunately I had forgotten just how naïve she was.

A few months later she talked about celebrating my birthday and commented that I was three years older than I really was. Surprised, I showed her my true identification, and that moment the big explosion began. "How could you be so insincere as to lie about something as small as your age!" she said. It didn't matter what I said, she wanted me to leave and not come back. If she couldn't trust me, then she didn't want to be around me. I looked at Geoff with a grin as I rubbed his head and told him, "I'll be back, don't worry."

Weeks passed before I ran into Patti again and had a chance to talk to her. We went to a small coffee shop and talked for hours about her misunderstanding and my need to be trusted. She finally relented, giving me another chance to be a part of her life. I think that was the last time she ever distrusted me. Even with her trust I would always wrestle with being one person on the outside, then coming home and being the real person who was on the inside.

Eventually, Patti and I married and she became the strength in my crazy world. Her calmness and trust gave me a whole new lease on life. It didn't change my confusion of whom I had become though. I still lived in a body I didn't like and spent days and nights in a world that could take my life away in a moment, then never regret the loss. She accepted my role and stood behind me all the way. Of course, as in any love story, we had almost been torn apart by a silly misunderstanding.

She had worked incredible hours in the salon to provide for Geoff and make sure he had a good life. As a single mother with her own business and relying on nobody but herself, she had been the picture of strength and success. When we married, she finally had someone else to help and could take a breather from her long and demanding days. She had more time to be with Geoff and even started helping at his school as a volunteer.

Shortly after we got married, we decided to shop for a new house. We made the perfect couple, a pretty, petite blonde with a huge, long-haired dirtbag following close behind. We went from one model home to another without getting any attention or respect. The salespeople stayed away from me as if I had the plague.

After days of looking and finally becoming worn-out from the effort, we stopped at one more model home. When we walked in the door, I expected the same cold shoulder as before, but a middle-aged man walked directly up to me and extended his hand. "Moon Mullins," he said. From that moment forward he worked with us until he found us the home we wanted. When

I filled out the paperwork for the financing, Moon realized what I did for a living and started to laugh. I told him about all the problems we had been experiencing and he said he wasn't surprised. It hadn't bothered him to wait on me because he'd learned years ago that looks can be deceiving.

Moon had once waited on a long-haired, skinny, transient-looking man who wanted to see homes in the million-dollar range. None of the other salespeople would give the man the time of day, so Moon made a special effort and gave him his total attention. The man turned out to be rock star Alice Cooper, who paid in cash when the deal was finally completed. Moon said he'd learned a great lesson that stayed with him forever.

It wasn't an easy life for Patti, being with me through all the death threats that started to mount as the years went along. I didn't let it affect our relationship and really never talked about it unless she was directly involved. Some police officers make it a habit to remind their significant other that this may be their last day. "Treat me good," they say, "I may not come home tonight or ever again." "Danger awaits me around every corner and we never know what will happen" is another thing they say. Not me though. I wanted to talk about other things and make Patti believe it was impossible for me to die. It worked and we never really worried about any of the threats.

After a couple years, Patti began to feel ill regularly and we became concerned that something was seriously wrong. After a visit to the doctor, she returned home looking gloomy. "I have something we need to talk about," she said. All I could think to do was offer her all my support to combat whatever illness she had.

She looked ready to cry, but then she jumped up and screamed with joy, "I'm pregnant!"

"Oh my God!" I said out loud. I had never thought about children of my own. I was totally content with Geoff in my life and didn't think I needed anyone else. I had even legally adopted Geoff and changed his last name to mine. The shock was overwhelming, then I started to think about all the benefits and joy a child would bring to our life. Suddenly it all seemed all right.

The morning that our boy was born, we sat in the hospital and my mind raced a mile a minute. Life, college, girls, sports, and everything else that I could think of. I stayed with Patti through the birth and all the hospital-related activities. Finally, I needed to go home and get some sleep or I would be no good to anyone. Before I left, we decided on a name, Cody Christopher.

I walked inside our new house and went directly to bed and lay there thinking about Cody's future. Nothing else seemed to matter because I now had a son. When I couldn't sleep, I finally got back up and headed back to the hospital. As I drove down the freeway, my mind continued to race and thoughts darted back and forth. School, college, life, good parent versus bad parent. How was I to know what to do and what to say? My mind went faster and faster as my car stayed close to the same speed. Suddenly, and for no reason at all, I grabbed the gearshift and while driving sixty-five miles an hour placed the truck into reverse! The gears screamed and I thought for a moment the truck was going to explode. I got the gear back into place, but sold the car a day later.

I have always told Cody that he was my special gift from God. He gave me a new reason to live life and enjoy it better than I ever had before. I became the talk of the community as he grew because I would go to parent meetings and school functions looking like a convict, drug dealer, or mobster. Nobody knew what to think of Cody's dad at first, but they eventually accepted me without too many questions because I was nice to everyone.

The dark world that I lived in for my job continued with more and more trips to the edge, but my family became a lifeline that kept me grounded. My challenge was to never do anything that would embarrass them and always remember they were watching. It was my new conscience and became more powerful than anything else in my life. Whatever I did was laced with the thought that I must return home because they needed me. I didn't ever want anyone else to raise my boys. I now fully realized the power of family in a man's life and never wanted to lose it.

When I wasn't on the streets being one of my many characters, I was in the salon cleaning toilets and fixing equipment. Or I was coaching baseball, football, or a number of other sports. I knew I had to keep balance or I would lose everything to the other world. The challenge came in trying to juggle both worlds: being a dad and a husband that cared and loved, then leaving that security and becoming a monster that stole, cheated, lied, and confused those around him. I lived a lie every day, but did it for the good of everyone. Now tell me that's not confusing.

Finding myself was a daily challenge that sometimes became too much to handle. When I became overwhelmed with trying to survive in the dark world, I would roll back to the Little League park or the cemetery and sit. Those two places seemed to clear my head and make me fresh enough to carry on for another day. The best place, though, was always home with Patti and the boys. I could be myself and not have to pretend. That was more refreshing than anything else.

I had two sisters and a brother, who adored Patti from the moment they met her. This made my relationship even better because I always looked for support from my family. My mother wasn't around any longer to give her approval or disapproval, so the siblings were in charge of that department. My older sister, Judy, was an entrepreneur who made and lost more money than I will ever see. Jeff was my younger brother, close enough in age to me that we had similar lives and memories. Jana, the baby, was successful in commercial property and was probably the most loving of all our family. They would always remind me where I came from if they thought I was drifting, and they did it in a way that only brothers and sisters could.

To survive this undercover world you must surround yourself with friends and family that will help keep you in check. They must invest themselves in your life and monitor how you develop and how you change. Everyone must understand where the line is and be willing to draw my attention to it when I seem to be coming close to crossing it. If the team works together, then a safe return is guaranteed. The help won't make everything better, but it will keep you focused and act as your personal reminder. Temptation is a strong emotion and has taken many undercover cops down a dangerous path. You need all the help you can get to lead you through the many tempting obstacles.

Every night I returned home, I walked into Cody's bedroom and sat next to him for a while. I would think about his laugh, his smile, his sense of humor. I would also remember that I was doing the job I was doing so his life could be safe. When I couldn't get home and was out at some flea-bitten hotel, I would pull out my bag and put a picture of Patti and the boys on the counter. That picture was a reminder of what was important. I also used it to prevent me from making decisions that would be life-changing. Someone needed me now and I had to keep that in mind. I didn't want my children to be part of a law-enforcement statistic of fatherless children. And I didn't want my wife's only memory of me to be a folded American flag.

No matter how hard I tried to keep my family sheltered and separate from the dark life I lived, a time came when my luck ran out. Once you completed a case, everyone was inevitably going to know who you were. If not through public records, my real identity would come out during the trial. Some defense attorneys prided themselves in outing me and felt it was their duty to inform their clients. Those defense attorneys were the minority, but nonetheless they were a danger to my family and me.

My wife and I decided to build our own home and contracted with a builder to manage the subcontractors. Everything worked really well and Patti seemed to become friends with every one of the workers. When the house was completed, we decorated everything. In the den we hung pictures of my career and the stories that had been written. After twelve months, we invited the painter back to do an annual touch-up around the house. As he stood in the den, he struck up a conversation with "Miss Social" and quickly remembered who I was from his days with the Dirty Dozen Motorcycle Gang.

When I returned home, Patti told me, "Jake, this really nice guy came and painted the house today. If you saw him, you would have never guessed he was so nice, kinda like you."

"Really," I slowly said.

"Yeah, and he said he even knows you."

When she said this stranger knew who I was, the hair on the back of my neck stood right up. He knew me all right, from my days with the Dozen and the time he hung around them. Within the month, the floor plan of my house ended up in a prison with the Aryan Brotherhood. It also fell into the hands of the entire Dirty Dozen Gang. I understand they talked about attacking me, but they were too scared I would have a camera around the house, or even that I would be sitting in wait for them. I also warned the painter of what might happen to him if they ever came after me.

The more cases I worked, the more high profile I became and the bigger the target. Even though I remained undercover as a hit man, I would do interviews for news outlets, both print and television. The only stipulation was that I remain hidden during the interview by their changing my voice and disguising my features. The benefit to the department was in letting the public know that someone like me was out there. If knowing I existed prevented someone from making the mistake of hiring people like me, then it was worth the risk.

It became evident that I was becoming increasingly at risk when the Alcohol, Tobacco, and Firearms division of the federal government came to speak with me. Aryan Brotherhood member Eric Jesse had been released from prison and was ordered by ranking members in the gang to have me killed. The agents assured me that they were trying to locate Jesse.

The information was developed in the early-morning hours on a Thursday. By evening, the agents had located Jesse. When they took him into custody, he had all the components to make a pipe bomb, including the explosives. He was sent directly back to prison since somewhere in the rules of parole they have a clause that prohibits possession of explosives. Jesse must have missed that section when he was being released.

Nearly a year after the incident with Jesse, an article about my hit-man exploits appeared in *USA Today*. David Patterson, one of the best and most respected defense attorneys in Arizona, was interviewed, and the story noted:

> *Patterson says he's never faced Ballentine in court as a witness. But he was once the attorney for a man accused of trying to kill the undercover detective. "That gentleman did five years in federal prison," says Patterson, adding, "I guess Ballentine was getting too close to something he shouldn't have been close to. Someone hired a hit man to get the hit man."*

Then came an incident too close to home. Geoff was a student at one of the high schools in town and had become friends with a girl who would give him a ride to school every day. Upon graduation, she decided to serve her country and enter the air force and had to pass a physical and a battery of tests. Everything could be done in downtown Phoenix in one place operated by all branches of the military.

When she got to the medical portion of the test, she met a physician's assistant, with whom she talked at length. During her conversation she told the assistant that her friend's father worked for the Police Department. This assistant was, however, a member of the Dirty Dozen Motorcycle Gang . . . and hated me.

I knew the assistant by the nickname Baldo and was well aware of his intense hate for me. Baldo, though, wasn't very smart and told everyone he had met my daughter. He only heard what he wanted to hear and missed that she was my son's friend. Several days passed and word got onto the street and to me through my informants that the gang was planning to get to me by killing my daughter. They had finally located one of my family members, or so they thought, and would kill that person. The girl moved shortly after the threat came out, and the gang couldn't complete their plan.

The threats continued to mount, and Patti became close friends with the SWAT team as they protected her when I was away. She would bake them cookies and they would follow her to the store as she shopped. In spite of the inconvenience she knew they had her welfare at heart.

If it wasn't the gangs trying to kill me, it was hired hit men from soldier-of-fortune groups. A hefty contract was placed on my head, and the Aryan Brotherhood green-lighted anyone who could find and kill me. I would constantly get prison mail or tips from informants alerting me to the next attempt on my life or the most recent contract floating around to have me killed. However, I changed my looks so often they couldn't give or get a clear description of me. They were also chickenshit and feared that I would kill them before they got to me.

No matter where we went or what we did, the cloud of being killed became routine for us to deal with. We all became careful when starting the car, opening packages left at the door, and answering doors or phones.

Fear became my dragon, but I refused to let the threats control my life. This time, though, I had more to think of than just myself.

15

A Massage to Die For

It isn't often that I find myself so involved in a case that I can place myself into the position of the victim. Being a guy gives me some insight into how accusations and behavior can affect a man and his family. I have seen too many manipulative women during my time in the criminal underworld and watched how these women destroy the men in their life for personal gain and greed. When they want something, it doesn't matter who is in their way or who will be hurt, they are going to get it. *It* could be another man, more money, expensive jewelry, or the mere fun of destroying a man and anything that means something to him.

Debra Mounla was the epitome of that woman. I had the chance to see her through the eyes of her husband, Nabil Mounla. I saw firsthand the hurt and pain a woman can cause in a man's life. I also saw how she could single-handedly destroy a family while trying to manipulate everything around her. Debra was an attractive but sadistic woman who would stop at nothing in her quest for wealth and self-serving happiness. To succeed in that quest, she developed elaborate plans to destroy Nabil that also destroyed her children and her world.

Nabil and Debra had three children of their own, and Debra had come into the marriage with one child from a previous relationship, a boy named Austin, who was twenty. Their own three children included their daughter, Millie, who was fifteen, and two younger boys, Justin, who was seven, and Steven, who was five. They all lived in New River, a small community outside Phoenix. This small town was known for two types of residents—those who loved horses or the large lots associated with horse property, and survivalists who didn't like to be around or bothered by the government. Nabil and Debra were in the horse-property category.

The Mounlas had a close friend in the community, Avery, who fit into the antigovernment category, but understood right from wrong and abided by the law. He had become a friend and confidant to both Nabil and Debra. Whichever Avery was with, he would open his ears to their complaints and give them someone to vent to. Nabil talked of day-to-day issues and ways to make a better government. They would share their ideas, with no threats and no plans to overthrow the government, just constructive criticisms and ideas.

Debra was different. She used Avery as a sounding board for her unhappiness in her marriage. Avery became somewhat of the "other man" in her life without the obligation of sex. Their friendship was simple and clean for Debra, and Avery was easy to manipulate. She was attractive and charming and could make men like Avery fall all over her. Avery didn't mind listening to Debra because she was easy on the eyes, and she kept him on a short leash by making him feel special when he was around her. He did the same for her because he made her feel pretty and desirable to another man.

Avery bragged frequently to Debra about his military experiences and survivalist expertise. He made her believe that he had special qualifications that the military used on important missions. Most important, he claimed he knew other killers and kept in contact with those that had retired or moved where they didn't have to be part of society. He made himself larger-than-life, and both Debra and Nabil believed every word he said.

After months of complaining about her marriage with Nabil, Debra decided to take matters into her own hands. To everyone who became a part of her plan, she seemed to be acting out for the first time, but in reality she had been doing things to destroy Nabil for several years. It was just enough to make Nabil look like a monster or a man losing his mind. While she manipulated Nabil's every move, she began to fill Avery's head with her desire to have Nabil killed. She also manipulated the children into thinking that their father was a bad man and had molested them when they were younger.

Austin was the easiest for Debra to manipulate in her plan to destroy Nabil. She convinced Austin that Nabil had molested him when he was a small child. After months of Debra's planting this seed in Austin's head, he suspiciously recalled the abuse. One day he told his mother that after years of not realizing he had been abused, he now recalled his father molesting him when he was three. This repressed recollection was just what Debra needed to go to the police and have Nabil arrested.

To destroy a man, you accuse him of molesting a child and he is forever finished. Even if he didn't commit the unforgivable act, he will be labeled a child molester for the rest of his life. It is completely unacceptable in our society to molest a child, and Nabil knew this well. So did Debra.

Debra wasn't satisfied with breaking Nabil by reporting him as a child molester. She wanted to destroy him. A broken man can get up and rebuild himself. A man destroyed will never recover. Debra had tired of Nabil and wanted something different. Her fire for Nabil had long been extinguished and she was looking for a new torch. Divorce wasn't going to work, according to Debra, because Nabil's family was too wealthy and would win the child-custody battle in court. Without the kids she had no pawns to play with. It wasn't love that made her fight for her children.

Part of Debra's plan was to drive Nabil crazy through an assortment of acts that would confuse and distract him. On one occasion Debra called Nabil at work and told him to come home after noon and they would go on a special family picnic. She would make a picnic basket with everything Nabil loved, and she and the children would spend the day in the park with him. She promoted the idea as a chance for them to rekindle their love and relationship. This was enticing to a man who still loved his wife, but saw his marriage and their relationship slipping away with every day.

Nabil was overwhelmed with excitement at the thought of his family being together during a whole afternoon in the park. So he hurried through his workday and rushed to be home by one in the afternoon. As he drove into the driveway, none of the children came outside and Debra's vehicle was gone. When he stepped inside the house, he nearly passed out. Everything was gone, the furniture, television, the dishes. Everything, not even one member of his family was left at home. Debra had lured him home under false pretenses only to have moved out and taken the children with her.

Nabil loved Debra so much that he accepted her back home after each time she moved. It became an emotional seesaw for him and he would never give up. Each time Nabil would have a little more of his heart ripped out.

Then, rather than moving away, Debra decided to remove Nabil from her life permanently. She had read of ways to seduce Nabil and then kill him during a moment of passion. This would be easy enough for Debra because she knew she owned Nabil's heart and he would do anything to keep her. Nabil also knew she was right about the power she had over him, but he couldn't help himself. If Avery hadn't made Nabil realize how manipulated he had become, I might never have intervened.

Debra told Nabil that she had planned a wonderful evening for the two of them and had taken the kids to a sitter for the night. No interruptions, and no witnesses. In her research she discovered that a chemical used in equestrian medicine could open the pores on Nabil's skin. She asked Nabil if he wanted a massage after dinner. He agreed and went to the bedroom, which Debra had decorated with candles and other sensual items to help set the mood. Erotic music was playing, and the vibe was perfect for a night of lovemaking after Nabil's massage.

While Nabil lay on the bed nude, Debra began her "black widow" performance. She sprayed the chemical DMSO on Nabil's back to open up his pores. Then she massaged in pure alcohol. Her plan was for Nabil to die of alcohol poisoning. When he became sleepy from the alcohol and passed out, she placed liquor bottles around the room to make it look as if he'd drunk himself to death. Debra then closed the bedroom door and left Nabil to die alone.

The next morning, Debra was preparing herself to cry and be emotional when Nabil was found dead in the bedroom after the children returned home. However, Nabil eventually woke and came into the kitchen for breakfast. He said he felt as if someone had hit him with a hammer and he had a major hangover.

Debra stared at the man she had just given her best shot and listened as he talked about the weird ending to their perfect evening. She had failed in her attempt to kill him. Now it was time to get a real professional.

Debra's next move was to contact her good friend and confidant Avery. She told him she wanted Nabil killed. She didn't have this conversation just once; she mentioned it several times. Avery had by now begun to tire of Debra because he had seen Nabil in action and respected him for being a great father. He was nothing like what Debra had described in her many conversations with Avery. He also paid closer attention to how Debra didn't care for the children and paid increasingly more attention to her personal needs.

After Nabil and Debra separated for the final time, she failed to pay her utility bills. Even though Nabil had been thrown out of the house, he still gave Debra $1,200 a month to help—which she spent on other things. Avery also tried to help her so she could keep the children comfortable, but that failed too. Avery saw how abusive Debra was to the children and how she forced them to live without any amenities. He became more and more upset until he went to Nabil with the story of Debra's trying to kill him.

When Nabil learned of Debra's plot to have him killed, he told Detective Dave Lucero of the Sex Crimes Unit, who was investigating the accusations against Nabil. Lucero was young but had gained great respect as an outstanding investigator with unusual insight into his cases. Lucero arranged a meeting with both Nabil and Avery to determine if the story was true. Lucero became convinced that Debra had made up the entire molestation story and was trying to destroy Nabil. Knowing my reputation as a "hit man," Lucero he reached out to me.

I needed to be 100 percent sure that Nabil hadn't molested his children or I wasn't going to take the case. I interviewed Nabil myself for several hours until I was convinced that he was telling the truth and would never harm his children. It was time to squish the Black Widow.

First, I needed to determine whom Debra was looking for and summon up that character. I spent a lot of time with Avery because I wanted to give Debra the person that Avery would most likely associate with. I became a disgruntled Vietnam veteran who hated society and now killed for a living. When I wasn't doing murders for hire, I was living secluded in the hills and as far away from people as I could get. I was seriously mentally ill and believed in what I was doing. No regrets for me if I took someone else's life. It made me money and the people probably deserved to die. Hell, the government had trained me and paid me to do it legally. I was just striking out on my own. From everything I saw in Avery, I think I hit the character head-on. From the moment I met Debra I knew I did.

Avery revisited his conversations with Debra to show that killing Nabil was her idea and not his. I had to make sure that his attraction for Debra, and her refusal to engage him sexually, hadn't led him to fill her head with ideas on how to have Nabil killed and get him out of the picture. I needed to be sure Avery didn't entertain the thought of Nabil's being gone and then moving in to be Debra's new toy. Avery convinced me that wasn't the case, but I wanted to be completely sure. His conversations also had to be taped so the jury wouldn't question his motive and give Debra any credibility. I knew right away that her defense would be that she was the battered and abused wife. What I didn't realize was that she would try to seduce me when we first met.

A case like this is touchy, and you can't go into it with the idea that she is guilty and you are going to get her. You have to give her the benefit of the doubt and let her prove her guilt: innocent until proven guilty, not guilty until proven innocent. This wasn't an easy thing to do after hearing all the pain she'd caused Nabil, but nonetheless I had to work that way.

The contacts between Debra and Avery had to be done on the phone because Debra had moved to Tennessee before letting anyone know. She grabbed the kids one day and went back to her parents' home, where she would have an easier time getting a divorce and custody of the children. In Tennessee the court system is sympathetic to women in a divorce. Without any hearing they would believe Debra's story of Nabil's child molesting and instantly give her custody. Nabil would have a much more difficult time regaining his children as long as they stayed in Tennessee.

Several phone conversations ensued between Avery and

Debra after I gave him his marching orders. Debra told Avery she wanted to have Nabil killed by someone other than herself. She had tried to do it herself, but failed. She now needed help. Debra used her most manipulative skills to plant a seed in Avery's head, hoping he would respond and supply her with a killer.

When looking for a sign of commitment to have someone killed, you always look at access. She no longer had access to Nabil, and he had no access to her. Why not let the courts settle the custody issue and live your life unharmed? Any person who was sound of mind and avoided greed would think rationally and feel victorious. Not Debra. She was safe, far from Nabil, and had her children. Not good enough for her. Nabil must still die.

Debra told Avery on tape that she had become obsessed with finding ways to kill Nabil. After she spoke at length about her desire to have Nabil killed, Avery told her he had run into an old friend who would do it. She immediately perked up and confirmed that wasn't a bad idea. Someone who could do it for her! It was as if her wishes had finally been answered. She could finally stop her search for a killer and now focus on the job for a hit man.

In each contract killing I would tell myself to question the client's commitment, and I would always use the same standard to evaluate that commitment. "If not for me, someone else" served me well as an evaluation tool. If the client would definitely look elsewhere if I turned the job down, then I knew I must press forward. Debra answered that question over and over. She had tried and would continue trying. When she failed, she reached out in hope of someday finding someone to do it for her. This was her big chance. If she really wanted to have it done and distance herself from the murder, this was the moment. I was the guy.

While my murder-for-hire cases were progressing, I would always give the clients an opportunity to escape unharmed. I called those opportunities "doors and windows," a time for clients to change their minds without feeling that I would kill them for backing out. If they refused to take that opportunity, I knew they were committed. I told Avery to do the same thing. Don't push and make Debra come to me. Give her a chance to think it out and maybe come to her senses. He did just that, but she chose to march forward.

Avery told Debra to think about what they talked about. If she decided she wanted to do it, she should call and say, "This is Debra . . . go ahead." Or, if she changed her mind: "This is Debra . . . forget it." She called a short time later and left Avery a message: "Go ahead."

A new problem arose as the case continued: jurisdiction. Debra was in Tennessee and I had no jurisdiction in that state. I could do the case there, but it would complicate things and I would have to do the trial there as well. The courts were obviously sympathetic to her because they were allowing her to keep her children. They were also prohibiting Nabil from seeing the children, and all this on a statement by Debra. No hearing and representation for Nabil. If they were that simple and biased toward men, then I didn't need to work my case through their courts.

I decided to convince Debra to come to Phoenix and meet with me. A face-to-face meeting on my turf or I wasn't going to play. I didn't like to come out of the hills very often, I told her, and a trip to Tennessee wasn't in my plans. To my surprise, she agreed and said we would make arrangements to meet soon.

My phone conversations with Debra before we met were friendly and easy opportunities for me to interject difficult questions. I needed to make sure she wanted me to kill Nabil so there would be no confusion for the court. As hard as it was for me to ask, it was that easy for her to answer. I posed the question along the lines of "Is it your ultimate goal to have Nabil die?" She responded, "That is my plan." She was ultimately glad that he hadn't died when she was giving him the massage because she had been obsessing too much about his murder. Because of her obsession she might have done something wrong and eventually been caught. Having a professional like me would keep her from making mistakes that would catch the eye of the police. All she cared about was herself. Whatever it took to help her accomplish her goal of self-gratification was going to be done.

After Debra had agreed to come to Phoenix and meet with me, she started to complain she was short on cash and tried to get me to come to Tennessee. I told her if she really wanted Nabil killed, then she would have to make the effort and drive to Phoenix.

After a week passed and I didn't hear from Debra, I called her house and spoke with her daughter, Millie. She was friendly as could be and loaded with personality. "Mom has left for Phoenix," Millie said. I told her to give her mom my pager number and have her call me when she checked in.

I didn't know if Debra was for real or just playing out a fantasy. What would she do when she got to Phoenix and had to commit? Two days later she called and said she was in Phoenix.

She had to visit her oldest son, who had been arrested for a probation violation, and then wanted to meet with me. I agreed and set our meeting for 7:00 pm.

I decided that the best place to meet Debra was in a parking lot at La Quinta Hotel, at Thomas Road and the freeway. This was probably my favorite place for doing deals. The parking lot was hidden away in a small, quiet cove between the hotel and a restaurant, making it easy to control the clients and keep them contained. It was also a great place to recognize a setup or countersurveillance. I had learned a lot from a previous client about how easy it was to be countersurveilled in a large, uncontrolled area. This parking lot was also a great place for the video-surveillance people to set up and blend in. They could get uninterrupted video that was never blocked and could quickly respond in an emergency. I never knew what to think with the people I dealt with and didn't want to be unprepared if they were setting me up.

Before I met with Debra I had to switch gears and become a father for Geoff. A young man by this time, he had a great enthusiasm to work to help people. He had signed up for lifeguard training and was the youngest student in the program. Both Patti and I were so proud of him and his determination to succeed. All I needed to do was show up at the training and let him know I cared and supported his efforts.

The swimming pool at the training site had bleachers because it was a competition facility. I quietly snuck into the arena and took a seat at the top of the bleachers. I watched as the instructor tested each student for technique in saving a drowning swimmer. The main instructor was a pregnant female, who brought along her husband, also a lifeguard instructor, to be the drowning victim.

Each student performed the lifesaving technique and easily subdued the mildly uncooperative drowning swimmer. Then came Geoff's turn. He got into the water and readied himself for the instructor to act as if he were drowning. Geoff swam to the rescue, but the mildly uncooperative swimmer had now become a violent man who intended to drown the smaller lifeguard. He forced Geoff underwater and became a completely different person. It was all I could do to stay in the stands and not jump in to kick the instructor's ass. I was shocked at his behavior and concerned about what he was doing to Geoff.

Finally the exercise ended and Geoff slowly swam to the side of the pool and climbed out as he tried to collect himself. The male instructor also climbed out of the pool and stood on the deck like a peacock and looked around as if to say, "I am so cool!" To my surprise he came over to the stands and took a seat right below me. Suddenly, the switch inside me turned on!

I slowly walked down the steps, then seated myself right next to the instructor. He looked at me with a smile as he continued to dry his hair and wipe his face.

"Nice job out there," I said.

He laughed and said, "I about drowned that kid."

"I know. How about you and me go out to the pool and you try and save me?" I stared at him for a few seconds and he stood up to walk away. "Ready?"

No," he responded. "I am really sorry, man." He walked away, then disappeared into the shower room.

I was so mad that I didn't even know where I was supposed

to go. Geoff looked up at me and knew what I had just done. He smiled, and that was all it took to calm me back down. He knew I cared and that I was there for him. Nothing else needed to be said, and I headed back to see Debra.

Debra arrived in an off-white Mercedes that seemed to be running rough as she pulled into the parking lot. I stayed in the shadows of a breezeway to make an obvious entrance for her to think about. How did I get there? Where did I come from? I wanted to be in control from the very beginning. As I approached her, I could tell she was a bit uneasy. Who wouldn't be? You are about to meet a guy that you plan to hire to kill someone. You believe he is a killer and can't help but wonder if he will kill you. I made sure Debra held on to that thought when I told her I would hunt her down and kill her if she told the cops about me. Nice way to make a new friend, I thought.

Debra was dressed in a cute outfit and had her hair down, but nicely styled. She wore some sweet perfume and immediately started playing the innocent girl with me. I wanted her to be at ease so I mentioned that her car was running rough. She giggled and shuffled around me, saying that it might be low on oil. When I checked the engine for her, I found it wasn't just low on oil, it was dry. She was really glad that I had taken an interest in her car and wanted to help her. She giggled more and positioned herself close to me as she complimented me on the size of my arms.

I stepped off the sidewalk and into the street. I didn't want the jury to see me towering over Debra and claim that I was too intimidating. Everything I did was an attempt to diffuse her defense that she was too intimidated to back out. I did all these things while still trying to be believable as a killer. I already new she was manipulative and expected her to try to manipulate me. She didn't disappoint.

Right before Debra came to our meeting she called Nabil's new roommate and confidentially asked him what vehicle Nabil was driving. When she met with me, she told me he would be driving a Jeep. Not only that, but she described him in complete detail and gave me a picture of him. Without hesitation, Debra provided everything that I needed to find and kill Nabil, including the payment.

She was short on cash so she brought me jewelry as payment: a necklace she valued at $1,200, a ring that she valued at $300, and a gold medallion she got while in the Middle East visiting Nabil's family. I later learned that all the items were wedding gifts from Nabil and his family. Didn't mean anything to her anymore.

After she gave me the jewelry, I asked if she had any cash. Debra looked a bit stunned and said that she had used all her money to bail her son out of jail. I looked at her for a minute, and I'm sure she thought my next request was going to be for sex, a normal thought for someone who thought she was irresistible to men. I looked a little harder at her, then said, "What about that watch on your wrist?" Her expensive watch looked like a Rolex. Debra looked at her wrist, pulled the watch off, and handed it right over to me. I asked her if she was sure, and she began to twist her shirt and sway back and forth like a little schoolgirl, batting her eyes seductively.

"How do you want me to kill this guy?" I said. "Do you want me to bring back something like an ear or just let him know it was from you right before he dies?" I also gave her several chances to back out and forget we ever met. If she didn't back out and I killed Nabil, she better keep her mouth shut. When the cops start coming around and asking questions, she better stay silent. I stared at her and said, "If you give me up, I'll find you and kill you too." She calmly looked at me and said, "Fair." Debra just wanted Nabil to know right before he died that it was from her.

Tomorrow I was going to take Nabil back to the mountains with me. I knew of some great mine shafts in the area and he was going to one of them. I liked baseball bats to the kneecaps. Debra just laughed sadistically and said, "All right!" I would continually hit him on the side of the head with the baseball bat, then break both his arms. He was going to suffer for the entire night. Debra stopped me and chimed in, "He's going to start crying, 'I didn't do it!'" Her face was all crinkled up and she showed me how Nabil would beg for mercy.

Nabil was going to beg for mercy because I was going to keep him in pain for a long time, I told her. She called her attempt at killing Nabil "a massage to die for." I told her that I would be calling my event "a night to die for." After Nabil suffered for an entire night, I planned to end his misery by shooting him in the head. Then I would drop his body in a mine shaft deep in the desert and full of rattlesnakes.

"Listen to me, by the time anyone finds this guy Nabil, he will be nothing but bones and nobody will care."

She replied, "Nobody out here would care." Everything I described to Debra was perfect for her, and she was ready for me to take care of Nabil. She wanted him out of her life and unable to breathe the same air as her children.

The arrest team was poised to take Debra into custody as soon as I gave them the sign. When my hat came off, the team was on Debra and forced her against her car to handcuff. "Are you Debra?" the sergeant said. "No," she lied. I quietly walked away and slid off into the dark breezeway before anyone could realize I had left. A reporter on the scene described it as "almost Batman-like."

Debra Mounla was charged with conspiracy to commit murder, and her defense was exactly what I expected it to be: the battered and abused wife. I hardly recognized her in court as she sat at the defense table. Her hair was frumpy and she wore no makeup. A far cry from the woman who'd tried to hire me. She told the jury and the judge that she wanted to stop what she had started, but she was scared I would kill her. She was changing her mind, but got arrested before she could tell me.

My biggest surprise was the support she got from battered women's groups and church clergy. Not a single one of them read the report and knew the facts. They just took her word and threw all their support behind her. They would sit in court during the trial and stare at me as if I were on trial. Not once did any of them even call me to ask about the facts of the case. Finally, toward the end of the trial, a minister in the group came up to me after hearing the audio of my conversation with Debra. "I'm sorry, son," he said. "I rushed to judgment and came to her defense without really knowing what she did." I then asked him if the other women understood the whole story now, and he said, "I don't think you will ever convince them she did wrong." He shook my hand and moved on through the hallways.

The women hated Nabil without ever knowing the story and threatened to keep him from ever having his children back. Even while the children were in Tennessee, they poisoned the mind of the court there with unsubstantiated facts about the children's sexual abuse. They never once advised the court that the Phoenix police had "unfounded" the claims and cleared Nabil. Just as I had said, Nabil was marked as a child molester, and Debra ruined his life.

The judge in Debra's conspiracy-to-commit-murder trial didn't buy what she had to say and neither did the jury. She was convicted and sentenced to twenty-five years in prison without any early parole. Before she left the court, the judge scolded Debra for flirting with me during the deal. The judge said it was hard to believe someone so flirtatious was scared.

The Black Widow was gone, but in her wake she'd destroyed everything around her. Greed was a powerful and intoxicating drug for Debra. If you have it, you can't get enough. Satisfaction is really never within reach.

Nabil has continued to struggle with the accusations Debra brought against him. She continues to haunt him and recently field a complaint against him from prison when she discovered he was working as a teacher. Nabil said he will forever be considered a child molester, thanks to Debra.

16

The Scar Face Chase

Time seems to fly by when you live in two distinctly different worlds and are raising a family. My love for Patti continued to grow with each day, and the children were growing like weeds. Every day included the juggle of family life and my work undercover. I always had to concentrate on separating the two worlds in order to have some success. One minute I'm playing baseball with the boys, and the next minute I'm on the phone negotiating a deal to kill someone.

For instance, Mortimer Hylton made me work at clearing my head and finding my true self. He always seemed to catch me at the most inconvenient times and normally in a family moment. He spoke to me on the phone one day while I was standing in the middle of a baseball field throwing batting practice. Mortimer was calling from jail and needed me to kill some friends of his because they'd disrespected him and his family in a business deal.

Mortimer and I talked at length about my going to a restaurant and delivering a package that contained two pounds of the explosive C-4. Then it would be detonated and an entire city block would be blown apart. A tremendous number of lives would be lost and huge structural damage was expected. Mortimer was just sending a message, he said. No concern for lives, just a message that you don't mess with him.

That was pretty heavy conversation when you're standing around a group of kids who are anxious for you to throw the next pitch. I'm not sure how I got through all the challenges of instant personality changes except by separating myself from the moment and becoming someone else. When it's all over, you have to gather your senses and try to find yourself again. I was always hoping and praying that I didn't forget who I was and be unable to return to that person. It's easy to do, you know. Play around with your mind long enough and the wires are going to cross and short-circuit. That's why most police departments place mandatory three-to-five-year rotations on their undercover officers. Too many have been lost, and the departments feel it is directly related to the time an officer spends under.

The FBI is filled with undercover agents falling in love with their new identities and never returning to their old ones. Some of the agents that infiltrated the Mafia got intoxicated with the lifestyle of a Mafia member and never came back, only to stay in Italy and play the role for real. These losses led the FBI to rewrite their undercover policy and give the agents routine psychological evaluations. Closer monitoring of the agents and their families also made for a healthier situation. Over time their program has become a model for other law enforcement agencies to use in their undercover programs.

In the case of Mortimer I had a difficult time forgetting about what he said and how cavalier he was about a mass murder. He didn't care about the families torn apart by his desire to make two people pay for disrespecting him.

As I began to pitch again, my phone rang. "Jake?" the caller said. "This is Jillie from the salon. Patti isn't available right now so I thought I could call you and get some help."

"Sure," I said. "I'd be glad to help with anything." No problem for me, I thought. I could take care of the salon's problem while Patti was out. Hell, I'd just spoken with a potential mass murderer. What could be harder to deal with than that?

"One of the lightbulbs in the bathroom has blown out and we were wondering if you could come in and change it," Jillie said.

I stood stunned for a moment and tried to contain the language that was about to come out of my mouth, especially with a group of impressionable kids around me. This self-centered hairdresser wasn't going to take one minute from her busy schedule and unscrew a lightbulb. She would rather call me and have me come over and drop everything I was doing to change it for her. "I'll see what I can do" was all that I could get out of my mouth.

I spend my days and nights dealing with murderers and thieves. Then I regroup and throw baseballs to a group of kids just looking to have some fun and get a little attention. It all ends with me walking through a salon changing lightbulbs and cleaning toilets. Somehow this is a bit different from the lives of the undercover cops I always watched on TV.

My mother and I on the night I graduated from the police academy.
(Author's Collection)

Tommy (third from left) and I (in doorway) in front of a social
club after we began riding as partners. *(Author's Collection)*

My first days undercover: working with Detective Billy Didio and buying stolen property. *(Author's Collection)*

Senator John Mc-Cain and Captain Kurtenbach award-ing Billy and I Police Officer of the Year for our early undercover work. *(Author's Collection)*

Sitting on a desk in the safe house and trying to hide from being photographed. Still pictures were normally never taken. *(Author's Collection)*

Police are trying to take my picture after I was stopped in a car full of suspected armed robbers. *(Author's Collection)*

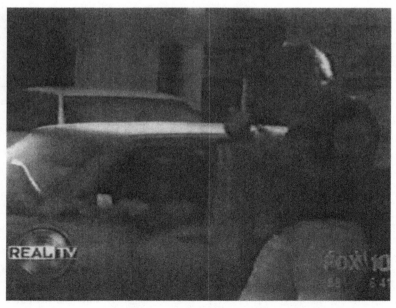

Waiting as Ma and Pa arrived to hire me to kill their boy before they were evicted from their trailer. *(Phoenix Police Department)*

At the beginning of my meeting with Debra Mounla. I'm checking her car oil to lighten up the initial moment. *(Phoenix Police Department)*

Convincing Debra Mounla that I kill for a living, and that I can kill her husband if she has the right payment. *(Phoenix Police Department)*

Debra Mounla describes the jewelry—gifts from her husband and his family—that she planned to use as the payoff to have her husband killed. *(Phoenix Police Department)*

On the way to my meeting with Jan Solomon, dressed as the mafia character. *(Phoenix Police Department)*

Jan Solomon gives me the big mafia hug when we finally meet to arrange the murder of his girlfriend's husband. *(Phoenix Police Department)*

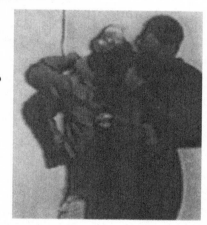

Discussing and planning the murder with Jan Solomon, and negotiating the payment. *(Phoenix Police Department)*

Invading the personal space of Alan Disomma to intimidate him and gain the tactical advantage in our first meeting. *(Phoenix Police Department)*

My last day undercover. Most of my hair was cut and I was taking one last ride before beginning my new life. *(Author's Collection)*

Patti and I after I had totally
cleaned up and left undercover.
(Author's Collection)

Awarded Police Offi-
cer of the Year from
the American Legion.
(Author's Collection)

My partner Alex and I after we both moved to the Homicide Unit.
(Author's Collection)

After I got through with the baseball practice I ran Cody home and slipped back into my biker clothes for another night in the underworld. It was time to make my way into the Candy Store and show my face so everybody remembered that I was still alive. Kristie had kept calling for several days and leaving messages wondering where I was. They missed me and a guy known as Scar Face had continued to bother her trying to get a meeting with me.

The great thing about Patti was that she was so completely secure that Kristie didn't bother her. She knew I loved her and that Kristie was just a means to an end in my business. I never used Kristie as a pawn in my relationship with Patti, and she trusted that I would never leave her for Kristie. It wasn't easy for any man to say no to Kristie. An incredibly beautiful brunette, she seduced all the men around her with her style, figure, and great looks. I worked hard to stay focused on my goals and never fall prey to her seductive charm.

I always got a kick out of watching all the guys who came into the club wearing their expensive suits and flashing big money. Kristie would completely mesmerize them from the moment they walked in the door. Each would pay her unbelievable money to dance at his table and give him some attention. Every one of them believed he could spend his money on her and she would be impressed. So impressed she would go home or to some hotel with him at the end of the night. In reality, her only plan was to take his money. When he realized she wasn't leaving with him, she would use her charm and leave him feeling that "maybe next time she'll go home with me." The guys kept coming back and always left wanting more.

I didn't spend a penny on her and never asked her to go

home with me. That was the answer with Kristie. Play hard to get and never act totally interested. It made her want you more. Those other guys could have played the same game, but didn't think about it. They were used to buying girls in the dance clubs, and in their minds this was no different. In a topless bar most of the girls have an "old man" and most likely a couple of kids at home. They just want to make their money and get back home after their shift.

I also kept Kristie on my team by never indicting her customers until the day I was ready to move on to another area and change my appearance. Eventually I would be forced to move because it became dangerous if you stayed in one place for too long. One to two years was about the extent of any stay. I stayed longer at the Candy Store because Kristie made me believable with future clients and she never compromised what I was doing. By having her validation, I was rarely suspected of not being the criminal I portrayed.

It was harder and harder to tell Kristie that I didn't have time for her, though. It didn't make sense that everyone wanted her but I continually refused her advances and could have had first choice. I had to just keep making her believe I would be there someday, but for now I needed to stay with the rich lady paying my bills. All my effort with Kristie went into keeping her wanting and willing to help. That was the only way it was going to work. When that stopped, I would surely have to move on.

As I rode my scooter toward the Candy Store, I looked along the side of the road for new places that might be rich with crime. My head was moving from one side of the road to the other until I saw a sign on the sidewalk at Greenway Road and Cave Creek: PERMS FOR JESUS . . . $10. "Unbelievable!" I thought to myself. I had wanted to change my look for a while, and what better way to do it than with a perm? I turned the bike around and drove up to the front door. Inside was a nice old lady that confirmed she would perm my long hair for $10 and donate the money to the church of my choice.

Even though Patti was a hairdresser, I thought this deal was too perfect to pass up. Patti did a great job taking care of my hair and routinely gave me the look I needed for each character, but I knew she would appreciate my concern for her busy schedule. And best of all . . . doing it for Jesus. At least that's what the lady said.

The lady had me sit in the chair and began to preach from her Bible as she permed my hair. The whole thing took about an hour, and when the preaching stopped and I got out of the chair, I was shocked. My hair was so fried that it looked as if I'd stuck my finger in a socket. My scalp was burned and so was my forehead. I looked like a mess and started to freak out. I paid the lady and went outside to figure things out. That's when it hit me. I'd get a hair pick and pick out the new style. I'd be a big-hair guy until it settled down. To my surprise it worked and gave me a different look. I fit in better in the rock-music clubs and attracted more attention from the younger generation.

After going to the store and getting a comb to pick out my hair, I wrapped my head in a bandanna and continued to the Candy Store. As I walked in the door, I brushed past Scar Face and he tried to talk to me. I ignored him and went to my table. Kristie and the girls ran over screaming about how cool my hair looked while Scar Face stood at the door dejected. "You need to speak with Scar Face, Jake," Kristie said.

"Not now. Maybe in a week or so," I told her. "Tell him I'll definitely get with him later, but I have a lot on my mind now."

She went over and told him the news.

I stayed at the Candy Store long enough to make my presence known, then I made my rounds to several other bars and clubs. I was hoping I could get done early because I had to be back at the baseball field early the next morning for some routine maintenance on the field. A few more clubs, I thought to myself, then back to the office to close out for the day. Just then my cell started ringing—Sgt. Dave Pennington wanted me back for a quick meeting. "Don't forget I have to leave early tonight, Dave," I said. He remembered and promised he would get me out in time.

Back at the warehouse I sat with a group of robbery detectives who wanted my help in finding one of their high-profile, violent suspects. I listened with the toothpick in my mouth moving from one side to the other. They described a guy, Shane Deaton, who had been on a robbing frenzy. He was wanted for murder, seventeen counts of armed robbery, nine counts of kidnapping, three counts of armed assault, two counts of aggravated assault, and one count of being a fugitive from justice. This man had robbed an off-duty police officer and a thirty-one-year-old woman pushing her grocery cart in a parking lot. He worked closely with his girlfriend, who had worked as a stripper in the past. Shane was a bad guy and they needed me to look for him in the topless clubs because that's where he hung out.

I asked for a picture so I could recognize him if I saw him in one of the clubs. With one glance at the photograph, I realized Shane was Scar Face! I couldn't believe my eyes. I told everyone this guy had been trying to hook up with me for weeks and I had been ignoring him.

"Maybe you ought to make yourself available," one of the detectives said.

"Maybe I ought to make myself available, shut up!" I sarcastically spouted back.

"Tell him I'm ready," I told Kristie. She was as giddy as a kid at Christmas when I gave her the go-ahead. I almost thought she might be getting some cash from Scar Face if she hooked us up. I told her to have him meet me at Cheers bar around seven o'clock tomorrow night. I wasn't going to meet him tonight and end up never getting home. He could wait one more day, especially since he had waited this long already. I had made a commitment to take care of the baseball field where Cody played and I coached. If I didn't keep my word, then what kind of message would I be sending to the boys? Always keeping my word was one of my primary rules to live by.

I remember being in a bar one time when a group of tough-guy crooks I had known came inside. These were guys who knew I was a cop after they had been arrested for dealing with me. I was just getting ready to leave for another game of Cody's, and they were blocking the door while they talked. If I went out the front door, I would be seen and end up in a brawl that would make me late or miss the game. Or I could head to the bathroom and squeeze out the small window. Nobody knew any difference when I didn't return. They were all too drunk.

Getting this body out the bathroom window was no easy task. I'm still not sure how I pulled that one off. I would have done anything to get out of the bar and be on time for Cody's game.

I knew now that Scar Face was a bit dangerous, but I had him so wrapped up in meeting with me that I didn't care. I planned to meet him by myself, then report back with what I found. The bosses were having none of my plan and once again began to whisper that I was becoming too much of a risk-taker and they were concerned. But to my benefit, nobody had time to worry about me because they were focusing on a plan for Scar Face. For sure, though, they would deal with me when things cooled down.

I knew I could seize the moment and insist on a plan I felt most comfortable with. In spite of what the bosses might be thinking, I wasn't going to meet with this nut if I didn't feel I was in control. Anything could happen with him, and he had proven it time and time again. He had also proved he could elude the cops. They finally agreed to let me meet him inside the bar by myself, but surveillance and a tactical team would be waiting outside. They would take him when I gave the sign.

The big day came and I got to Cheers about fifteen minutes before seven. I positioned myself at the end of the bar with my back to a wall. Everything was in front of me, and nothing could sneak up from behind. The bartender rolled me up my favorite drink, schnapps and soda. I drank, watched the door, and waited. Shortly before seven the door opened and in walked Scar Face. He was always a stylish dresser, obsessed with his appearance and clothes. At times he would wear a suit, but now he was in nice slacks and a neatly pressed dress shirt.

He smiled as he walked over to me, and when he got close,

he held out his hand to shake. I looked at his hand and kept chewing on my toothpick. I just nodded and he turned toward the bartender and ordered a beer. We made small talk for quite a while, and I finally told him to tell me what was so important that he had been bothering Kristie to arrange a meeting with me.

I've got an offer for you that I don't think you can pass up, Scar Face said. You and I go to certain houses that I have picked out. I already know the ones that will have a lot of money. I'll be the first at the door and make them think I'm a cop. You bust in behind me when they're distracted and beat the hell out of everyone. I'll get the jewelry and money, and you kill the owner if he doesn't cooperate. We can hit a bunch of houses, then move somewhere else.

He was completely serious.

What made it believable to me was the increase in home invasions around the nation. As part of the trend, criminals were pretending to be police officers to gain entry to houses to rob them. Really no different from what Scar Face had suggested, except he incorporated murder into his plan.

I must have had a completely uninterested look on my face because he quickly said, "Half the money is yours!" I still looked uninterested as he reached into his pocket. I could visualize a gun coming out with Scar Face thinking I'd disrespected him.

No gun this time though. He looked nervously around the bar as he pulled his hand out of his pocket and grabbed my hand. I looked him straight in the eyes and looked at the scar running down the side of his face. Then I looked in my hand at a Phoenix Police Department patrolman's badge. The real thing, not a fake. "Where did you get this?" I asked.

"It's a long story, but the cop is lucky I didn't kill him."

Tell me about it, I hesitantly said.

He began describing an evening not so long ago at a Pizza Hut restaurant when he was robbing the clerk, and a man walked inside to pick up his pizza. He opened his wallet to pay, and there lay a police shield. The off-duty officer didn't even realize what was going on. Scar Face seized the opportunity and threw the young officer to the ground and started screaming at him as he stuck a gun in his face, "I should kill you, motherfucker! I should kill you!"

Scar Face began to sweat as he told me the story, and I noticed that he had drifted from me and was back at the robbery. His face changed, as did his mannerisms, and he began to sweat even more. "I screamed at him that I was going to kill him," Scar Face said. "Then I just stopped and got off the ground." Suddenly he snapped back to reality and said, "I could have killed him but I didn't. . . . I don't know why. I just don't know why. I had the chance."

I did everything I could to look as if I were cool and still unimpressed, but this guy was totally freakin' me out. I had never seen anyone seem as if he'd left his body and emotionally placed himself somewhere else. It was if he were possessed and his head were about to spin off. "Take the badge," he said. "It's yours so you know I mean business. I also have credit cards and checks at home that we can sell for more money."

I told him to go get those things and come back. We'd go to my man and sell them before we did anything else. If he didn't come back, I'd keep the badge.

"Fair enough," Scar Face said, then walked out of the bar.

As soon as he left, I collected myself and called Dave Pennington to make plans for someone to buy the cards and checks. I always trusted Dave and knew he would work with me on a good plan. Dave, I said, this nutcase is coming back to sell his stuff. Let's have the robbery guys back off and we'll take him someplace where we can control him. Oh, yeah, and, Dave, this is going to be a shoot-out . . . I have no doubt about it.

You could feel Dave's stress level ratchet up a couple notches and he said, "I'll make the calls. You get him to La Quinta when he gets back, and I'll have Gray Beard do the buy." Gray Beard was Gary Davis, a longtime, successful undercover detective who looked like a crotchety old man. He was experienced, fearless, and knew how to make a deal work. The plan was to get Scar Face to La Quinta and have him cornered. Once we got the deal done, we would take him off. The site would be controlled, and if he started shooting, we could handle it with minimal or no casualties.

I sat back at the bar for about an hour and waited for Scar Face to return. While I waited, Scar Face drove back to his apartment and got all the goods we had discussed. On his way back to me, he was suddenly blocked in traffic by cars driven by members of the Robbery Detail. Scar Face accelerated his car back and forth until he freed himself and sped away, reaching speeds of 100–110 miles an hour.

Just when I was thinking he wasn't coming back, my phone rang. Dave was on the other end. "Get out! And get out now! Robbery tried to jump him and he got away. He got into a big crash down the street, and it looks like he's on his way back to you." You ever leave some place and feel the hair on the back of your neck is standing up? That's exactly what I felt. I didn't know if he was back to me yet or not. If he was, did he think I set him up?

Minding her own business amid all this chaos was Virginia Rhymes, who was driving west on Indian School Road approaching Seventh Avenue. Also in Virginia's car was her thirteen-year-old son, Mark Tang. She didn't see Scar Face coming north on Seventh Avenue, and he didn't see Virginia driving west on Indian School through the green light. Of course he wouldn't, he was driving at a blinding speed and entered the intersection against a red light. They collided in the middle of the intersection, and the horrific crash left Virginia dead and her son with a severe head injury that left him in a coma for four weeks.

Scar Face crawled from his overturned car with both vehicles on fire and somehow fled from the scene before officers could catch him. He was eventually caught when a K-9 officer and his dog found him hiding under a car near the bar I had been waiting at. Just as the officer and his dog were about to subdue Scar Face, he raised a .357-caliber handgun at the officer. The dog attacked Scar Face before he could fire even one shot. Once he was in custody, they searched him and found firearms, knives, and enough ammunition on him to last through a heavy gun battle. Scar Face even had a knife taped to his ankle for use if he was caught.

He went to jail after being treated for the injuries he sustained in the fiery crash. They held him on all his robbery charges and a murder charge from his home state of California. It didn't take him long to call his girlfriend, Tara, and tell her to hook up with me and get money for an attorney. After all that had happened, he still didn't know who I was and never suspected me, as I had worried.

Tara was another stripper and friend of Kristie's. They worked at different clubs but were considered by most patrons to be the two top dancers in the city. Tara also began to hang around me, and rumors started to fly that she was my new "old lady." It doesn't take long for people on the street or in the bars to think someone had picked up with someone else in a bar. There were always rumor makers, and relationships were the hot topics for them to pass around. Good for me, though, because I had instant credibility wherever Tara went too. Just another person saying I'm someone that I'm not.

Tara agreed to fly back to California and get five ounces of meth for me to sell to pay for Scar Face's attorney. When she got back from California, she sat in my truck in the airport parking lot and reached under her skirt. She was wearing no panties and pulled out a bag of meth from her vagina.

"One hell of a purse," I thought to myself.

Before we could even talk about her trip, Tara was arrested, and word quickly got back to Scar Face through his court-appointed attorney that I was a cop. Hours later he was found hanging by the neck in his cell, dead.

Tara was sentenced to prison and did her time. When she was released, she married the president of the Dirty Dozen Motorcycle Gang and they had a child. For some crazy reason, some of the old-time members in the gang think the child is mine. Just because she and I ran together for a short time, they assumed I, not her new husband, got her pregnant.

The family of Virginia and Mark sued the Police Department because of the pursuit. They claimed that the police had several chances to arrest Scar Face on foot, but chose a pursuit instead. The courts found in favor of the Police Department, saying it had a plan, executed it, and provided a surveillance in case of an emergency.

Now came the most difficult decision. Should I tell Kristie who I was now that Tara was arrested? Or should I chance that she would never find out. Tara was every bit as dangerous as Scar Face and could easily have had Kristie killed by making one call. If I told Kristie, I'd be done with the Candy Store and all the work I had done up to that point. If I didn't, she would very likely die.

This was a difficult decision that could impact all my other current cases if the clients had ever met Kristie. Deep down inside, I knew I only had one choice.

17

Just Like a Kid in a Candy Store

The night after everything ended with Scar Face and I knew that Tara was locked up, I was at a boiling point emotionally over what had happened. Dave and I had known exactly what it would take to get Scar Face into custody. We were ready to risk ourselves if it meant he would be arrested and no other innocent people would be hurt. The whole plan was snatched right out from under us, and now I had to live with what happened to Virginia and Mark, what to do about Kristie, and what about me.

I spent the whole night riding around from place to place and thinking about things over and over. I sat at the cemetery for over an hour in the dark and prayed for an answer. Then I went home and stayed up for hours bending Patti's ear and looking for an answer. Then Patti made me realize something that I had never considered. I had no choice but to tell Kristie.

I owed it to her, she said. I also had to think about my safety. Everyone knew who I was and Tara would get the word out. If I showed up at the Candy Store or Bourbon Street where she worked, I was a dead man. Someone was going to kill me just to say he was the one that did it.

If that was the case, then I needed to change everything and move my game to another part of town. Reinvent myself and start over. It would be a new challenge and a chance to explore some new characters. To this point I had limited myself because of my hair, clothing, and mode of transportation.

First thing, though, I needed to go to Kristie and let her know what I had been doing and who I was. Sounds easy, but it was almost like divorcing someone. Telling her you are leaving and don't want to be with her anymore. Difficult for me and traumatic for her. She also had the burden of explaining why she'd vouched for me regularly, and people were going to hold her responsible for any arrests that were tied back to me. That meant she would have to relocate and change her lifestyle.

While I had been running around with Kristie, we had done a workup on her and learned where she lived. I went to her house, walked up to her door, and knocked. The feeling in my stomach was like a Mexican fiesta in full swing. The door opened, and there she stood with boys holding tight to her side. She met me with a big smile, and when I told her we needed to talk, I knew she thought I had finally decided to come stay with her. She told the boys to go inside and wait, than stepped outside.

"What's on your mind, Jake?"

I didn't know any other way to say it except right out front: "I'm a cop."

She laughed out loud and told me to quit messing around and tell her what was on my mind.

"No, I'm really a cop."

She looked hard at me and started to hit me over and over. "Why didn't you tell me!? I wouldn't care! I would still love you!" Then she broke down and cried for what seemed like an eternity.

I had tricked her all this time and she would be in big trouble for having introduced me to so many people. I had made her feel like a fool, and she still loved me.

After the crying stopped, we talked for the rest of the night and tried to figure the best way to keep her and the boys safe. Bottom line was that she had to leave the stripper business and move. She knew they would kill her once everyone found out. It was almost as if she was relieved and had finally found a reason to move on.

"Can we get together now?" she asked.

"No, Kristie, I'm married."

"I knew." She laughed in between the tears.

I planned to help her and her boys relocate and start a new life, but I also needed to begin mine. The first thing was to get a haircut and find some new territory. That meant going to the salon and letting Patti know what I had planned and what I needed from her. A new look with shorter hair. Not too short, though, so I could put in hair extensions if I needed that look too.

I had Patti work her magic on my hair before I could change my mind. Then I told her she was done for the day and we were going to do something fun and exciting. "What?" she excitedly asked. I just told her to wait and see. I didn't have any idea what we were going to do, but I knew I would come up with something. I called a friend and made sure Geoff and Cody were covered for the night, then I called another friend with a limo. Billy owned his own limo service and was always begging me to let him take us out. I told Billy to pick us up at the salon in an hour.

The first place we went was to the Biltmore Plaza, where we could buy each other something to wear that the other one really liked. It was incredibly fun watching Patti try on all the different outfits, then helping her change while we both stayed in the dressing room. Then we made our way to the Camelback Resort, where they gave us "his and her" body massages. We lay on the tables next to each other and talked about each other. Then out to the pool, where nothing seemed to matter as the day lingered on and we just hung out and played rich people.

When the afternoon turned into night, we changed into the clothes we'd bought for each other and went to dinner at our favorite restaurant. We finished a couple bottles of wine, and I knew we couldn't end the night without a stay in one of the rooms back at the Biltmore. The whole afternoon and night seemed like a dream adventure and ended with making love to the woman I loved the most. When we got back home the next morning, I thought long and hard about changing my job and moving into something safer. I decided to give it more consideration in the upcoming days.

Patti got ready for work and I had Billy drive both of us back to the salon. The adventure was over and it was time to step back into reality. While I sat in Patti's chair at the salon, I went through the messages on my phone and found one from Frankie. He was one of my informants, the epitome of the Rambo informant. Carried a gun on his hip in a low-slung cow-

boy holster and always looked for business. Frankie made everyone believe he was Mafia and connected to a family out of New
York. His message said he met another mobster who was trying
to get someone killed and needed a "hitter." That's apparently
where I came in.

Frankie had been driving down the freeway coming back
from Tucson when he saw what he thought to be a fifty-five-
year-old guy broken down on the side of the road. Always a
pushover for meeting new people, Frankie pulled over to help
the guy out. As they talked, he learned the man's name was Jan
Solomon, who had recently turned fifty-seven. His car had broken down while he was coming back from the state prison visiting a friend, and he had no idea how to fix it. Frankie was a
mechanic and realized immediately that Jan's freeze plugs had
blown and he needed the car towed back into town. He ordered
a tow truck for Jan, then offered to fix the freeze plugs for nothing. Frankie also planned to give Jan a ride back into town.

The two men quickly found out they had something in
common. Frankie spoke with bravado on how he was mob-
connected and did collections for the family. When he said this,
Jan's ears perked up and he told Frankie, "Me too." Jan explained his former involvement with a Detroit Mafia family and
said he wanted to get back in. Then he told Frankie the stunner.

Jan had gone to the Arizona state prison in Florence to meet
with a mob boss and get his permission to have someone killed.
He not only wanted permission, but he wanted the name of
someone to do it. Frankie remained quiet and decided to bring
my name up later when it didn't seem so obvious. He knew he
could stay in contact with Jan because of the car repair and he
thought patience might be best. Always thinking like a cop

made Frankie feel good about himself. Sometimes he just took it too far. Getting to Jan with a name of someone to do the job was important. We didn't need him getting it done for real by someone who truly killed for a living.

Jan Solomon was a pathetic man who had spent his life trying to be someone he wasn't. A brief stint as a minor league baseball player and an attempt as a professional boxer were a few of his highlights. His athleticism and punching power made him a great candidate for the Mafia, who regularly needed muscle to make collections on gambling debts. As Jan got older, he married a woman named Cindy. They had been married for over thirty years when I met Jan. They had one child, who later gave them their only grandson, who adored Jan and thought his grandfather was the greatest man in the world.

When the Mafia business and professional sports didn't work out for Jan, he took his family to Tucson, Arizona, where he started his own furniture business. Tucson was a great place to go because Jan had spent part of his teenage years living there. As did everything Jan touched, the business failed and so did his manhood. He began to experience problems sexually and soon became impotent. Not only was he a failure in life, but according to him, his wife had also begun to humiliate him for his inability to please her. I'm not too sure that was the case, though. Jan had a natural ability to blame everyone around him for the things he did wrong or went wrong in his life. Blaming Cindy was a perfect excuse to justify his illicit affairs.

He finally landed a job with another furniture company and became a traveling salesman. He would go to Tucson during the week, then return home on the weekends. During one of his weeks in Tucson he stopped at a Mail Boxes Etc. to mail a package. To his surprise, his high school sweetheart was behind the counter. Jenny Moore owned the store with her husband and instantly recognized Jan. How they recognized each other after having been apart for nearly forty years was beyond me. They had both aged painfully and didn't look anything like they had in their youth. But somehow they knew it was the other one and instantly fell back in love with each other.

Jan and Jenny met regularly after that chance meeting and told their tales of woe in their marriages. Jan felt Cindy disrespected him, and Jenny claimed to be mentally and physically abused by her husband, Jordan. Jan and Jenny spent days secretly meeting and entertained themselves by kissing and cuddling. No intercourse, because Jan couldn't participate. Finally, Jan pushed Jenny to leave her husband, and he would divorce Cindy. They could be together for the rest of their lives and finally find some happiness. It all sounded good to Jenny, except for one thing. She told Jan that Jordan was a madman and wouldn't accept a divorce. If he knew about Jan, he would kill the both of them, divorce or no divorce.

So began Jan's quest for happiness, at all costs.

Frankie told Jan that his cousin from upstate New York was coming into town for a few weeks. I knew that Jan claimed to have past Mafia ties and wanted badly to be respected and back in that life. He obviously lived in a dream world and would jump at the chance to be with a real mob guy and work in that world again. I knew if he got a meeting with me, he would try to position himself to do collections again. Maybe then he could once again be someone special. Or so his twisted mind thought.

When Frankie called Jan to tell him about his cousin, they talked about how close they had got and how they had become like brothers. This was everything to a man like Jan, who had lost his confidence and craved a friend like Frankie. Someone Jan could brag to about the old days when he was tough and all the world respected him.

Frankie told Jan he would give his cousin Jan's phone number, and when he got into town they could talk. No promises except for a phone call for a "brother."

Plans for Jan ran through my head, and I found it easy to develop the right character. The mobster was a great character for Jan, but I had to slip into my Dad role for about an hour before turning into Jan's new best friend. I had to rush over to the pizza parlor and pick up ten pizzas for Cody and his little pals. I'd promised Cody that once a week I would come to school at lunchtime and bring pizza for him and his pals. Those pals included both boys and girls because kids at that age didn't differentiate between the two sexes when forming their friendships. I would sit in the lunchroom with all these little kids around me, and we would eat pizza and I'd listen to all their stories. The chair was too small for me, but I didn't care or really think about it.

Cody felt like the big man on campus and never tired of my coming to school and hanging out with him. He looked right past my constantly changing appearance and always saw me only as his dad. Our bond started the day he was born, and I took care of him and got up in the middle of the nights with him. I told Patti that I wanted to bond with him because she had an automatic bond through birth. Everything I did in my life from the day he was born was impacted by the thought of my caring for him. It worked because he never lost his love for me and I knew it. When he was born, I swore I would never let him down or disappoint him. It took a lot of work and perseverance to make sure I kept my word.

My plan with Jan was to play him at a distance. I wasn't going to rush and act excited to do business with him. I didn't want some old-time mobster falling back into his old habits and ordering me around or controlling how the deal went down. I wanted his respect and fear and wanted to keep him from hiring someone else. I really didn't want Jordan coming up dead on my watch. This meant that every phone call would lead to another, and we would drag it on for weeks. I pretended to never really have time because of all the other murder jobs I had scheduled, and I purposely forced him to anxiously await my decision on whether I wanted the job. In my phone conversations I wanted to become his drug of choice. Other drugs were out there that he could use, but I was the one he craved. He would wait for me until he could have me, never looking any further, just waiting patiently for the right moment.

The big problem was how I was going to be believable. I was an Iowa-born guy and didn't have an ounce of Italian in me. The stereotypical Mafia guy was Italian, so I had to get over that hurdle. I also worked for a city police department, not the feds. The Phoenix Police Department was incredibly supportive of me and what I did, but they had budget issues. The money associated with being a Mafia guy was big and demanded equally big props. Two chiefs had taken over for Kurtenbach when he retired, Chief Kevin Robinson and Chief Mike Frazier. Without their support throughout my career, I would never have succeeded in doing the things I did. This case was no different.

Robinson and Frazier gave the order: do what I had to do and they would sort out the expense later.

I knew I had the support of the department, but I wanted to be creative and take advantage of all my resources, the first being Patti. With Patti I could get the mobster-style hair and have her grease it back. I watched several mob movies and developed a character that was the image of those TV personalities. I also hung out with Joe Stedino, a Mafia member from Reno who later became an informant. Joe taught me the walk, the talk, and how to ooze being a mobster. The best thing he ever taught me was how to carry my money. Joe said that mobsters never carry money in a wallet or on a money clip. They carry hundred-dollar bills rolled together and wrapped in a rubber band. Carry the money in your front pocket, Joe said. When you pull it out, flip the hundreds off one by one as you count them for everyone to see. Count the money as if you are making love to each bill, he would say. Then walk away with all the confidence that money and power can buy.

Joe would tell me stories of how members of the different crime families in New York became the stars of their neighborhood. Everyone respected them and gave them the best of what they had. Of course, it was because they were feared and nobody wanted to end up with a broken arm or in the river. They controlled the areas they lived in. They were bigger than sports stars and movie stars. The only person they listened to was their mother. It was an unbelievable life, Joe said, until you got caught.

The final thing I needed to "sure-up" was how I dressed and traveled. I needed jewelry for flash, expensive suits for the look, and a limo to get around. That was going to be rough, I thought.

But then I remembered my friend Bill Mack. He donated every waking minute to community charities, such as Scottsdale Rotary, Phoenix Thunderbirds, and Citizen's Police Academy. One day Bill had told me that if I ever needed his help or support for one of my cases, he would be there. This was finally the time to ask.

I called Bill and reminded him about his offer to me. "I'm here whenever and for whatever you need," Bill said. Okay . . . I need a limo, an expensive suit, and jewelry that says *money.* Bill said, "I'll call you back in two hours." The phone rang a few hours later, and Bill just said, "Could you have the limo back by tomorrow morning at ten a.m.?" Of course I could, and he gave me an address where to pick it up. A $3,000 Italian suit and all kinds of jewelry to make me look like a mobster with a lot of money was ready. Each item was located by Bill, provided by one of his Rotary brothers and sisters with a related business.

The night of my first meeting with Jan was going to be a hit. I went to the address given to me by Bill, and as I drove into the parking lot, I started to laugh uncontrollably. Bill had gotten the limo from his buddy Dave, a funeral-home owner. I needed to get the limo back by tomorrow morning because they had a funeral planned for 11:00 a.m. and needed it for the family of the deceased. I thought to myself how this was real, but could as easily been straight from the movies. It was almost too surreal to believe. My driver and bodyguard was to be Ronnie Red.

Every mob guy needs a beautiful woman hanging on his arm and every word. I wasn't going to be any different. The analyst at my office was a tall, dark, and beautiful African-American female. The mob guys are normally racist, but I was going to buck that trend and bring my girlfriend, Donna. When the deal was nearing the end, I was going to tell Jan that I'd tired of her and killed her. Until then she would make him uncomfortable and not sure of what to say to me. Another edge that would make him think I didn't follow all the rules. Another thought in his head that maybe after I finished his deal, I would kill him too. I wanted him completely off-balance and afraid to check on me. I didn't want Jan calling Chicago or New York to see if I was for real. If I convinced him I didn't follow all the rules and was a bit of a renegade, then he would be more careful about questioning me and accept me for who I said I was.

Periodically I would call Jan and check in, or he would call me. I would explain about being on the road taking care of business for the family, and he would convince me to wait for him for the right time. He also worried that God would punish him if he had Jordan killed. I routinely gave Jan opportunities to back out, but greed overpowered his fear of God.

The day finally came when Jan and I spoke on the phone and he had obviously made his mind up and was nearly ready. I explained how I had been busy in Vegas taking care of family business. Work had to be done at Caesars and some of the other "joints." I had family running the casinos, and they took good care of me. Of course Jan wanted me to know that he completely understood the business and knew most of the names. He wanted me to believe he was the same as me, just older. His people were Detroit and mine were Chicago and New York.

To make sure he didn't question my not being Italian, I came up with an elaborate story about living on the streets in Buffalo, New York, and hanging out with the kids of Mafia families. They saw how I operated and soon took me into their families. I eventually became one of them and was accepted as family.

I didn't pull Buffalo out of thin air and decide to use that as home. I went there periodically over several years and would stay for two to four weeks at a time. I learned everything I could about the city and its people. I knew where the money was and I knew where the ghetto was. Every mob guy that was killed in a neighborhood became my business, and I learned all their families and what kind of work they were in. Then I went to the jails and prisons so I could later talk intelligently about the places I claimed to have stayed. Don't ever lie about something you know nothing about. You may run into someone who was there and will catch you in the lie. You can lie about circumstances, but not locations.

I got tired of the small talk with Jan and stopped the chitchat. "So you need some business done?" I asked. He explained how he needed something done, but wasn't quite ready. It was good to know, Jan said, that I would be around. "You're wrong about that, buddy. I'm not around much at all. If you need me, then you better take advantage of it right now. Otherwise, I'm moving on," I said.

That was all Jan needed to know. He felt he might have made me mad and didn't want me alienated, so he completely opened up. He had a guy he wanted "eliminated." The guy was accessible and not the least bit jittery about his surroundings. We discussed a number of ways that I could make the guy disappear. Blow him up and make sure everyone knew, or quietly kill him and make his body disappear. He was a small guy according to Jan and wouldn't be any trouble. "Not a boxer, not a wrestler, not a heavy-duty dude," Jan said. Just a guy. A guy who worked in Tucson at a Mail Boxes Etc.

When Jan finished describing the guy he wanted killed, I

told him to get me something on him so I could follow him around and figure out how he operated. He would never know I was on him and I could pick the best spot to do my hit. Killing the guy and making it look like a suicide was Jan's idea. His target had a bad heart and was depressed. Suicide would never be questioned by any of his family and friends. Jan also had a heart condition, he told me. He didn't have long to live and wanted his final months or years to be happy.

"Call me when you're ready, Jan. I'll be here a week or two and then I'm off to other business. I like the weather here," I said. "That's the only reason I'm staying longer. If you change your mind . . . cool. Just forget about me and ever talking to me."

A few more days passed and Jan and I spoke again. Every time we spoke he opened up even more and told me more facts about his plan. He finally gave me the target's name: Jordan Moore. He was the husband of Jan's old girlfriend, with whom he had fallen in love again. She had told him how Jordan beat her and pistol-whipped her. Jan wanted Jordan dead so he could be with Jenny. Jan saw himself as her knight in shining armor who was going to save her from the beast. According to Jan, Jenny wanted Jordan out of her life too, but didn't want to get involved with me. She was leaving everything to Jan and protecting herself in case something went wrong.

At least that's the way Jan made everything sound. He was waiting until Jenny told him the time was right to give me the go-ahead. Jenny never popped up in any meetings or phone conversations, except through Jan. I thought about it many times and wondered if Jenny's only mistake in the whole mess was her infidelity to Jordan. Or was she a smart and manipulative woman who wanted out of her marriage, but wasn't going to dirty her hands? She had her puppet in Jan and would direct him to do everything for her. Either way, she was going to have to live in her own hell when this was over, either in prison or in the eyes of Jordan.

A couple more weeks passed and Jan called again with an idea of how I might be able to kill Jordan. Jan had been thinking about it and decided he wanted it done so Jenny didn't know. That way she could act surprised when they told her Jordan had died. Everybody would believe her because she would truly be surprised. Jordan was an avid bike rider and raced in cross-country meets. He trained for his long-distance rides on the back roads. Jan thought this was a great way to kill him. Run him over as he rode down the highway and leave him to die. Nobody would think anything except what a terrible accident.

In my phone conversations with Jan, I continued to make him believe I wasn't comfortable with meeting him and was constantly out of town on business. In this racket, the longer I waited, the more it would convince someone that I was for real. But wait too long, and the person might go somewhere else. It was a fine line. Time would tell me when Jan was ready, and it wasn't time yet. My plan to extend Jan over time seemed to be playing out perfectly. He would call me and never once indicate that he was looking somewhere else. I was his guy now and he was sticking with me.

I would sit in my home down the street from Jan and make him think I was in another state doing business. Too busy for him and tied up with real moneymaking opportunities. Patti would laugh as she walked past the room I was sitting in. I would be talking to Jan on the phone and acting as if I were getting a drink from my girl. Patti said it sounded as if I had multiple personalities. In a sense she was right, today I was the mobster . . . tomorrow, who knew.

Then the time came when Jan wanted to meet me in person so we could finalize our deal.

"If I'm going to do this, then I want four to five hundred and then more when I'm done," I told him.

"I'm good with that," he said. "I know how much of a favor you are doing for me and I appreciate it. Frankie has done me good."

"Just make sure I get what little money you are paying me before I leave town. I plan on leaving right away."

"I will, and maybe I can pay you back more by doing some work for you later."

"Friday evening at the Coffee Plantation in the Biltmore."

The Biltmore Plaza makes everyone who knows about it excited at the thought of being there. Historic, because of all the presidents who had stayed at the resort, and exciting for those who enjoyed shopping at high-dollar stores with exclusive name brands. The Coffee Plantation was in the middle of the outdoor Biltmore Plaza and played host to everyone who wanted to be seen. Music at night and mimes during the day. This was a perfect place for me because I could make a stunning entrance and not be totally out of place. Everyone seated outside could see me when I arrived, and Jan could allow his fantasy to rise to a new level. I would finally be for real and arrive just as his mind dreamed I would.

Everything was in place before we showed up at the Biltmore. Ronnie Red was dressed in an expensive suit and looked like a monstrous bodyguard. Donna was dressed beautifully and was sure to turn eyes as she got out of the limo. Ray Roe was seated in the video platform and ready to capture all the night's events. Ray was a successful undercover detective in his own right and also an expert in capturing good video and audio for cases. Better people couldn't surround me, and I knew we were in for some fun.

Ronnie Red pulled up directly in front of the Coffee Plantation as a single guitar player sang for the outside crowd. As soon as the limo came to a stop, I watched the people start moving closer, trying to catch a glimpse of who was inside. Red got out first and went to the back door where Donna was seated. She slithered out of the seat and stood for everyone to admire how she looked. The crowd started to grow thicker, and I sat inside the limo to give it a chance to grow even bigger. I wanted as big of a show as possible for Jan. I couldn't see him while I was seated inside because the crowd of people blocked the view. It was as if they were expecting some rock star to come out next and didn't want to miss the moment.

Finally, after waiting long enough for the excitement to grow, I stepped outside the limo and stared at the crowd. Hair slicked back, gold on my hands, and a $3,000 Italian suit and shoes to match. You could see all their faces as they stood in awe and wondered what was going on. Nobody moved, and suddenly I could see Jan running from one of the tables calling out, "Jake . . . Jake!" Red stepped right up to Jan and told him, "Back off!" I looked Jan in the eyes as I pulled my suit jacket together and hooked a button. Then I pointed for him to go back to his table: "I'll be there in a minute." He ran back to his seat and sat still, just like a kindergarten boy waiting for his snack!

I turned toward Donna and reached into my pocket, pulling

out the roll of hundred-dollar bills. Counting them just as Joe had told me to do and periodically hesitating to look at the crowd. I gave Donna a couple thousand dollars and told her to go buy herself something. Totally impressed with the show, the crowd moved apart and let Donna walk through to the stores. Turning to Red, I said, "Pick me up in thirty." Our plan was that I would call him when I was ready; he would sit in the back of the plaza waiting.

No way was I going to the table I'd sent Jan to. Instead, I walked to the other side of the patio, and when I got to a table, I motioned for him to come to me. Jan jumped from his seat and almost ran to me. As he got to my table, he gave me the Mafia hug and nervously sat down. I looked around first, then took my seat. Everyone continued to watch the show, and I sat with my hands folded in front of my face. I gave the I'm-in-control-here posture, and Jan knew I meant business. Before we even got far into our initial conversation, he secretly passed me an envelope. As I looked inside, I could see he had given me a description of Jordan's truck, Jordan's name and physical description, and where he lived and worked. While I looked through the envelope, I stopped for a moment and looked Jan directly in the face. "I hope I can help you, Jan," I said.

He responded right back, "I hope you can too, and I will really appreciate it. Jenny has a very important request for you, Jake."

"What might that be?"

"She wants you to wait until the twentieth to kill Jordan. She has a bunch of things happening at work and doesn't want to impose upon her boss by taking off for a funeral."

Jan loved Jenny so much that he saw this request as being

completely considerate. He described the entire relationship, and everything he was doing for Jenny, as a "beautiful love story." He claimed that Jenny wanted Jordan killed, but needed to get her decks cleared at work so she didn't burden the boss. Pretty strange for a gal who owned her own business and worked with the intended victim. Love is blind though, and Jan didn't seem to see through the story.

The more we talked, the more Jan wanted me to believe how he was tough and could still do collections or any other work the family needed. He even stood up in front of me and dared me to hit him in the stomach. See how hard the stomach muscles were, then check out the biceps. He was so preoccupied with my size that he continually compared himself to me and tried to make me think he could do the same job I did. "I have the body of a twenty-five-year-old, the mind of a twelve-year-old, and the insides of a seventy-year-old," he said. Jan explained that years of vascular problems had taken a toll on his heart. Though, he was getting stronger and better with each day.

This broken man suddenly began to flower and grow with every minute he was with me. It was if I had validated his manhood for another year and he could carry on. He was empowered and saw a new lease on life, even if it was at the expense of someone else.

The deal was for me to find Jordan riding his bike down the back roads of Tucson and knock him off the bike. Make it look like an accident, Jan said. Once Jordan was lying in the road, I would drive over him again and again until he surely died. When I finished killing Jordan, then I would take my vehicle to some friends of the family and have them dismantle it. I'd immediately leave town for Vegas, and after a couple of weeks I'd send for Jan. A limo would pick him up and get him to Vegas. When he arrived, we would party and celebrate for days. Jan was so excited about the opportunity of being with me in Vegas that he immediately began to devise a plan for his boss that would surely get him excused from his job.

The hard part was yet to come, with the discussion of money and whether Jan could afford me. I never knew how far to go with someone until I was in the middle of the deal. Ask for too much and they might leave and find someone cheaper. The law of supply and demand can really put a crimp in one's charges. Charge too little and you send up a red flag that you aren't for real. Only drug addicts kill for nothing, and based on this night, I obviously wasn't a drug addict. I knew Jan had money problems and was expecting to deal along the lines of "professional courtesy" or because of his friendship with Frankie. I had even promised I would take care of him. So I knew much more than $500 cash was going to tap him out. He even told me that Cindy held the purse strings and knew every penny he spent.

I sat and looked at Jan in a way that was obviously making him feel nervous. People around us were craning their necks trying to hear a few words of the conversation. Then I glanced at his wrist and noticed a beautiful gold bracelet and a Rolex watch. How much? I asked with an evil smile. A thousand dollars for the bracelet and $6,000 for the watch. He begged to keep the watch, but took the bracelet off and handed it to me. Fourteen-karat gold, but he sure would like to keep it too. I just handed it back to him slowly and stared.

I told Jan that if he wanted to give me the bracelet as partial payment to show me his commitment, I would gladly accept it as full payment. I would make up the rest of the money after I killed Jordan by selling his jewelry and taking his money.

"I'm a bastard, Jan, but I show you respect because you have it coming," I told him.

"You're not a bastard, Jake, you're a nice guy."

What Jan worried about most was that he had upset me over the money talk. He was nearly shaking over the idea that I was mad and would get up and leave. When I finally convinced him I was fine, he held out his hand and handed me the gold bracelet. He sat upright in his chair and with a smile said, "Let's call ourselves square." Jan extended his hand to shake on the deal, and we continued to discuss our plan.

My limo pulled up to the front of the Coffee Plantation and Red got out and went to the back and opened the door. As Donna walked by me, she brushed my hair, then strolled to the limo and slithered back inside. I told Jan I had to leave and we would meet in one week to finalize our deal. In the meantime I would learn everything I needed to know about Jordan before he died.

"She was beautiful when I first met her. He has stressed her out so much over the years that she is now full of wrinkles. She still has a nice body and a heart of gold," Jan said with a devilish smile.

I got up, rebuttoned my jacket, and walked away. After a few steps I stopped and turned back toward Jan. "See you here Saturday at one." Then I smoothly slid into the limo and we drove away.

Saturday came quickly and I made arrangements to have D. P. Davis and Alex Femenia sitting at one of the tables near where

I was going to meet with Jan. Their job was to arrest Jan as soon as I got up from the table and walked away. That sign would tell them that I had all I needed, and he was good to go. It was never a good idea for me to make the arrest because it would give other people too much time to see me and place me as a cop.

Alex and D.P. were perfect for the deal because they had both worked years of undercover and knew how to make this situation work. Alex totally looked like a mob figure himself with his svelte appearance and distinguished head of combed-back, gray hair. D.P. looked as if he belonged to money and walked with an arrogance that demanded respect. But Jan never noticed them because he was too busy trying to impress me to pay attention to his surroundings. I knew I was in good hands with D.P. and Alex if Jan decided to try anything stupid.

Many people will question why I let Jan walk after the first meeting. He paid me for the job and gave me good information on who needed to be killed. Jan even helped develop the plot to kill Jordan. All the elements of the crime were there for me to arrest and charge Jan. But the jury pool always has a hard time believing that anyone is capable of killing someone, let alone hiring someone to do it. I wanted to eliminate Jan's only defense—that I scared him so much that he couldn't back out. Let him walk and get away from me. Give him plenty of time to rethink his decision and go to the police. Or to call me and say he had changed his mind. He wouldn't have any fear of intimidation because I was not in his face. I had already told him it was okay to back out, just don't tell the police. None of that rational thinking came to Jan. He was ready and wanted to be with Jenny no matter who was hurt.

At one in the afternoon I arrived at the Coffee Plantation in the Biltmore Plaza. This time I gave Jan a completely different look. I arrived on foot and walked to him from the other end of the plaza. When I arrived at his table, I caught him by surprise because he was looking for me to arrive in the parking lot. It gave me the element of surprise from the moment we got back together. Once again he was off-balance and not sure what to expect from me. I arrived from behind him and laid my hand on his shoulder. I thought to myself, "I got you Jan and you didn't even know it!" He jumped with surprise and babbled about looking for me elsewhere.

As I sat at the table, I asked Jan if everything was still a go and if he still wanted Jordan killed. "Absolutely," he said. Jenny had already left for California, he said, and was staying with her sister. This would keep her far away when Jordan was killed, according to Jan. A perfect alibi for her, one that would keep the police from questioning her too hard. He was so proud of himself for being "cool" and making all these arrangements so everything would go off as planned.

Before I stood up from the table to leave, I told Jan that by this time next week his mental health was going to be good. "I'm a happy man," he said with a giggle. "I'm like a kid in a candy store." He told me one more time how this was turning out to be a beautiful love story.

I stood from the table and excused myself to go to the bathroom. Jan stayed seated with his hands folded on the table. I made eye contact with D.P. and Alex as I passed and went straight into the Coffee Plantation. Then I stood at the glass picture window that overlooked the patio where I had been sitting with Jan. D.P. and Alex calmly walked over to Jan and showed him their badges. "Jan Solomon? You are under arrest for conspiracy to commit murder." Jan stared and looked as if he had just been punched in the stomach.

Everyone in the restaurant stood at the window and watched as handcuffs were placed on Jan. They looked at him, then at me, confused and a bit scared because they knew we were just together. They moved a little farther from me as I stared at each of them with the toothpick dangling from my mouth. I gave a cocky smile from the side of my mouth, then disappeared out the back door into the crowded plaza.

At the end of every deal I went to the intended victims and sat with them, to answer any questions they might have. Before the suspect even gets to jail, the media are all over the story and airing it on the earliest news. If I didn't go directly to the victims, they would find out about their near miss while watching television. I never wanted that to happen. If it did, then I would have failed in my compassion and concern for the victim. That's what it was all about in the first place. I wanted to do something for the victims so they didn't get hurt or die. Even if I risked my own life by becoming known by too many people.

In my quiet time I started thinking about who the victims really were. Of course, in this case the intended victim was Jordan, the target of a murder plot. Even though he didn't die, I'm sure he considered the possibility when he found out about his wife's infidelity. The forgotten victim in this scenario was Cindy. She sat at home waiting for Jan to return from his normal Saturday shopping trip for his ailing mother. She didn't even consider that her husband of over thirty years might be plotting a murder with a hired killer. His grandson, who looked up to Jan, would never have imagined his hero was on the verge of going to prison for the rest of his life. The entire family had no idea. I had to go to Cindy right away and tell her before she found out from the news. A reporter would surely be knocking on her door within an hour.

I didn't even take time to change and went directly to her house in my mobster appearance. I knew she wouldn't believe me if I met her at the door alone, so I had a police officer go to the door first and prepare her for how I was going to look. I knew I was imposing and I knew I would scare her. She invited me inside after learning I was one of the good guys. She was a sweet elderly lady who had a beautiful home that she obviously worked hard to keep neat and orderly.

We sat at the kitchen table, and just as a good grandmother would do, she offered me something to eat and drink. As I looked at her trying to please me and make me comfortable, I found myself hating Jan for what he had done and the position he had placed me in. Having to tell Cindy that her husband wasn't coming home, that he would be in prison for the rest of their lives, just didn't seem fair. Cindy sat across from me at the kitchen table as I told her what Jan had done. Tears began to flow and her breath was short as she tried to understand the devastation Jan had caused.

Then I looked at Cindy's wrist and wanted to reach across the table and hug her. She wore a bracelet just like the one Jan had so quickly given me as payment for the murder. I pointed to it and said, "Tell me about your bracelet."

Oh, this, she said as she fondled the bracelet and looked deeply at it. Jan has one just like it. They were companion bracelets that they had bought together to wear to remember each other by while apart.

"I have his," I said with a pause. "He used it as payment for the murder." Cindy didn't believe me and said he would never part with his bracelet. It meant too much to him. I slowly pulled the bracelet from my inside coat pocket and held it in front of her. "He isn't coming home, Cindy." She cried even harder.

I sat, thought, and held her hands as she cried and cried. She'd never recover from this, I thought to myself.

Jenny was never personally involved in the negotiations with me, and Jordan retained an attorney for her right away. He never believed that Jenny was involved and always thought that Jan made up the whole story about Jenny.

Jan died of a massive heart attack six weeks into his prison sentence.

18

Lost in Nightmares

As the murders for hire mounted, I found it harder and harder to be me. Everyone in my department and even the press was expecting me to continue my string of successful cases and to invent new characters each time. The pressure didn't come with being successful; it came with making sure each case was correctly done. I didn't want to get so caught up in the hype that I began to manufacture cases that shouldn't have been done in the first place. I had to begin with managing myself and questioning everything that I did. A good self-evaluation never hurt anyone, and I had promised myself from day one to do just that. After I evaluated the merits of a case, I would run the case by Patti and get her honest opinion on my true motivation for taking the case.

The murder-conspiracy conviction carries an incredibly lengthy prison sentence, and the guilty verdict not only impacts the defendant, but also the jury that handed down the decision. I had to be extra careful to consider the impact of my actions on other people, including the players' families and friends. That's why I made sure each suspect that hired me was completely committed to killing someone.

I had to believe in my heart that if I didn't agree to do the murder, the client would go elsewhere. I had to be convinced of this commitment 100 percent of the time or I refused to participate. If not for me, someone else; that's what I lived by.

Then I had to deal with another interesting addition to my role, which further blossomed with each case: attention from the media. The media can be sneaky, especially if they smell a titillating story. A story about parents killing their son or a man blowing up a restaurant with people inside is definitely titillating. It's exactly the material that news organizations want to lead their evening news with. My cases became the six-o'clock lead story regularly and fodder for sensational newspaper articles.

APPARENTLY, HE HIT ON HIRING THE WRONG HIT MAN said the *Arizona Republic* of one case. "'She's made my whole life miserable. I've been looking for someone [like you] for ten years,' Di Somma told Detective Ballentine during their meeting Sunday night," the article recounted. Another article in the paper described me as looking like "a real Mafia hit man—complete with silk suit, oiled hair, flashy pinkie ring and a fat bankroll." Some clever headlines on stories about my cases included REACH OUT AND KILL SOMEONE . . . DRESSED TO KILL . . . MURDER, HE THOUGHT . . . LOVED TO DEATH . . . KILLER FOR HIRE: CAN BE BIKER, MOBSTER— OR COP. Even papers across the globe covered my cases, such as the *London Independent*, which declared DETECTIVE BALLENTINE MAY BE AMERICA'S MOST ACTIVE GUN FOR HIRE.

If it wasn't enough that articles were regularly being written, the cameras tried to follow me and capture my daily movements. I would do interviews after a successful deal and conceal my identity by having my face blurred out on camera and my voice electronically altered. As I would leave the interviews, I found cameramen and reporters lurking in the shadows to try to follow me. It became a game to lose them before they could figure out where I was going. Businesses also profited from my deals by making T-shirts to promote the murder for hire done at their business. UB's bar was where I did the Mortimer Hylton case. At its end, after I told the owners what had transpired, they went right out and made a T-shirt that flew off the shelves. I GOT BOMBED AT UB'S was emblazoned on the front of the shirt.

A typical police-beat writer will go to the department's headquarters and scroll through all the arrests during the day and night. From a short description attached to each case, the reporter gets a taste of whether he wants to pursue the story. The major newspapers usually have an owner who is closely connected with one of the local television stations. The TV station shares its breaking news with the paper, and the reporter shares his breaking news with the TV station. Both sides immediately request a copy of the full report and associated tapes. They also request an interview or a staged press conference. You can say no, but the Freedom of Information Act protects the media and forces the department to cooperate. Refuse the interview and the media will put whatever spin on the story they want. If you cooperate, you have much more control over how the story is told and may be able to protect those who could unnecessarily be hurt. When one network shows the story, every other station demands it. That's why press conferences are so popular. Everyone hears the story and you only have to do it once.

Over the years I found a couple of writers and reporters that I trusted and knew would never write an incorrect story. Paul Rubin from the *New Times* and Bill Herman from the *Arizona Republic* were the best I ever met. They were fair and never had their facts wrong. Both were extremely skilled writers that I trusted with my stories. I would even give them a story before any other outlet to repay them for their honesty. Bill Herman was once allowed to ride with the video crew and watch a deal firsthand. He's the one who started calling me Batman because I'd slip away into the darkness.

Of the television news outlets I found two other journalists that were good as gold. Mike Watkiss from Channel 3 and *Current Affair* fame was amazingly understanding and trustworthy. I would never have guessed it when I first met him. He had the Hollywood-tabloid style and I thought he would be a snake. I was so wrong. He truly was a friend of law enforcement and one of the best in his business. Then there was John Daly from *Real TV*, one of the most honest and sincere reporters I ever met. He never got caught up in the hype of his fame and stayed a true friend to me for years. John and his show continually donated to a slain police officer's fund whenever I completed a story for them.

On all my cases I determined which television outlet was the most interested in doing the right story by placing a price tag on each release. I never personally took one penny for what I was doing, but I did make them pay. All the money was donated to funds supporting families of police officers or firefighters that had lost their lives in the line of duty.

It's tricky and stressful when you deal with the press during an ongoing undercover operation or lengthy investigation. Some editors want the story aired or printed as soon as possible with no concern for the undercover operative or the ultimate success of an investigation. I understood they had their job to do, but I had mine too. That's why I selected honorable reporters and TV personalities to bring the stories to the public. I brought them into my confidence, and in return they protected me and my family at all costs. At times it would lead to knock-down, drag-out fights with their bosses, but in the end they would refuse to do the story if I or my case was jeopardized.

As the pressure from the press and my success began to increase, I worried that I would become too popular and be moved out of my assignment. The staff would consider my job too dangerous since I was getting too well-known. I did everything I could to not let it bother me or change my style of doing business. I just knew that the more I became known, the more I would need to change my character and physical appearance. I had done it over and over for years and never been discovered. Change my name and get a new look. Go to a different area of the city and start all over again. The same recipe worked over and over and never failed me.

I worried most that the people I respected would start to question me and think I was doing the hits for personal attention. That was the furthest from the truth. I became successful because of the style I incorporated in my work. I never compromised a thing and never ever crossed the line. The thought of being questioned for what I did would hurt more than anything else. I could only continue to be honest and make each case as important as the others. Either people trusted me or they didn't.

My stress level increased and I began to worry more about the staff's concern that I had been taking too many chances. If they were concerned about the amount of attention I was getting, this would be an ideal excuse to move me out. "He's taking too many chances and could get himself killed. Let's get him out for his own good," they would say. Politics are powerful in law enforcement and can be a daily battle for the investigator. I knew that all too well after years of watching the wars.

Success breed's jealousy, and jealousy leads to bad management decisions. If someone became jealous over my notoriety, then I was finished. I just kept telling myself to ignore the paranoia and stay focused on what I was meant to do. My mother always told me that if you are doing the right thing, never stop, forge ahead. That's what I planned to do, I told myself. But I never let anyone know that all this was happening, and I never exposed my feelings to outsiders.

I was sitting around the house one day, playing with Cody, while all this was going through my head. We decided to go outside to the park, and I hit him grounders and fly balls as he worked on his third-baseman skills. Cody and I did this whenever we could get a moment. The more I worked with him, the better player he became. It was so rewarding watching him get better and better, becoming a competitive player. Then it hit me! A pain in my stomach and lower back that was worse than any other pain I had felt in a long time. It was even worse than the first time I had experienced kidney stones.

I started to sweat and felt that I was going to pass out. I had no idea what it was and only knew I was at stuck in a park and things didn't look good for getting back to the house. I looked like some transient with a young boy, and this wasn't a recipe for a good outcome. The pain felt similar to the last kidney stone, but then it didn't, because it was much more intense. I didn't know if my appendix was about to rupture or if I was experiencing some other internal problem. More and more people in my life were dying from cancer and heart attacks, so that definitely went through my mind. We had just run around pretty hard for the past hour, and that could have stimulated something. I couldn't saying anything to Cody because I worried he would freak out. He only knew me as a strong man who never showed pain or fear or got sick.

When I could finally catch my breath, I told Cody we needed to wrap things up and get home. I was feeling a little "puny" and needed to rest and take a break, I told him. When we got back to the house, I called Patti at the salon and told her to get me to the hospital. You would think that I would have called the paramedics, but that never crossed my mind. I would never have done anything that brought attention to my being weak out in public. In my business you never want to expose yourself so people know who you are. Especially in the neighborhood and to people you don't want knowing anything about you.

When Patti got to the house, I picked myself up and made it out the door to my truck. Once I got to the hospital and saw a doctor, I found out the pain was from another damn kidney stone that was stuck and wouldn't move. This time though I had waited too long and hadn't got myself treated early enough and had gone into renal failure. As I lay in the hospital bed the pain got worse and worse and I started to bleed. Concern ran throughout the emergency room as I got even sicker.

Patti knew I was struggling, but she also knew I wasn't

going to complain. She had got use to my hiding my pain and disguising my fears. She also knew the only way I was going feel any comfort was if she made the doctor juice me with a strong dose of morphine. She disappeared for a while, and when she returned, she had the emergency-room doctor in tow and he was holding a syringe loaded with morphine. After a few minutes the pain was gone and I slipped into dreamland. I remember feeling strange as I lay there and allowed the stone to move. I was now out of my own control, and the only person I could count on for my safety was Patti. My, how times had changed and how I had finally become vulnerable. Everything was in Patti's hands, and I could only hope that she would make all the right decisions.

A kidney stone makes you so sick that all you want to do is throw up and lie on the ground curled up in a ball. Intense pain radiates through your back and around your stomach. No position really helps. Morphine is about the only strong drug they have found to take the edge off the pain. A kidney stone is just no fun at all, and renal failure makes it that much more dangerous.

When a part of the stone finally passed, I woke up from the drug-induced sleep. I was given the okay by the doctor to go home, but he ordered rest for several days in hopes that the remainder of the kidney stone would pass and no surgery would be necessary. I was to return in a few days to determine if the stone and the renal failure had caused any permanent damage. I knew right then the follow-up visit wasn't going to happen. I was too busy and only had a few days to rest before I had to get back on the street.

I got back to the house and made it upstairs to my room, where I could lie down and rest. After a while I walked down to the kitchen to get something to drink. As I walked into the kitchen, I looked up to the glass ceiling and watched as a man-size rooster crashed through the glass and onto the floor. The rooster jumped to its feet and started to fight me as a man would. The fight was like no other I had ever had, and blood started to fly everywhere, along with feathers. I thought to myself, as I fought for my life, that this bird was not going to be the one thing that finally got me.

The fight seemed to last for thirty minutes until I finally slew the rooster and stood over him trying to catch my breath. Blood and feathers were all over the kitchen, with glass from the ceiling sprinkled about. Then I opened my eyes and looked around. It was all a dream. The stress and pain medication had done it all. I was fine and the rooster had never existed. The remainder of the kidney stone passed during the dream, and I was able to go on without any future surgery. The doctor later told me that the pain of the kidney stone's moving, along with the drugs, had made me hallucinate. That was why I never used any drugs. I'd never have survived. Too many fights with roosters would have been the end of me.

Things seemed to simmer down at work, and the feelings that I might be moved out for my own safety calmed down. I always felt that a group of chiefs acted as my guardian angels and protected me from the forces I worried about. Chiefs Tim Black, Kevin Robinson, and Mike Frazier were there when I needed them, and obviously when I didn't know I needed them. Because of them I continued on my path and survived the dangers of jealousy. Fortunately for me, these powerful decision makers didn't have jealousy in them and led with a clear mind.

When I was relocating to another part of town and changing my identity, I would travel from bar to bar until I found the right fit for me. I wanted a mix of dirtbags and people with jobs. The dirtbags were my source for criminal activity, while the people with jobs played the part of my mouthpiece. All the things that I did would be so outrageous to the people with jobs that they would do all my bragging for me. They had never met anyone like me in their lives and made me bigger than I really was. But, the most important person for me in every bar was a barfly. She was the girl or woman who made the bar her home and all the patrons her family.

The barfly wanted to know everyone's business, and once she knew it, she told everyone else. Of course she made each person feel like the only one with whom she shared this inside knowledge. The great thing about being in a bar was that if you hung out regularly for about two weeks, you automatically became a regular who had been coming in the bar for years. The barfly made sure of that. She would tell anyone who would listen that she had known you for most of her life and had either had sex with you or loved and trusted you like a brother. Normally she loved you like a brother after claiming for the better part of a week to have had sex with you.

The barfly also needed to be extremely good-looking or she would have no credibility with the other men. If she was ugly, they would write her off as a drunk and not pay her any attention. If she had a great body and looked really good, she could say or do anything and have the ear of all the men. Men in bars are wolves and only listen to a great body or an outstanding set of tits. It's the same in any bar, whether high-end or a dump with a dirt floor. The only thing that differed from place to place was how the men defined "good-looking." The rougher the bar, the lower the expectation.

I finally wandered into the Dunes bar on the west side of town, and the minute I got inside I knew this was going to be my new home. Before I went into the Dunes I'd changed back to my biker attire and started to grunge up again. Put on some more pounds and began to shed the personality that was the mafioso. Walking into the bar through the back-alley door, I immediately spotted a little blonde shooting pool and looking fine. One look at how she was running her mouth at the pool table and I knew I had my barfly. I ordered a drink and sent one directly over to her while she stood and waited for the other guy to shoot. She got the drink, looked at me with a smile, and I knew from that moment she was my ticket to quick validation in the joint.

Coon Dog showed up shortly after I had started talking to my new friend, Kim. We usually met at some point during a night and would let each other know by phone where we would be going. That way we could help each other with not looking too out of place in new joints. If you had a friend, then you looked like a regular real fast. I looked at Dog, then back to Kim. She asked me my name and I said, "Sonny." Then I said to her:

"See that Charles Manson–looking guy over there?"

"Yes."

"I got some business with him in the parking lot. As soon as I get back, I'm buying you another drink."

"I'll wait right here, Sonny." She smiled and titled her head flirtatiously. All these women seemed to use this mannerism as they tried to get their way.

I knew she wouldn't wait one minute past the moment I went outside. She was going to gather everyone to look out the door and watch what I was doing. She knew it wasn't going to be legal. I didn't look as if I did anything legal. I went outside and Dog followed me out the door. We stood to the rear of his car and he opened the trunk. I did all this in view and for the entertainment of the bar patrons. Dog and I looked in his trunk for a minute, then moved a pile of rifles from his trunk to mine. I peeled off a bundle of money and handed it over to Dog, then we went back inside the bar. I didn't have to say a thing. They'd all soon what had happened and Kim was going to take care of the rest. Before the week was over, Kim had told everyone that her new man Sonny was an "outlaw."

Felt pretty good to be back on the scooter and really good to be outside, where I felt better in the fresh air. It also felt good to be back in a place where I could run my business and be part of the crowd. I dropped my car off after leaving the Dunes that night and rode around on my bike for a while. Then I got a call on my pager from the OCB. This time the case called for a biker, and the source was a "professional" that would be a pain in my ass before everything was finished. I threw on the WARLORD jacket for the motorcycle gang for instant respect throughout this deal. A visual was worth a thousand words. The new target was in for the scare of his life.

It's hard to explain the emotional pressure that comes with constantly living a lie and changing your identity as frequently as you change underwear. When the rooster dream came, I passed it off as caused by the pain medication. That turned out to be partially wrong since I started dreaming weird dreams almost every night.

As I fell asleep in the upstairs sitting room, someone suddenly attacked me from behind, grabbing me around the neck and strangling me until I nearly passed out. I was thoroughly pissed off that the little bastard had got me from behind and not in my face, where I would have had a chance. I remember grabbing the guy's arm to relieve some pressure from around my neck and to hopefully get control of him. No matter what I did to get away it was not working, and I began to feel more and more faint. I struggled back and forth while seated in the chair and thought this was not how I wanted to die. It just couldn't happen like this. I hadn't had time to make all the wrong things right. It's absolutely crazy how your minds runs through a hundred thoughts as you are in a battle or think you are about to die.

Then I opened my eyes and realized it was all another dream. I was breathing heavily and my adrenaline was flowing from the fear of the fight. I had all the emotional strain related to a fight without ever lifting a hand. Everything seemed so real that it took several minutes for me to calm down and fall back asleep. The dreams continued and worried me because they were so real and I was always being attacked or nearly killed.

So many triggers were playing a part in my stress and difficult sleep. More stressful than the job or dodging the press was the journey with my father as he fought his own battle with cancer. I would spend as much time as I could with him talking about normal day-to-day topics. I would travel with him to the doctor or take him back and forth from his hospital stays. All this as I watched the giant of a man that I loved wither away to nothing. When I would go home to sleep at night, I would lie awake and think about him and what he had meant to my life. Struggling to sleep, I would finally close my eyes and drift back to the dreams.

Every night came with a series of more dreams, and some dreams returned for several nights in a row. My father's battle with cancer was finally lost and he died with me and my brother and sisters by his side. Moments before he died, he woke from his sleep and started rummaging through the dresser drawer by his bed. I asked him what he was doing and he only said, "Looking for my stuff." Finally, he lay on the bed and rested for a minute to catch his breath. My dad then closed his eyes, fell back asleep, and never awoke. I remember that during the final week of his life I would bring in the newspaper to his hospital room. We would read the sports page together and talk about the stats. How strange it must have felt to him knowing any day now he would be dying, yet he was carrying on normal conversations.

In all of my dreams I started getting visits regularly from Tommy, my mother, and my dad. They would show up in each of the dreams and stand back from the action watching intently. I would remember going to them at times and talking, but never being able to remember what those talks were about when I woke up. It was as if they had their own little gang now and were running together in heaven. That confused the hell out of me because I never expected Tommy to hang with my mother and dad. They had made two completely different choices in life. My parents lived their lives doing good for everyone they met. Tommy snuffed out another man's life and destroyed friends and family along the way. Then it hit me. As I said before, after Tommy killed Ray, I never made the time to speak with him again once he went to prison. I told myself that he wasn't the same person any longer. The Tommy I'd respected and loved like a brother was dead. He died the day Ray was killed. The dead Tommy, I realized, was the Tommy with my parents.

The strangest dream would be when all my characters showed up at the same time. I would stand in the shadows as they mingled. The characters would all be standing in a bright light, and I just watched from outside their circle. This recurring dream never seemed to change. It just came with more frequency and intensity if I was in the middle of a deal and being one of my characters.

I had had the same dream problem earlier in my career, and then I'd considered it to be related to stress and fighting. I worked in the housing projects as a walking beat officer right before I went undercover. You would drive your car to the projects, then get out on foot. My shift was from 3:00 to 11:00 p.m., and most of the time was spent in the dark. My partner and I walked through the projects from building to building and through every alleyway or backyard. All the project apartments were single-level, and families lived there for generation upon generation. A family of criminals would train their children, and those children would eventually train theirs.

The drug PCP could be found everywhere in the projects. Dealers carried the liquid PCP in jars and dipped brown-colored Sherman-brand cigarettes in the "juice" or "water." The users would buy the cigarette for $25 and smoke it around a corner in the projects or in a burned-out apartment. If they didn't have a vacant apartment to smoke in and deal from, they would chase a family out of theirs and use that one. Smoking one "Sherm" cigarette was like opening the cell to the Incredible Hulk. You got instant incredible strength when your adrenaline was tapped, and you fought to the death. I had never encountered people so strong in my life and so unwilling to quit a fight.

They didn't feel any pain. Every night a series of fights challenged your intestinal fortitude. Never one to show fear, I internalized the constant angst. Then at night my dreamworld would unfold and I would begin work even in my sleep. I became more tired because of the restless sleep and even considered leaving the job. Then came the undercover assignment at Special Projects, and I was off again and forgetting about the emotions brought on from work in the projects.

Dreams or no dreams, I had to carry on and finish what I had set as a goal for myself. I would pay close attention to what was happening to me and avoid the things that would make me surrender to the confusion and pain. I would always remember what waited for me at home and how I never wanted to disappoint my family. That was my driving force and how I fought all my demons.

All of a sudden I remembered the professional informant who had been trying to get ahold of me. I knew whatever he had was going to be good, but would be laced with problems. Those guys never come without baggage and a truckload of demands. I sat for a moment, then thought it should be interesting to see what lay ahead of me.

19

Waiting a Lifetime
for You

The earlier phone call was from Pete, a "top-shelf" informant. He had no other job except working for the federal government as a snitch. He made unbelievable money, primarily working with the DEA. This time, though, he had decided to reach out to me and bring me his new friend, Al. They had met in a club and started palling around. Pete told Al that he was involved in drug manufacturing and sales. Al said he loved the idea and wanted to get involved with Pete, but first needed his help in killing Al's ex-wife. Pete and Al had done some petty one-ounce drug deals together, but this was a whole different story.

For Pete, this was everything the little rat had dreamed of. He had always wanted to be a federal agent but got regularly turned down because of his shady past and questionable psychological condition. Being an informant allowed him to play cop and get paid for it. Someday, he thought, he would get hired for real and be sworn in as a special agent.

Pete, however, seemed to embellish things for sheer excitement and wanted to control the deals he brought. That wasn't going to happen with me, and he was going to have to follow my directions or move on. Controlling Pete became a constant problem the entire time I dealt with Al. I never once found myself trusting or liking Pete. I thought he was a snake that would sell out his own mother for money or notoriety. Because of that I questioned everything he said and revisited any conversations or statements he claimed were made by Al. That wasn't easy because Al would look in wonder at some of my questions because he thought Pete had already handled it. Most people dealing in crime want the middleman to handle the entire deal. They want to keep their hands clean. Let the middleman do all the talking and negotiating so they can feel completely removed. I always thought it was like being two-year-olds who believed they weren't being looked at if they didn't look at you. You are still looking at them, but since they don't see you, they think they are safe.

I had to know that Al had dreamed up this scheme on his own and that Pete hadn't planted the idea in his head. If I found out that Pete did really plant the idea, I was going to arrest his ass for false reporting or hindering an investigation. I didn't like him, wasn't going to like him, and didn't care to ever see him again once this deal was done.

The whole time I dealt with Pete he pressured me for money and bragged how he'd made federal agents the success they became. According to Pete, if not for him, the federal government's undercover division would have fallen flat on its face.

I had to deal with him though. I'd learned years ago that you can't get close to criminals with saints. This was just another time I felt as if I were selling my soul to the devil. I made sure to question everything Pete said to make sure I didn't get duped.

Pete set the tone for the entire deal because he got me so fed up with dealing with his bullshit. The anger he brought out in me also transferred into my personal life. I was getting ready to hook up with Al when Patti called and said we had a big problem at home. I didn't really have time for a big problem at home when I was in the midst of meeting someone who wanted me to kill another person. "What's going on, Patti?" I quickly asked. The hot-water pipes under the kitchen floor had burst and we had no hot water. In fact we had no water at all. The plumber was planning on taking a jackhammer to the kitchen floor and tearing it out so the leak could be fixed.

I was about to meet Al and couldn't leave to fix the problem. If I didn't meet with Al and convince him I was the guy he had been looking for, then he might go elsewhere and get the hit done for real. I told Patti she had to deal with this on her own, and whatever she did, not to let the plumber tear up the floor. She wasn't too happy, but I had no choice and she had to do it on her own. Unfortunately I had to end the call and direct all my attention to Al.

I had spent a majority of my time schooling Pete on how to talk to Al and stay clear of entrapment issues. Then how to get Al to me so I could take over and decide if he was for real. Of course, Pete always knew of a better way and would try to interject that into our plan. Because of my mood, I felt the outlaw biker in me come out and I became a no-nonsense ex-convict that was now a Warlord in the Dirty Dozen Motorcycle Gang. Complete with the gang colors and gear. I was everybody's new nightmare with a huge attitude, and it wasn't going to be pretty.

I reached into my trunk and put on my old, tattered Levi's and a T-shirt that showed how big my arms were. The trunk of my car was like a treasure chest of costumes for whatever character I needed to play. I always carried the trashy clothes for the biker and the ex-convict because they worked better when they were wrinkled and dirty. I planned to intimidate the hell out of Al and chase him down the road. If he didn't run, then I knew I had the guy, in spite of Pete.

The gang colors was a sleeveless denim jacket with the emblem of the Dirty Dozen on the back. The front had a patch below the collar with the word WARLORD. Other items were also sewn onto the jacket to show racism and sexual preferences. I wouldn't have to say anything about who I was or what I was capable of doing. The jacket would say it all. This would be a huge test for Al right out of the box. He would know from the very minute when I walked up to him that I was for real. Everyone in criminal circles knew that you didn't wear that jacket unless you belonged. If you didn't and and you wore the jacket, that was a death wish. A death wish that had been fulfilled time and time again.

I planned to meet with Al in the cove at La Quinta so I could control him and Pete. I knew from talking to Pete that Al had visions of being a badass, and I didn't want him to try it out on me. If he was looking to have someone killed, then I already knew he was unstable and could be capable of any number of other goofy ideas. If he had a gun and thought about robbing me, then I wanted a good place to beat his ass. I still hadn't started carrying a gun regularly, so Al was going to feel some pain if he got stupid. I was ready for his action and had my head on right to jump him in a second if this was a setup. If I got into his head right away, and he truly wanted to hire me, then all would be well.

Our meeting at La Quinta was set for late in the evening when few cars would be around and most people would be settled into their rooms. I knew I would attract attention with my jacket and wanted to minimize the number of spectators who would watch our business. The later the better, and I could control the crowd with harsh stares if they started to look.

On the east side of La Quinta was another parking lot that was concealed from the area where I told Pete and Al to meet me. By this time I had Pete under my control; I warned him to keep his mouth out of my deal or he would pay a severe price. He wasn't sure how to deal with me because the federal agents had kissed his ass. Now he was being treated like a second-class citizen and was scared to say anything about it. I didn't want him to help Al answer my questions. I wanted to hear everything from Al.

I entered from the east and walked to Pete and Al through the breezeway. Coming out of the dark and suddenly upon Al was just the right start to an intense evening. I slowly walked toward Al with all my gear on and a toothpick hanging from my mouth. He stared intently with each step I took and seemed to cower toward the back of his car's trunk for comfort. Pete just backed out of the way and waited for me to acknowledge them. As I walked in their direction, I scanned the area and looked at the rooftops. I wanted to make Al think I didn't trust him. Getting him scared and off guard was my first step.

The night was really perfect for intimidation, complete with a dark parking lot and dim lighting. Clouds overhead with the chance of rain. It had already rained and a thin layer of mist hung in the air and almost made it feel cemetery-like.

When I got to where Pete and Al were standing, I walked right past Al and over to Pete. I didn't even acknowledge that Al existed, other than a hard stare as I passed him. The hard look is almost like a punch in the stomach. I hugged Pete for a moment, then turned to Al. "Sonny," I said, "what about you?" I grabbed Al's hand with our thumbs interlocking and pulled him into my chest, wrapping my other arm around his back. I held Al for a long moment and squeezed him so he could feel the strength I had compared to his. I felt the size difference and knew that Al definitely felt he was undersized.

I kept the toothpick in my mouth and moved it back and forth, in and out, without ever touching it with my hands. Then I would pull it from my mouth when I wanted to make a point and point it inches from his face. I later learned from Pete that Al told him he thought I was going to poke his eyes out. He said he was so scared with the toothpick that he couldn't stop watching it in my mouth. Al would consciously tell himself not to look at me and the toothpick for fear that I would get mad.

I didn't mince any words with Al. I wanted him to believe that I was one badass dude. He believed I was a killer, and if I killed for him, I could just as easily kill him. Best price and best deal, that's my perfect client. No personal attachment was the impression I wanted them to have.

I made it a point to invade Al's personal space and make him as uncomfortable as possible. I hoped he realized he had made a horrible mistake and wanted to take it all back. This would definitely be a way to determine how committed he really was. Then I just blurted out, "Let's cut through the bullshit. You tell me what you need done." He immediately said he needed me to get rid of someone. "You have any money?" I asked. Al had $500 with him and would be willing to make payments for the difference. I laughed out loud at the thought of making payments for a murder. I envisioned myself wearing a long trench coat with a charge-card slider hanging from the inside lining. Charge your murder at the "one-stop killer."

I already knew that Al was dabbling in sales of meth and cocaine, so I made him another offer for payment. How about his paying me the remainder in coke or meth? That was a fantastic idea for Al, but he needed to talk to Pete about it first. I quickly jumped on him when he mentioned Pete. "Don't bring his ass into your business, punk. Either you take care of it by yourself or find someone other than me to do your shit!" Al didn't know what to do at this point and told me he would work through a couple of his guys and arrange for the dope. That was a good start toward my being convinced that Pete didn't have a hand in this deal. Throughout every deal with informants, I had to continually test their involvement. When I determined the informant was the reason for my participation, then I would end the deal abruptly and not return. I would also fire the informant as soon as we met again.

Once all the questions were out of the way, Al began to explain what he needed. Al wanted his ex-wife, Tina, out of his life. She had custody of their ten-year-old daughter and had driven him crazy for the past ten years. Al said, "I have been looking ten years for someone like you." He wanted sole custody and didn't want Tina telling him how their daughter should be raised. That wasn't all, though. Al was a full-time U.S. postman and had started to hate his boss. He also wanted her killed. Then he had two business partners who had done him wrong on a business deal, and he wanted them visited by me. The partners had sold Al a retirement home that was completely occupied by elderly residents. Once Al took possession of the business, the partners opened another home nearby. All of the residents, except one, left Al's home and moved to the new home. Al couldn't fill his rooms and lost the business.

For ten years Al had been in and out of court with Tina fighting over visitation rights. According to him, Tina had made his life miserable, and now she must pay the ultimate price. With her out of the picture he could have his daughter without any interference. The problem with his plan was that the court didn't trust him as a father. He was considered too violent and short-tempered. The court ordered him to have only one visit every two weeks with his daughter, limited to three hours. Additionally, the court ordered a family counselor to be present during the visits. No unattended visits for Al.

Al was prepared to take me to the apartment where his daughter and Tina were living. I would have a picture of her and a complete description to make sure I had the right person. The best time to make my move was when Al had his daughter for her visit and Tina would be home alone. He didn't want his daughter to see or experience any of what I had planned.

Suddenly he became more excited, and I think it was because he thought I was going to help him. To that point he wasn't sure what I was going to do. Then he told me he had a great idea of how I could get a good look at Tina. Follow him to his visitation, and when she handed over his daughter, I would know Tina and could then follow her.

Really intelligent idea, Al, I thought to myself. Take a murderer to see your daughter.

Just as Al was beginning to relax and not be a hard-ass in front of me, two marked Highway Patrol vehicles drove through the parking lot. Al started to stress out and I told him, "Knock off your shit and act normal!" Then I slowly removed my Warlord jacket and rolled it up, placing it under my arm. Just as I did that, the officers got out of their patrol cars and walked into the restaurant, never giving me another look. "See!" I said to Al. "Don't ever shit yourself in front of me again, or I'm out!"

When everyone seemed to have calmed down and stopped worrying about the cops, I wanted to get the deal moving along.

I needed to know how Al wanted his ex-wife killed and if killing her was what he really wanted. I needed to get him personally invested in the plan by telling me how he wanted it done. This was no time for confusion and giving him the defense that all he really wanted was to have Tina scared. At trial he would use either the defense of I scared him and he couldn't back out, or all he really wanted was for me to scare Tina. Al said he didn't care how I did it, just, to let him know when it was going to happen so he would have an alibi. Al thought that he would be the first person the cops came to when they found her. He wanted to be ready when they came.

Pete was behaving himself, even though he wanted to be in the middle of the conversation. When Al mentioned that he was

against meeting me in person and wanted Pete to do the negotiating, I saw Pete look at me as if to say, "Can I talk now?" But I
didn't give him the chance and looked deep into his eyes as if to
slowly say, "Keep your mouth shut!" I said, "I don't care, Al, I
wanted to see you face-to-face so I know who to come after if
you tell the cops about me. If you really want to do this, you better be as serious and committed as I am. When I get the green
light, this thing will be done and there won't be no turning
back."

"I'm good with it," Al said. "Like I said, I've been waiting to
do this for ten years."

Al had obviously given a great deal of thought to how he
wanted Tina killed and knew the best way to do it was make it
look as if she'd walked in on a burglary.

"Shoot her or blow her up?" I asked.

"I don't know exactly yet," Al responded. "When we meet
again in a couple of days, I'll have it all figured out."

In the meantime he gave me her name and the address
where she was living. I would be able to sit on the apartment
and watch her every move. When he gave the green light, I
could take her.

This wasn't going to be nice, I told Al. "I'm going to fuck her
up in a very violent way." I'd follow Tina to her apartment and
go inside once she was in the door. When I got inside, I would
hurt her badly and rape her. Then I'd beat her to death and stab
the hell out of her. Finally I would cut her into pieces. But before
I left, I would take all her jewelry and pawn it to make up the
difference for what Al was not giving me. For my doing this, Al
had to give me $250 up front and $250 with an ounce of meth

when I finished. "The apartment is going to be a bloody mess," I told Al. "Don't let your daughter back in there."

Al worried about how he was going to keep his daughter out of the apartment if I did the murder while she was in school.

"Don't worry, Al. I'll make a call to the police from a pay phone before I leave. I'll tell the cops I'm hearing a lot of screaming and fighting in the apartment. The cops will be there in minutes and block off the whole complex. Your daughter will never get inside." I told him that I didn't want his daughter hurt or seeing the mess either. He wouldn't have any worries about that.

We eventually agreed that Tina was going to die in a couple days while she was in the apartment and her daughter was at school. We also agreed to meet again at this same place and same time in two days to seal the deal.

No matter how many times I did these cases, it never ceased to amaze me how cold and cavalier people were about murder. Take someone's life violently and that would touch me for the rest of my life. But Al's hate for Tina was so incredible he didn't care if she was raped, stabbed, beat, murdered, and cut into pieces. He arranged to take his daughter's mother away from her and force her to live with the memory that she died a violent death. Just so he could have her to himself. But the courts would have prohibited that, and she would have been put in a foster home. Al never thought that far. He was too obsessed with Tina's death.

As soon as the meeting with Al ended, I headed out to the complex where Tina lived and to do some surveillance. I needed to sneak into the gated community because the vehicle gate was closed and only allowed residents entry. I waited in an open space until one of the residents used the code to open the gate, then followed behind as if I belonged in the community. It was really dark and the apartment community wasn't well lit. I also had darkly tinted windows, so none of the residents knew who I was or what I looked like. This helped me blend in as a resident and didn't alarm anyone to call the police. That was the main reason I left my motorcycle at home and took the car.

I sat back in the shadows and waited for Tina to come outside and throw out the trash, or to come home from being out. Before long the door to her apartment opened and out she came. Shock! Not once in my conversation with the lily-white, Italian Alan Di Somma did he tell me that his ex-wife was black. It never crossed my mind to ask about her ethnicity. I should have got a picture during our first meeting, but I had settled for a description of her size instead.

I wondered to myself if it was a test and Al was waiting to see if I really followed Tina. If I did, then I would know she was black. If I didn't, he would know I was a fraud.

I followed Tina to the community center at her apartment complex and watched as she met with some of the other residents. Then I quickly got out of there before I started to attract attention because I looked so out of place. This was good stuff for me. I would embellish my story by telling Al that I hung out with Tina when she was at the apartment complex's weekly barbecue. "That's how close I get," I would tell Al.

Just something else for him to think about when dealing with me.

I want the people I deal with to be so afraid of me that they have only two choices. Run as fast as they can to get away and never look back, or be excited that they had found a true killer to do their dirty work. Dirty work they were too cowardly to do themselves. My goal was also to make them so afraid that when they left me, they erased any thought of doing harm to me. I always felt that I was one step away from being robbed or shot and needed to make them question that decision. They needed to think that robbing me would only end in their death. If they walked away with that thought, then my job was done.

Al made the decision that would change the course of the rest of his life. He returned two days later with $250 in his pocket and another $250 in his car. When I got to court, I'd testify that I gave Al many chances to change his mind and back out. I'd explain that I tried to scare him out of his awful decision. I'd tell the jury how I told Al he could leave now and I would forget we ever met. And more important, I told him how vicious his ex-wife's death would be. With all that information for them to discuss, the jury would find it hard to believe Al wasn't committed to the murder of Tina.

I began our conversation during the second and final meeting by describing Al's ex-wife's appearance. "While I was at the complex the other night, I mingled through the community center, Al. Before I left, I read the announcements on the notice board and saw there was going to be a housewarming for all the residents." I not only met his ex-wife, but I hung out with her at the housewarming party. "See, Al, I reached out and touched, just like I can do to you. It doesn't matter to me, everyone is a potential target . . . even you." Al just stared at me with his head nodding and put his fingers to his mouth, looking scared.

Given the green light to kill Tina, and with $250 in my hand,

I thought we were about finished. Then Al explained how he had arranged to get me the meth and would have it ready when I completed the job. "Just be aware," Al said, "the guys I get my stuff from have a reputation of selling stuff that isn't great."

I looked back at him and said, "That's your problem, Al. I'm sure the stuff you get for me will be very good!"

Everything was completed in our agreement to kill Tina, and then Al wanted to talk about me killing his boss at the post office. She had caused so many problems for people at work, he said, that she wouldn't even be missed. Then when she was gone, he needed me to work on his business partners. The partners included an elderly lady and her son, who, Al believed, owed him $20,000, the amount he'd lost when he had to close the elderly care home he'd bought from them.

"If I do that job, Al, I'm going to 'tax' them." I said. "I'm going to the door of the trailer and telling them they owe you twenty thousand dollars for a bad business deal. Pay up or I'm pulling a truck up and taking shit until I get twenty thousand dollars' worth."

Al loved the thought of being a collector and asked if he could go to work with me. He had Fridays and Saturdays off and could work for me anytime on those days. I'd think about it I said, but first I needed to kill Tina. When she was dead, I would take a week's vacation and wait for things to calm down. I'd come back and kill his boss, then we'd work on his partners. With everything accomplished with Al, I positioned him at the back of his car where I could distract his attention as the SWAT team approached.

The code for the SWAT team to arrest Al was my taking my

boot off. I did that as Al and I talked about what I was going to do sexually to Tina. His total attention was on me as the SWAT team converged on him without a moment's notice. Fred Spitlar yelled, *"Police—put your hands on the car!"* Al jumped on top of the trunk in his surprise and the team took him into custody.

Once again, I slithered into the breezeway and disappeared into the dark.

When the deal was completed, I called Tina by phone and identified myself. I told her I needed to talk with her about Al and asked if I could come over. She asked if she could come to the police station and talk with me there. A short time later I met with Tina and explained the whole story. She said she wasn't surprised and had always feared he would eventually try to kill her. There weren't any tears, and she asked how this would affect her applying as a detention officer in the jail. Tina's reaction to the whole situation seemed odd, but I figured it had to do with her personal management of stress. She had dealt with Al for so many years, this may have come as a relief.

A few years later, after Al was sentenced to prison, Patti and I attended a party hosted by a close friend. I was in one room with the guys and Patti was in another with the women. Patti called me into the room where she was and introduced to me to a middle-aged woman. "You have to hear this story," Patti said.

The lady kept attendance at her school and noticed a young girl was called in sick by her mother several days in a row. The staff at the school were already concerned that the child might be a victim of abuse by her mother.

After the girl had not returned to school for several days, the truant officer made a visit. The officer went to the girl's front door and knocked. After several knocks, the officer finally heard the door unlock and it slowly opened. There in the doorway stood Al's daughter, severely bruised and with her front tooth missing. Tina had beaten her daughter so severely that she couldn't go back to school until she healed. Tina had an uncontrollable temper and her daughter had set it off. Apparently not for the first time.

The police were called and Tina was arrested and went to jail while her daughter went into foster care. This little, innocent girl tragically lost both her parents to unthinkable crimes. This incident with Tina never justified what Al did, but it made me feel even worse for their daughter. She had no role models or true love in her home, and that's the one place it needs to be. Every child needs to be able to go home and be loved at the end of a rough day in school. Home is the one place a child isn't supposed to be subjected to ridicule or harsh words from other children. It should be a place where she is accepted for being a special little girl and never beaten.

A couple more years passed and I was sitting at my desk when the phone rang and a young girl's voice was on the other end. The young girl had got permission from her counselor to call me and ask about her father. She was going to prison to see her father for the first time, and he had been giving her conflicting stories. She wanted to know if he had really tried to have her mother killed or if he was wrongly accused, as he had told her.

My heart went flat at the sound of her voice and the thought that this young child had to deal with this so early in her life. Al was still manipulating his child and would probably do so for the rest of his life. I'm sure she wanted her daddy so badly that she was willing to believe most anything. But then I thought, how smart to ask and learn the facts first. Maybe in spite of her parents she would have a chance.

20

Time for a Change of Scenery

It never ceased to amaze me, but I had this weird sense to find the right bars to hang out in and conduct my business. No matter what bar I chose, it was always perfect for enhancing my reputation and validating the person I was trying to convince people I was. I used bars in the undercover world to meet shady characters and hopefully have them spin me into their illegal enterprises. And bar patrons would validate me. You needed to have one good bar to entertain potential clients and have everyone know who you were. If you slipped off to the bathroom and left the client alone, you wouldn't fear being discovered. The client could ask around the bar about you and if you were as bad as the client thought. The bar patrons would gladly speak up for you if you had done your job right and laid the groundwork.

Finding the Dunes bar and homesteading the place for my

enterprise proved perfect and reaped great rewards for me. I brought countless clients into the place, and Kim continually confirmed I was the man and had been in the bar for years. She was constantly making everyone believe I ran the bar and my rules were etched in stone. If anyone tried to come in and take over, she threatened him or her with a visit from me. And of course my close personal friend Charles Manson, in reality my buddy Coon Dog, would also pay them a visit.

One night we were in the joint and trouble broke out around the table with a new guy who had been getting drunk and breaking things. Kim and the owner went to him and told him he had to leave, but he refused. I whispered in Dog's ear to take a gas can from his truck and set it on the guy's trunk. Come back in, I said, and go to the corner by yourself, lighting matches one after another.

I let some time pass, then went over to the new guy and told him it was time to leave. I still have a quarter on the table, the drunken guy with little common sense said. "Listen, buddy," I told him, "my pal over in the corner is a pyro." Everyone in the bar started to pay attention, especially Kim. "When he was in prison, he got mad at his cellie and sprayed him with hairspray while he was asleep. Then he burned him to death after lighting him with a match. If he wants to send a message that he plans on burning you up, he puts a gas can on your car. Looks like he's decided you're next, bud."

The guy ran to the front door and saw the gas can on his trunk, then looked at Dog in the corner lighting matches. The guy ran out the door at a sprint, jumped in his car, and sped away.

I looked at Kim with a mischievous smile and walked over

to Dog. Looking at Kim again as I walked Dog to the door, I said, "I'm getting him out of here before he does something he'll regret." Kim nervously nodded and Dog and I drove away laughing and planning our next visit to the Dunes.

Two ready-to-go cases were waiting for my attention at the office the following day. One involved a punk who molested kids, and the other a lady who had finally had all the abuse she could take from her husband. Tough way for me to make a living, and in these cases I wasn't sure I could make everyone happy. The child molester was going to be an easy gig, but the abused lady would be tough. If she was really abused, then maybe I could talk her out of her decision and get her some help.

I needed first to tend to my new business at the Dunes before I threw myself into a couple of other characters. As I headed to the bar, I thought that the abused lady was almost like going back to the beginning for me. I got into law enforcement in the first place to help abused and bullied people. Now, after all these years, I was starting to realize I could never change some things and had to learn to accept them. I could also impact some circumstances and needed to direct all my energy to them. Years had passed since I'd left college for this life, and I was finally learning I must prioritize and choose the things I had the best chance of correcting.

I returned to the Dunes one evening after hanging out in a few of the stripper clubs and a pool hall. When I walked through the front door, my radar immediately focused on two burly bikers standing at the bar. They zeroed in on me immediately as I came through the door and followed my every move as I walked to the end of the bar. The end of the bar was always my comfort zone because there I could place my back against a wall and have a clear view of everyone in the place. I didn't have to worry about some coward sneaking up behind me and stabbing me in the back.

In bars, small men get artificial courage from a bottle. When that happens, they find the biggest guy in the joint and try to take him down. I'd never quite understood that process, but from firsthand experience I knew it existed. I was always the one they got in their sights and planned to challenge to enhance their reputation. It never took long to adjust their attitude though, and it really made me look good to everyone else in the bar. "Leave Sonny alone," they would say. "If you don't bother him, he won't bother you. Start something with him, he'll beat you into next year."

I continued to remain different in the underworld though and kept people guessing as to who I was. I was nice to all, until someone did something that jeopardized my safety. Then a caged animal was released and I beat people until I felt safe again. I never really liked the fighting, but I knew I had to protect myself or be killed. It became strictly a survival mechanism. It was different for me though because I never grew up beating people. No matter the situation.

The girls would always whisper about how different I was. I knew it was because I didn't physically or verbally abuse them. I only beat the men who were a threat to me and my safety. Fear continued to haunt me though, but I had learned to use it to my advantage. It became an indicator of how unsafe my environment really was. If I felt fear, then I knew it was important for me to be aware and prepared for anything that might happen. I should probably have been that way all the time, but it was too much work. That's probably the reason the bosses thought I was a risk-taker.

The two burly bikers stayed to themselves while Kim came over to me and wondered if I was okay with them inside. I said, "I don't care, Kim, as long as they leave me alone."

"What about me?"

"They won't bother you, trust me."

She loved that and scurried off to play more pool.

After about an hour, the bartender came down to me at the bar and set me up another drink.

"Not now, Joey, I gotta ride out of here."

"It's not from me, it's from the guys at the other end of the bar."

"Give it back to them!" I ordered. "I don't want anything from them."

"Okay," Joey said, and went back to the bikers.

Nice move, I thought to myself as they looked straight at me and stared, insulted that I'd refused their drink. I could feel the pressure mounting and saw that two against one could be a losing situation for me. They obviously had plans for me that didn't appear friendly.

I got on the phone and called Dog to have him arrange a traffic stop from the patrol officers for my two new friends. I needed to find out what their story was so I knew how to handle them. I just didn't like the feeling they were giving me and felt uncomfortable around them. It was as if they knew me from somewhere, and I didn't want them to have that edge.

The boys finally left the bar and got on two Harleys parked outside the front door. They stared at my scooter parked by theirs for a long time and talked among themselves, never coming close, making note of it. I even started to think they were going to snatch the bike when I wasn't paying attention, or wait for me to leave and follow me. They looked awhile longer, then rode away. I waited about thirty minutes and said my good-byes before I hopped on the scooter and rode away. As I drove down the street, I saw the two pulled over and sitting on their seats as an officer was giving them tickets. I slowly rode by and nodded my head to each of them. They nodded back, then looked at each other.

Another hour passed and I met up with Dog behind a shopping center to get the rundown. Dog said, "Bad news, Sonny." The two guys had big issues and it wasn't good for me. Then he burst out laughing and yelled, "They're fucking cops!"

The two were undercover cops from another city, working as narcs. They saw the Dunes as prime dope land and were trying to get into the joint to make some deals. Their main concern was how to get me out of the picture. They thought that as long as I was there, they had no chance. Get me on a drug deal and they could lock me up. The whole bar would become theirs. They were working just like a snitch that works to eliminate competition. I never experienced anything like this before, but I'm not too sure it wasn't happening more frequently than I realized.

Dog arranged for a meeting between me and the two where we shared a few laughs at how they thought I might try to kill them. Kim and others in the bar had warned them that I was dangerous and not to cross me. Those cops had no idea how to deal with me other than trying to get a drug deal on me. I always wondered after our conversation how they were going to make that happen. The only way would have been to plant dope on me.

They asked me to introduce them to everyone in the bar to vouch for them as good guys to deal with. All they wanted was the dope deals in the bar, and I could have everything else. That seemed all right to me because I never liked doing dope deals. It was never challenging enough because anybody could, and did, buy dope. I worked with the two for a couple weeks until they quit showing up and wouldn't answer their phones. When I started checking around about them, I found out some disturbing news. One of the guys had taken drugs from the drug locker at his police station and replaced it with fake stuff. He'd got so addicted to cocaine that he couldn't stop his nose from bleeding. Everyone believed his partner knew what was happening, but failed to report him. As a result, their careers as police officers were forever changed.

The line I always refused to cross had been crossed and stomped on by those guys. I had told Dog during the weeks we were around them that they were loose cannons and had too much freedom. They were staying out too late and never had a handler that kept them in check. It was all a recipe for trouble. Boy, was I right.

Kim was a huge asset for me in the club, but I had to keep her under control by bringing in undercover female officers. When she got the message that I had my own group of ladies, she toned down and accepted being with me only at the bar. She became a lot like Kristie. It was a challenge to always come up with another excuse why I couldn't be with her. Before it became too big of a problem my worries ended because I took a huge burn—street slang for having your identity exposed—and had to leave the bar for good.

To help maintain my image as a "bad guy" biker on the

streets, I would "multitask" by working myself into every aspect of the criminal underworld. Kim had set me up with a drug dealer by the name of Denny Kidd, who was the supplier for all the major motorcycle gangs in town. He loved me when he got to know me and accepted me into his house because Kim approved. I could come over anytime and be a part of his family. Eat his food and drink his beer because he instantly liked and trusted me.

Over several months, Denny and I arranged an elaborate plan for him to supply cocaine and meth to me to put into transistor radios. The radios would then be shipped to my contact in Buffalo, New York. That was all good until he was driving to me with the product and discovered he was being followed by the police. Denny had been monitoring the police surveillance on his police scanner and realized he was being followed.

Denny called Kim right away on her cell phone and told her he thought I was the police. He then directed her to keep me at the bar and the gang would be coming to kill me. I was never to leave the bar alive.

I was sitting at the bar and Kim came over to me with big tears in her eyes. "Sonny," she said, "you have got to leave and never come back." I knew right then I had serious problems. "They're coming to get you and you are going to die."

"Tell me, what's up?"

She cried harder and asked me if I was a cop. "They say you're a cop, Sonny, and they will be here any minute. Leave now or your gonna die!"

I knew she was serious and I had no choice but to calmly walk out the back door and ride away. No backup and I was a sitting duck with no chance if they got me cornered in the bar.

No sooner did I start to ride down the alley then I heard the roar of what seemed like a hundred bikes. No doubt, all of them for me.

Kim saved me and probably didn't even know why. If she had not warned me, I would surely have died that night. It seemed as if someone was trying to tell me something, and maybe it was time to listen. I thought about it as I rode away and felt like shit. I had never walked away from a battle, but this one didn't seem like a battle I could have won.

Denny was arrested later that night, and when he went to trial, he was found guilty and sentenced to thirty-six years in prison for his drug trafficking. I had always stayed away from drug deals because they were easy. I did the deal with Denny because of his relationship with the gang, and I thought that would make it challenging and dangerous. I got that one right, but I never felt good about it. I almost felt ashamed for the position I'd placed Kim in. That was the first of many signs that I may have been "under" a bit too long.

When you start to like the people you are doing illegal business with, you begin to lose judgment. Without good judgment, you make bad decisions. I learned a good lesson from it all that stayed with me for the remainder of my career:

Nothing is black-and-white. Even the bad people have some good in their heart.

21
Wayne's Strange, Twisted World

I had become so popular for doing murders for hire that several awaited me back at the safe house. This time, though, I was going to take my time and not rush right over and get started. I was starting to feel the pain of all the hours and constant personality changes. Patti was starting to tire of putting in hair extensions or styling my short hair to fit one role or another. I still loved everything I was doing, but I was feeling some strange emotions more frequently. The one big release I found was coaching Cody's baseball and football teams. Then I would go back into the underworld and feel a ton of bricks weighing down my shoulders. New personal choices started popping up in my life, and being normal was beginning to look better and better.

It made me laugh to see how different my two worlds had become. On the street I had obtained all kinds of respect from the outlaws as a crime figure, but on the Little League field it was a different story. The competition between the kids is normal and no different from when I was growing up. The parents are a whole different story. Many of the parents think their five-year-old has the ability to turn pro, and they expect preferential treatment from the coach. If Johnnie isn't getting enough playing time, they become nasty. The respect I had as a crime figure on the street didn't transfer to the angry mother or father living their adult lives through the five-year-old just trying to be a kid and have fun.

Cody suffered the most, and also gained the most, with me as the coach. I never wanted anyone to think I was playing favorites and giving him playing time he didn't deserve. He had to become an even better player so that concern never became a reality. We would work for hours on hitting, catching, and running. He got better and earned every minute he played, but I wondered sometimes if all the extra work was taking the fun out of the game. He never complained and always said he loved the practice, but I still wondered. I was lucky with Cody because he worked so hard to be good and he always stayed so humble. His personality stayed consistent and he continued his lovable ways. The thing I loved the most was that he never failed to hug me and tell me how much he loved me. He was never ashamed to be with me and just hang out. That was, and still is, truly special. Our time together in sports kept us close and continued the bond I started when he was first born.

I never stopped thinking about Cody while I worked and ran around with the scum of the earth. With every drug dealer and child molester I thought about how he could be impacting my child. Then I realized that my concern was what protected him from those people. I never left him in a situation that would jeopardize his safety, nor did Patti. Just when I'd started feeling good about myself and Cody's life, I learned about Wayne Wisdom.

If you ever have the chance to meet a police officer, ask what the number one most disturbing type of investigation is for him or her. I can guarantee 99 percent of the time officers will tell you it's the sexual abuse of a child. Most officers will even shy away from going to child-crimes investigative units because they can't psychologically handle the cases. All the heartache and all the pedophiles who've slipped through the system for years and years make the job unbearable. Each year the child molesters are free gives them more opportunities to offend. There is no true rehabilitation for these criminals, despite the medical experts' efforts in that area.

Wayne Wisdom is a typical pedophile and could easily have been the face on any poster for "stranger danger." He was a peanut of a man with crooked teeth, bad hair, acned face, and strong body odor. I'm not sure why any kid would ever come near him, or any parent would trust him, but it happened regularly. I was told by a friend of Wayne's that he laughed out loud about the stupidity of parents. He lived in an apartment complex with a pool and spent most afternoons hanging out and playing with the little children. All the mothers loved him because he was so good with their children and kept them entertained while the mothers hung out and tanned. What they didn't know was that he was molesting their children. Wayne would pretend to be helping the children swim and hold them in his hands as they floated on their stomach in the water. While with one hand he held a little girl above the water, the fingers of his other hand would be buried in her vagina. He loved it, the mothers loved him, and the children were violated and forever changed.

When your small children are finally old enough to go to kindergarten and first grade, they leave your protective arms and begin a new phase of their lives. Elementary schools are increasingly watchful of your children and do everything to protect them from predators that can abuse and injure them. One rule in elementary schools is the buddy system. When going to the bathroom or moving about campus while students are in class, a child must have someone from the same gender go along for support and protection. Most parents think it is a ploy to goof off, but in most cases it works and does truly provide protection.

From my regular visits to Cody's school, everyone on the campus knew me. Every teacher, janitor, and teacher's aide knew who I was in spite of my outrageous and ever-changing appearance. Even with that notoriety I was still forced to stop in the main office before entering the campus. I had to sign in the visitors' log and wear a name tag. When I left, I had to sign out or the office staff would be calling me back. Waiting for Cody and his friends to be released from class for lunch, I routinely witnessed the buddy system at work. Two girls or two boys would be walking together hand in hand. They traveled throughout the campus as a team. I thought to myself how cute it was, but also how great an idea.

On one beautiful afternoon at the Ingleside Elementary School, two young girls left the classroom for the bathroom. Each entered a separate stall with the doors closed and latched, but Wayne Wisdom was waiting in another stall after sneaking on the campus. As the girls pulled down their panties, Wayne crawled from under the stall wall and tried to touch one of the girls. They ran back to their classroom and the police were called. The campus was locked down in an attempt to find the predator. A description of Wayne was released to all the sur-rounding schools, and everyone immediately went on high alert.

The following day Kathy Grossinger was walking her normal tour of the campus as a teacher's aide at Desert Cove Elementary School. Kathy is a wonderful lady who was liked by everyone and truly cared about the children at the school. She had an equally wonderful and supportive husband, Jeff, plus two loving and pro-tective teenage boys. On her tour, Kathy spotted Wayne near the bathroom looking around suspiciously. When Wayne saw Kathy, he took off running, and she followed him without any concern for her own safety. Wayne got into a vehicle and drove away, but not before Kathy got his license-plate number.

Phoenix police officers responded to the call of a predator on the campus and tracked Wayne down and arrested him. The li-cense number was the key, and if not for Kathy's keen sense of danger, Wayne might have survived another day to molest. He was taken to jail and charged with several child-sex crimes that kept him from being released. The main witness: Kathy Grossinger. Wayne's new number one enemy: Kathy Grossinger.

Two rules reign supreme in the jails and prisons that dictate how inmates are to manage one another. The first rule is that inmates will not snitch on another inmate to better themselves. This rule seems to make a great deal of sense in the primitive world of inmates, but it's the most violated rule they have. Al-most every inmate will snitch at one time or another if it means a better deal or preferential treatment. The other rule is that child molesters will suffer in pain whenever another inmate can get to them.

So, snitches and child molesters are put into PC or protective-custody sections of the jail or prison. The snitches end up there when word gets out they snitched, or the other inmates start a rumor to be vindictive. They are placed in PC for their safety. Child molesters go to PC when their records are reviewed upon their arrival, since word travels quickly through the institution. Most of the time the information is released by the correctional officers, who hate child molesters and don't care what happens to them. If they get stabbed, beaten, or killed, nobody cares because they deserved it.

When Wayne went to jail, everyone knew him because he had requested and participated in a press conference where he cried like a baby about wanting to go home and be with his cats. He whined and whined to the judge asking for release and making a disgusting display of himself. Because he was so well-known after his press conference, he was sent to protective custody and housed with another inmate named Jerry.

Wayne was a young, ignorant punk, and Jerry was an old convict who had been institutionalized for the better part of his life, minus a few trips into society when he married and had children. He was in protective custody to "lay down" and do his time without having to deal with the politics of prison life. He told me his wife was sick with cancer and he wanted to finish his sentence and get out so he could be with her before she died.

When Wayne moved into the cell with Jerry, he started to act tough to impress Jerry. Wayne was so ignorant about prison and jail etiquette that he began to brag about how he molested the children at his apartment complex. Not only did he brag about the molesting, but he also wanted Kathy Grossinger killed before his trial so she couldn't testify. If she wasn't available to testify, then Wayne just knew he would be free. Free to live his life, play with his cats, and of course hurt more kids.

Jerry didn't want any problems during the remainder of his time, so he ignored Wayne and his rants about Kathy. A little punk child molester was simple for Jerry to room with because he would cause him no harm. But Wayne wouldn't stop talking about it and began to ask Jerry to find him someone to kill Kathy. Wayne would pay the hit man well, he said. He bragged to Jerry that his boyfriend and "meal ticket" was very wealthy. He would give Wayne any amount of money he needed.

Jerry thought about it for several days and finally reached out to me for help. He knew about me from newspaper articles and television shows and sent a message from the jail to arrange a meeting. He would help arrange a meeting with Wayne and wanted nothing in return. Except maybe a chance to see his wife before she died. His only other choice was to kill Wayne himself, but that would only extend his time in prison. Letting me handle the problem kept Jerry in line with his newly discovered spiritual beliefs and faith in God.

Things became a bit more complicated once Jerry told Wayne that he could arrange for him to meet a friend of his, a friend who would take care of Wayne's problem for a price. Both Jerry and Wayne were locked in cells, and visits from the outside were limited. I had to make sure that Jerry wasn't forcing Wayne into his decision and also manipulating him. I knew that the defense attorney for Wayne would allege that Jerry was older and more convict-wise than the pitiful Wayne. They would say that Wayne went along with the plan to look "big and important." He had agreed with the plan to keep Jerry as a friend and confidant for protection in jail. Wayne was truly afraid of Jerry, the attorney would say, and would do whatever it took to please Jerry. Jerry also had plenty of time with Wayne to manipulate him because they shared the same cell day and night. Jerry's time with Wayne would be considered quality time and unmonitored. Plenty of time for Jerry to groom Wayne. Of course none of that would be true, but the defense attorney would make sure it's what the jury believed.

My ace in the hole was that Jerry had nothing to gain, and Wayne had everything to lose if Kathy wasn't killed. Wayne was a deceptive little rat and had a history of manipulating people to his benefit. That was exactly how he operated with his boyfriend, Jason. Jason always felt sorry for Wayne and showered him with gifts, such as cars, clothes, and a place to live. Wayne took advantage of this and played the role of an abused and weak individual who needed to be taken care of. Jason soon learned that Wayne was much smarter than he gave him credit for and had taken advantage of him.

While in jail, Wayne wrote a letter to Jason and cried about his love for Jason and need for his support. The letter became public information as part of the criminal investigation.

I haven't eaten tonight; I'm so much more scared than I was cause now I'm looking at 25 to life!!! I'm never gonna be free again—oh sob!!! Oh big sob.

I'm so sorry. Please don't hate me; I need you so bad. I need you you! I have no one else! I'm so scared! I'm so alone! I just wanna die!

After Wayne's arrest it appeared to everyone that Jason was trying to sever their relationship. He was doing his best to put distance between himself and Wayne and never condoned what Wayne had been accused of. But Wayne never stopped his antics to get Jason to pay attention to him. He was used to Jason providing for him, and when he wasn't there, Wayne was lost.

The other problem I had was how to get a meeting in the jail with Wayne and capture it on tape. The jury needed to see what kind of person Wayne was when he didn't turn on the tears and play the poor misunderstood boy. I knew when he was in my presence, he would become the true predator that he was. To make this happen, I had to visit him in the jail and get the help of jail staff. Not an easy task in the self-proclaimed "toughest jail in America."

The sheriff of the jail where Wayne was housed was known to many as Sheriff Joe. The self-proclaimed "toughest sheriff in America," he promoted himself better than most other politicians. I find it disturbing to have politics dictate decisions in law enforcement. From what I have observed, Joe would make all his decisions based on the publicity he expected to get out of them. Press conferences were regularly announced and attended by throngs of reporters. Everyone wanted to know what shenanigans Joe was up to that day. I didn't care for Joe because I felt he sacrificed the safety of his employees for the attention he got from his gimmicks. Outstanding and hardworking police officers had to fulfill Joe's wild schemes, schemes that constantly put them in harm's way as they walked the halls where the inmates lived.

The *Phoenix New Times* once wrote an article about my award as Police Officer of the Year. The guest speaker at the award ceremony was Sheriff Joe, who had every intention of using the moment to promote himself, as the *New Times* noted: "Everyone knows that Sheriff 'Joke' used to be a DEA narc. But in his case, *narc* is short for 'narcissist.' So it was fitting that onlookers cast wagers on whether the sheriff would bother to mention Ballentine at his award ceremony. It was generally suspected that if Joke did mention the honoree, it would be in the context of his own exploits."

Of course the public didn't care about his antics, they just liked how he handled the prisoners, most of whom had not yet been convicted and were awaiting trial. Joe wasn't going to like my doing a murder for hire in his jail and preventing him from personally getting the press for the case. The case would also go against his claims that he ran the "toughest jail in America" if a murder plot was planned and carried out under his watch.

For this to work I had to contact my close confidants in the jail and get their help without bringing too much attention to what I was doing. I was successful in that effort and also got their help with wiring the phones to capture Wayne's conversations with me. Everything I asked for, the officers provided. Like a well-oiled machine they arranged for me to visit Wayne and discuss his plan to have Kathy killed.

I went home at the end of a long day of planning for my meeting with Wayne on the following day. As I walked in the door, I noticed that Patti was lying on the couch and the room was dark. The boys were out at a movie, and the whole house felt rather empty. I walked over to Patti and sat next to her on the edge of the couch. She cried and then looked at me and blurted out, "Lee has died!"

Patti's dearest friend was Lee. She had been suffering for sev-

eral years with a rare lung disease and had been close to death
for the past couple of weeks. She was the one person who understood Patti, and they shared their innermost secrets. Patti
never believed Lee would die. She banked on Lee always being
there for her, and she for Lee. I had never met any other woman
like Patti until she introduced me to Lee. This woman made
everyone feel loved and cooked as if there were no tomorrow.
Every event with Lee was accompanied by a feast where everyone came together as one. Losing her would shatter the lives of
many people.

Patti's eyes were swollen from all her crying and she sobbed
as she told me, "I don't know if I can take this any longer, Jake.
I always had Lee to listen when you didn't come home or we got
a call in the middle of the night and you disappeared for days.
Who listens now when I find out someone is trying to have you
killed!" I always knew Patti had years of pent-up emotions and
fears related to my job that she never told me about. How could
she not? I just figured she had her own special coping mechanism to deal with the contracts to have me killed or the constant
presence of the SWAT team to protect her. Little did I know that
her outlet was venting to Lee.

I didn't know what to say and just grabbed her and held her
as she cried even harder. I knew the pain of her loss, and I knew
none of my words would help. I could only assure her that
everything would be all right and that I was capable of protecting my family and myself.

While I held her and she cried and sobbed, it finally sank in
that it was time for a change. Patti had waited long enough for
me, and she'd gambled on the belief that I would return home
every day. Enough was enough.

I'd wait and let this pass before I made such a big decision, I thought to myself. She would have to be a part of this and be sure it was what she wanted. If it was, I'd do it. Until then I could only be supportive and let her know I loved her.

The following morning I left early and Patti finally got some sleep. She'd had a restless night, but finally dozed off around 3:00 a.m. I headed into the office, then over to the jail for my meeting with Wayne. I thought about Lee the whole way to work and how we would miss her and her infectious smile. I also remembered that she had been the first of Patti's friends to tell her that I was the perfect man for her. Lee helped me open the door to Patti's heart and became my biggest supporter.

For the visit with Wayne I had completely changed my appearance and took on the role of an ex-convict. That character was a great fit for this case because Wayne would identify with me. If I dressed up as a mafioso or a businessman, he might have questioned me. I looked the part, walked the part, and sounded tough. It also helped that I was really sick the day I met with Wayne and my voice was totally shot. I sounded like ten days of hard road and a man who'd drunk whiskey nonstop for the past month.

When I arrived at the jail, I looked around the visitors' entrance and stared everyone in the eyes. Mostly I was trying to see if I knew any of them and if they recognized me. The same thing happened as I was escorted to the maximum-security visitation room for my visit with Wayne. I had sent plenty of people to prison and jail over the years and didn't want to see them again. That would have been just my luck: sitting in the visitation room making a deal with Wayne and being recognized by another convict who knew me from the past as a cop.

He would then tell Wayne and everyone else in the visitation room what was happening. That was the problem with any of these deals. You just never knew when they were going to go sideways on you.

I sat in a chair in a small cubicle that was divided by a window with another cubicle on the other side. Both sides had a phone hanging on the wall, used to talk back and forth. After a few moments Wayne was escorted to the seat across from me and the negotiations began.

He was obviously nervous about meeting me, and I sat slouched in the chair showing body language that spoke volumes of whom I was trying to be. It seemed as if he wanted someone to kill Kathy so bad that he believed in me within the first couple of minutes. Then I had to hear about how bad things were for him and how he couldn't survive in prison. He was too small he said.

It was hard for me to listen to Wayne whine because I was so disgusted with him for what he had done to those small children. But then I would remind myself that the more interested I appeared, the more comfortable he would become. The more comfortable he became, the more he would open up to me. It would all lead to my making a case that could keep him off the streets and away from children forever. This was the moment I had dreamed of for my entire life. A chance to help children before it was too late. Most people never get the chance to experience their dreams, and there I was living them.

I first had to determine from Wayne if Jerry had put him up to this and forced him into meeting with me. Through idle and unnecessary conversation Wayne discussed his trust in and friendship with Jerry. "I just bugged him and bugged him and bugged him and finally he said he could help me out." Like a gift falling from the skies, I knew I had Wayne before we even started to dance.

"Let me tell you something, man," I said. "This is all about money for me. I won't be staying here long, so I'll do what you need and be out of here."

"Okay, I understand," Wayne assured me.

"You can change your mind, but you must never snitch on me."

"Totally! Fuck that!"

Wayne said his dad had taught him never to be a snitch or a narc; he would rather have seen Wayne dead than know he was a snitch or a narc. Then Wayne surprised me by telling me that I reminded him of his father, who was a biker. I made Wayne feel comfortable. It also made me feel good that he believed in who I wanted him to think I was.

Wayne really started to open up and chattered about how he wanted Kathy killed and far away from his trial. She had seen his license plate and her testimony was going to convict him. He was offended that she'd even shown up at his initial-appearance hearing and told the judge how she didn't want Wayne to be released. Wayne saw her as his only eyewitness. It was either her life or his, and according to him, she lost that contest.

The money Wayne planned to use for paying me was tied up in a vehicle that he was arranging to have sold. Once it was sold, he would give me all the money. In the meantime he was going to have Jason put $100 in his jail bank account, then sign it over to me.

When we had some understanding of the payment plan, I set out to make sure Wayne knew exactly how I planned to kill

Kathy. "I'm not gonna pick her up and set her in a fuckin' motel room. I told you . . . I'll fuckin' kill her. If you don't want me to do it, then you better find someone else to fuck around with you. I'll fuckin' blow 'em up . . . I'll shoot 'em in the head . . . I'll cut 'em into pieces . . . I'll fuckin' punch their fuckin' lights out and step on their head. I will fuck them up!

"And best of all, Wayne . . . I won't get caught."

I told Wayne that in this situation I planned to follow Kathy when she left Desert Cove School. I was going to do that for a couple of days and see where she went and what she did.

Wayne said, "She gets out at three p.m."

I said, "Okay, Wayne, I'm going to grab her as she leaves school."

I also suggested that I would sit on Kathy and plant a bomb in her car when she parked it. When she left for school and got into her car, "I will blow her ass up. Or I could wait until she goes someplace, kidnap her, and shoot her."

Wayne laughed and was excited as he responded, "Whatever is easier." I wanted to know which one he wanted, and he told me to use my instincts and do whichever felt right.

That's how we left it, and I assured him I would complete the job before he went to court, but not before he gave me some money. Wayne assured me the money would be ready in a few days, and he already had all the information on Kathy so I could start following her.

I met again with Wayne four days later and confirmed that he would pay me the $100 before I left on this visit, and $4,900 when I completed the murder. He told me the car had been sold, so he had all the money.

The normal practice after completing a deal and confirming

the client's commitment has always been to make the arrest swiftly. That wasn't the case with Wayne because he was already in jail and wasn't going to run or attack me through the glass window dividing us. My only concern throughout the deal was that I would be recognized and Wayne would be informed who I was. Then I would have lost Wayne and he could eventually have continued with his predator ways. Wayne would be escorted back to his cell believing that I was everything he hoped for, and his dreams were about to be answered. It was kind of like giving a little kid a candy bar, and just when he was about to take a bite, snatching it from his hand.

The first thing I did when I left the visitation room was to make arrangements to have Jerry moved out of the cell with Wayne. I had him transferred to a completely different facility where he could live out the remainder of his time safely. Wayne would definitely make noise about Jerry's setting him up when he learned about me, and I didn't want Jerry around that mess. Some young punk in the jail would surely stab Jerry just to make a name for himself. Inmates make knives out of anything they can get their hands on. It may take weeks for them to sharpen the blade, but time is all they have. Patience is a virtue in prison, and the inmates realize its benefits.

After I made sure Jerry was safe, I changed all my clothes and left the ex-convict character in the shadows. Paperwork was completed charging Wayne with conspiracy to commit murder, and I contacted Sgt. Janice Mallaburn of the Jail Intelligence Unit to help me charge Wayne. Janice had always been a premier expert in jail and prison gangs and was a great resource for outside police agencies. She escorted me to the level where

Wayne was housed and had him brought out to be informed of his charges.

Wayne walked out of the pod section containing his cell and looked around as he walked through the open door. He looked at me inquisitively for a minute, but didn't recognize me. Then I spoke and my gravelly voice made Wayne suddenly jerk his head directly at me. He froze as I began to inform him of his charges, then he started to cry. When the tears were ignored, he became a loudmouth and claimed he had been set up. The pleasure of fingerprinting this worm was overwhelming and left me filled with great excitement.

While I was preparing all the arrest paperwork for Wayne, we stood in an open area where other inmates were being returned from court. They were all attached to each other by a chain and stood in a line. I was minding my own business, paying attention to Wayne, when one of the inmates yelled something offensive and interrupted our conversation. The outlaw character in me surfaced immediately, and I walked quickly over to the inmate. "Shut your mouth punk!" I said. Calling someone a punk in the jail or prison system is the worst thing another inmate could say, a sign of disrespect.

The inmate then went wild in front of his fellow inmates, and the others on the chain followed suit. They became so loud and out of control that I had to be physically removed to calm the situation. I refused to back down to a big-mouth convict who has probably never paid an ounce of respect to anyone in his life.

Most convicts have spent a lifetime taking advantage of anyone they can. Before I left the jail, I made sure the inmate understood the meaning of respect and how society looks at people who refuse to live by the accepted rules. He learned quickly that opening his mouth to me was not going to go unnoticed.

During Wayne's trial, the other inmates saw Wayne practice crying for the jury. The defense's strategy didn't surprise me. They claimed that Jerry planted the idea to hire a hit man to get a better deal for himself. Wayne had a dependent-personality disorder and always wanted to please. He did what Jerry wanted him to do to please Jerry. Wayne feared me, but also wanted to please me, so he agreed to the murder conspiracy, though he never wanted to get involved.

Surprisingly, Wayne testified and offered a number of excuses as to why he got involved: He had been rejected by his father. He was depressed and prone to panic attacks. He was self-medicating. He wasn't in control of his mind and depended upon Jerry to guide him. Wayne said he thought Jerry knew how the system operated and would teach him how to be nice to the guards so he could get something in return. Jerry even taught him how not to be a snitch.

While Wayne was on the stand testifying, he looked at the jury and said, "Snitches are bitches and they get stitches." I looked at the prosecutor in amazement at what Wayne had just said. I couldn't help but laugh.

Wayne also testified that he was indebted to Jerry because Jerry was understanding and kept everyone from hurting him. That was the single most damning statement made by Wayne in the trial. It contradicted everything he was saying about being afraid of Jerry and participating in the conspiracy to keep him happy.

The defense said that Wayne was inexperienced with the jail

lifestyle. According to his attorney, he was a naïve twenty-year-old, and I reminded him of his father and he wanted to please me. I should have discouraged him instead of making the case. Bottom line for Wayne . . . Kathy Grossinger didn't die. Since she didn't die and he was sorry, everyone should forgive and let him go home.

That didn't matter to the jury. When they finished hearing all the testimony, they sentenced Wayne to life in prison. He also received many more years on top of his life sentence for the child crimes. I don't think Wayne will be a problem for children ever again. He'll have a whole new set of problems just trying to survive in prison, because nobody likes a child molester. Not even convicted murderers.

22

Regrets? I Have One

After I finished with Wayne, I still had one more piece of business: meeting Nancy Olson, who wanted her husband, Robert, killed. But before I met with Nancy, I had some unfinished business with Cody and his school.

The kids in my community get to go once for three days on a science trip. They live in cabins, eat country-fresh food, and learn survival techniques. A select number of parents also go and work as guides and cabin leaders. To go, the parents have to apply and write a letter explaining why they want to go and what benefit they will be to the camp. I knew I had to go, but I'd be damned if I could explain why I would be a benefit. I had never been a Boy Scout so I knew nothing about the outdoors and common survival. All I could do was throw myself at the mercy of the selection panel and hope they rewarded me for all my earlier efforts at the school.

Shortly before the trip was to begin, I got a call from the principal telling me that I had been selected to be a cabin leader. It was almost as if I had won the lottery when she told me. Then she said I was also in charge of the knot-tying class. What did I know about knot tying? Not one thing!

I found everyone I knew that had ever been a Boy Scout and had them all teach me every knot-tying maneuver they knew. I even went to the library and checked out all the books on the subject. By the time I left for science camp, I was a knot-tying fool. I put together a class for the kids that I knew would be fun and give them a nice skill for the rest of their lives.

On the second day of camp we left the campground and headed deep into the woods for a long hike. We had been gone from camp for several hours when another camp guide found us and said he needed to talk to me. I laughed at how he was able to find us when we were so far into the woods. Nonetheless, he did find us and said I had an urgent message back at camp. He didn't know what it was about, but knew it was important.

It took me quite a while to work my way back to the camp, but when I did, I found out that the message was from work. I was irritated at first because I thought they could leave me alone at least for three days. Then concern rushed through me because I realized they wouldn't call me unless it was important. The news was surprising. The SWAT team was sitting on my house again and watching every move Patti and Geoff made. Some soldier-of-fortune nut had taken a contract to kill me. He was on the hunt for me and planned to take me out when he found me at home. I didn't really care about me, but I knew Patti would be shook up and irritated over the attention.

As I talked to Patti, I had to stop for a minute while she gave the SWAT team members more drinks and cookies. I could hear her say, "If you boys need any more sandwiches, let me know." I knew right then that she was all right and knew I didn't have any worries about her. She got back on the phone and said, "This has got to be the last time, Jake, I'm tired." I know, I told her, and promised it would change when I got back and finished one more deal. "Promise?" she said.

"Yeah," I said. "I promise."

When I got back home a few days later, I immediately sent the SWAT team back to other pressing issues. Then as I had always done, I took care of my family by myself. It was embarrassing for me knowing that someone else had to look after my family. It also bothered me that everyone in my family was forced into getting upset about the incident. I prided myself in not making them feel uncomfortable or worried about my job. Most times that worked and they lived their lives in bliss. I'd left town for a few days and everything I'd worked to achieve in making them feel safe had been snatched away from me.

The soldier-of-fortune guy never surfaced, and for some unexplainable reason I never expected he would. Most threats against me were just big talk. My plan was to never worry myself or my family about the threats. If they became real, and danger was imminent, I would take appropriate action and deal with the threat. Otherwise, we were not going to live in fear and be constantly looking over our shoulders. Living in fear that I might be killed was not in any of our plans.

All the deals and the undercover lifestyle had really taken its toll on me. I knew I had to deal with Nancy Olson, but I also knew in my heart that this would probably be my last gig. It seemed to be the right time to hand off the torch and consider other investigative assignments. Especially ones where my family and I had little to worry about.

This case with Nancy Olson was more than I had bargained for. She was an extremely nice lady who had been married to Reed, a disabled Vietnam veteran for sixteen years. If you believe the picture Nancy portrayed, Reed was an abusive husband and father. According to her, Reed lived his life looking for sympathy. He took advantage of mental-health ailments related to his Vietnam experience and wouldn't work. She provided for the family as he stayed home relaxing, drinking, and using drugs.

In return for all the attention Nancy gave him, she claimed he abused her both mentally and physically. Nancy said he also abused their two children. Their son told her Reed hit and kicked him regularly, and their daughter lived in fear of Reed. So much that she had turned to drugs, older men, and wanted to live away from him. Nancy couldn't allow any of this to happen anymore.

Her entire life with Reed was lived in fear of the next physical abuse or the next rant of demeaning verbal abuse. She said his excessive drinking triggered his abuse, which became worse when he coupled drinking with drugs.

I've known and respected many Vietnam veterans throughout my life and found the vast majority to be strong, caring, and driven people. They worked hard and cared for both their family and country, never expecting anything back for their service except respect. Nancy's description of Reed didn't come close to matching the Vietnam veterans I have known and admired.

When I met with Nancy, I found myself feeling sorry for her and doing everything I could to stop her from hiring me. It didn't matter what I did or what I said, she was committed to having her husband killed so she could enjoy a better life. Divorce was not an option for Nancy. The only thing she could see that would make her life better was having her husband dead. That way he could never abuse or humiliate her again.

Nancy said that Reed had been incredibly abusive with her and the children right before she'd left him. Everybody in the family, even her own father and mother, was subjected to his abuse, she said. According to Nancy, during a recent family fight Reed slapped her across the face and her daughter tried to help. The daughter first tried to karate-kick Reed, then tried to stab him with a kitchen knife. When Nancy gathered the children to leave, Reed told her he would see her in jail. The daughter countered with "I'll see you in jail for molesting me when I was nine!"

Nancy made plans far in advance of our meeting and convinced me she was going to have Reed killed even if I didn't help her. She went as far as taking out a life insurance policy on her husband that she would use to pay me. In her naïve, sweet way, she had me look at the policy to make sure I would get paid when Reed was killed.

The whole meeting with Nancy, and the idea of sending her to prison, was killing me. Nothing that I thought of to distract her seemed to matter. I had no alternative if she continued to pursue me for the murder. It broke my heart when she was arrested and broke my heart even more when she was sentenced to prison.

I had started out with the goal of saving the world. As I got older, I narrowed my goal to helping the abused, specifically children. Here I was years later being so naturally convincing as a murderer that this gentle woman hired me to change her entire life—not only to rid her life of her husband, but also to change her world forever. She didn't know she was getting two deals for the price of one. What I didn't realize was she would also change my life.

The day that Nancy was sent to prison was the day that I decided I could no longer be a hit man. I had been searching for the right time to fulfill my promise to Patti, and this was it. My time had run its cycle, and some new blood was needed. Fifteen years was long enough in this role, and my family had suffered more than their share. My energy had been sapped by Nancy, and the thought of how many people's lives had changed course by their meeting me was staggering. Every one was driven by greed, except maybe Nancy. Only Nancy felt she truly had no way out of her hell. I liked her, and when I met her husband, although I could not confirm all of her claims, I understood her heartache.

If only I could have intimidated her so much that she changed her mind. I tried like hell, but she was too focused on her goal. I felt responsible for Nancy's being in prison. My compassion for her gave me a great deal of guilt, and I tried to understand why she'd placed me in that position. I had always said these cases impact more people than the primary victim. They ruin families, destroy friendships, and ostracize the person committing the crime for the remainder of his or her life. And now they'd impacted the person that cared the most through the whole ordeal. Me.

I really never understood killing someone instead of leaving the person for good. I never understood that divorce was out of the question. If it was that bad, then run as far away as you can and start over. Because when you made a deal with me, you were left with no choice but to start over as a convict. Nancy explained that she feared her husband so much that she could never leave. She believed in her heart he would hunt her down and kill her if she ever left him.

If only she could have found a different way out . . .

23

Finally, Home Again

After all the recent events and with my concern for Patti and the kids, I knew the time had finally come. If I didn't get out of undercover work, I was going to make myself physically and mentally ill. The first thing I did was to go on an intense training program to lose seventy-five pounds and get me back to where my body became a temple again, not a cage-fighting venue. I also decided to switch over to the homicide unit and focus on an area where I could continue to do some good and still work my tail off. I could also start to dress like a normal person and maybe search for the guy who started the academy years ago and planned to save the world. My family and friends helped make the difference in my searching for myself.

After the change had taken place and I was getting more mainstreamed, I got a wonderful invitation to present a badge at the Police Academy graduation. What an honor and a great chance to see people I hadn't seen in years.

When I arrived at the auditorium, I met up with Alex, Coon Dog, and a number of other friends. Both Dog and Alex had made themselves icons in the law enforcement world and were respected around the country. Alex was still the funniest man on earth, and he had also groomed himself to be an incredible investigator. People came from all over the state and the country to hear him speak or ask for his guidance. Alex had an unbelievable ability to see things that nobody else saw. He had that gift from the first day I met him. It just got more advanced through the years. The Dog never stopped throwing himself into assignments that were the most dangerous offered. He ended his career hunting violent fugitives and was in several gun battles through the years. Each one ended with the same result: Coon Dog went home and the bad guy didn't. Through all the years Dog stayed true to our friendship. He never once wavered, staying by my side during the good times or in a crisis. My boys have always thought Alex and Dog were their uncles. I was always comforted in knowing that if I died, they would take care of my family. No questions asked, just pick up where I'd left off.

Everyone was there to see the new graduating class and welcome them into the law enforcement family. My whole immediate family was there, and so was my brother, Jeff, who had his older son, Mike, already on the force. That was special because Mike was also my godson and a young man I was proud of. I also knew that my mother and father were with me that night and knew everything I had gone through. They had stayed seated on each side of my shoulders after they'd died and guided me through the darkness. It had to feel good to them knowing their guidance had safely led me home.

We all got seated in a several rows and waited for the evening to begin. That's when I was told to come on stage and wait for the badge presentation.

I stood onstage as the new police recruits lined up to receive their badges and become sworn police officers. It's a dramatic moment in any police officer's life because the badge stands for everything that is good and just. They will die in the name of that badge and will treasure it, and what it stands for, the rest of their lives. I remember the day I was given my badge and sworn to the oath of a police officer. It was as clear in my mind as if I had been doing it right at that moment I was standing onstage. The emotions flooded back and I remembered how incredible it felt to have completed the Police Academy training. And how I realized my life would never again be the same.

The chief stated the oath and the new officers repeated every word after him. The cameras in the auditorium flashed as family members burst with pride. Any parents would be incredibly proud to know that their sons or daughters led lives that allowed them to be accepted as police officers. Tonight is the parents' recognition of a job well done, especially when so many temptations surround your children as they grow. The oath was completed, and one by one the newly appointed officers walked toward the center of the stage to have their badge pinned on their uniform.

As a guest waiting to pin on a badge, I stood quietly and admired each of them. I knew the pain and suffering they'd gone through for nearly twenty weeks to achieve this moment. I understood how hard it was to finish, and I knew what all their families had done to support them in this endeavor. Then the chief announced, "Geoff Ballentine!" I waited as he crossed the stage to stand at attention in front of me. As I placed the badge on his uniform, my eyes began to well up and the badass in me that had lived the life of a street thug had finally been put to rest.

My mind shifted to the exact moment that I'd stood in the halls of the South Phoenix precinct and listened to Sam Uptegrove tell how he was leaving undercover work. Too burned-out and couldn't do it any longer. I'd told myself that if I ever got a chance to be undercover, I would never stop. Funny how it all changes once you are in the battle. The day came for me when I couldn't drink another glass of alcohol, look at another stripper, or ride my Harley down the street. My life had been sucked from me, and I wanted to find the guy I knew before it all started.

With the badge snugly attached to Geoff's uniform I threw protocol out the window and passed on a salute. I grabbed him tightly and gave him a big hug, saying how proud I was. He marched back to his spot in formation and I quietly left the stage for my seat in the audience.

As I sat with my family, I thought about my travels and looked at Patti in awe of her ability to cope with and support me. I was lucky with her and never forgot that. She was the reason I could find myself when it was over. I remembered the first night I saw her and how beautiful she looked to me. The first time I walked into her house and smelled the candles and knew I had been reborn. Patti had stood by me for years and helped guide me through the darkness of the hell that I lived in. Then she gave me the greatest gift I will ever get in my life, the birth of my son Cody.

Cody stared in admiration at his older brother, and I'm sure his mind darted about, placing himself in the uniform. He has already committed himself to joining the police force if his planned acting career comes to an end. His plans are for SWAT and being a hostage negotiator. Until then, he's pursuing football at Mountain View High School and working on his studies and social life. A healthy teenage boy with all kinds of dreams. He's turned out to be everything I dreamed he would be, and even more. Loving, caring, and committed to making all the right decisions. I see myself as a young man in Cody and understand how his mind and heart work. He is my gift from God, a gift that keeps giving.

I looked around at everyone and took a deep breath as I realized the tightness of stress was no longer in my chest. I was with my family and living a proud moment for all of us. My mind once again flashed to my mother and how proud she would be that I survived the battle and never once crossed the line. My father lived his life admirably so I would have an example to follow. The lessons were many from those Little League years, and I still remember every one of them in the spring when the aroma of fresh grass and the dampened infield floats in the air as the first game begins. Lessons surrounded me from everyone that had helped in bringing me back to my home.

Then I thought to myself, I was back.

Index

Made in the USA
Las Vegas, NV
02 June 2023

72896582R00187